Praise for

Christ-Enlivened Student Affairs

"This is a landmark study of the lived experiences of Christian student affairs professionals in the 21st century. But it is not just a study. It is a guidebook, a map, and a manual for what it means to integrate the Christian faith into the field. In a world where the next generation is desperately looking for a sense of meaning and purpose, these authors challenge us not to check our faith at the door of our institutions and incorporate secular theories and practices uncritically. Rather, they challenge us to focus on Jesus Christ, who enlivens our work as student affairs professionals. This is a must-read for any new or seasoned professional!"
    —**Felix Theonugraha,** President, Western Theological Seminary

"Perry Glanzer and his colleagues are convinced that effective student development on Christian and secular campuses requires something more than caring professionals who understand higher education. Forming whole persons in ways that honor God calls for a coherent theology that integrates academic learning with a life of faith. The result of their research is a redemptive, Christ-centered approach to student affairs with biblically grounded principles and practices that will exercise wide influence on the field of student development and—even more importantly—make a real difference in the lives of college and university students."
    —**Philip Ryken,** President, Wheaton College

"In this much-needed volume, Perry Glanzer and his colleagues capture the current state of the journey toward a distinctively Christian vision of Student Life within the world of Christian higher education. This work also serves as a call toward a normative theological foundation for Christian colleges and universities that will enrich their capacity to speak distinctively and constructively—even beyond the world of Christian higher education—into the perennial student life challenges of residential life, alcohol and drug abuse, sexual integrity, and student discipline, as well as the contemporary challenges of race relations and Title IX. *Christ-Enlivened Student Affairs* inspires an incarnational approach to inviting our students into their full inheritance as created and redeemed divine image bearers."
    —**Shirley A. Mullen,** President and Professor of History, Houghton College

"For the Christian leader in student affairs, a thoroughly faith-infused perspective on our work with students and colleagues is at the core of our calling. Part indictment and part call to comprehensive theological faithfulness, the authors provide a well-researched, compelling, and articulate Christian vision for our profession and for our campus communities. We would do well to pay attention as we prepare and equip the next generation of Christ-followers!"

—**Brad Lau,** Vice President of Student Life and Athletics, George Fox University

"These encouraging words remind me why I chose a career in Christian higher education. I find myself reflecting on how my life was deeply impacted by key student affairs employees and their 'enlivened' Christ-like influence. This book serves as a rich resource for those of us that desire to imagine and live out a Christian vision within the academy."

—**Tom Middendorf,** Provost and Senior Vice President, Trevecca Nazarene University

CHRIST-ENLIVENED
STUDENT AFFAIRS

CHRIST-ENLIVENED
STUDENT AFFAIRS

*A GUIDE TO CHRISTIAN THINKING
AND PRACTICE IN THE FIELD*

PERRY L. GLANZER
THEODORE F. COCKLE
ELIJAH G. JEONG
BRITNEY N. GRABER

Abilene Christian University Press

CHRIST-ENLIVENED STUDENT AFFAIRS

A Guide to Christian Thinking and Practice in the Field

ACU PRESS

Copyright © 2020 by Perry L. Glanzer, Theodore F. Cockle, Elijah G. Jeong, and Britney N. Graber

ISBN 978-1-68426-500-8 | LCCN 2020005163

Printed in the United States of America

LIBRARY OF CONGRESS CATALOGING-IN-PUBLICATION DATA
Names: Glanzer, Perry L. (Perry Lynn), author.
Title: Christ-enlivened student affairs : a guide to Christian thinking and
    practice in the field / by Perry L. Glanzer, Theodore F. Cockle, Britney
    N. Graber, and Elijah G. Jeong.
Description: Abilene, Texas : ACU Press, 2020. | Includes bibliographical references.
Identifiers: LCCN 2020005163 | ISBN 9781684265008 (paperback)
Subjects: LCSH: Student affairs services—Moral and ethical aspects—United
    States. | Education, Higher—United States—Religious
    aspects—Christianity. | College students—Religious life—United
    States. | Universities and colleges—United States—Religion.
Classification: LCC LB2342.92 .G53 2020 | DDC 378.1/94—dc23
LC record available at https://lccn.loc.gov/2020005163

Cover design by ThinkPen Design | Interior text design by Sandy Armstrong, Strong Design

For information contact: Abilene Christian University Press, ACU Box 29138, Abilene, Texas 79699

1-877-816-4455 | www.acupressbooks.com

20 21 22 23 24 25 26 / 7 6 5 4 3 2

CONTENTS

PART FIVE
Current Issues in Christian Student Affairs

ACKNOWLEDGMENTS

As I (Perry) languished in bed for most of 2017 due to unforeseen health issues, my coauthors modeled Christ by coming to visit me at my home. During one of those bedside lunches with Ted Cockle, we talked about some of the innovative Catholic efforts to infuse faith into student affairs. As I remember, Ted simply asked something along the lines of, "Why don't we do something like that in the Protestant world?" That's how I thought this idea was born (but see Ted's dedication for the rest of the story).

Of course, birthing ideas is easier than getting them financially supported. Thus, we are extremely grateful for the financial support of the Association for Christians in Student Development (ACSD), which also made this study possible. ACSD gave us generous freedom and did not have a role in the study design, data collection and analysis, or writing of the report, and, therefore, cannot be held responsible for any shortcomings.

We dedicate this book to those Christian student affairs staff we interviewed and surveyed and the rest of the Christian student affairs contingent. Thanks for your devotion and sacrifice to educating students and your willingness to share your wisdom with us.

As a coauthored work, we also have additional sources of inspiration.

Perry—I dedicate this book to all the Higher Education and Student Affairs (HESA) students I taught over the past decade. You seek to live out what it means for Christ to animate student affairs. Thanks for your inspiration and commitment.

Theodore—I dedicate this book to my wife Kate, who—over chips and queso—helped raise the initial questions that inspired this study. Thanks for your encouragement, questions, and wisdom through it all.

Elijah—To my immigrant parents, who gave their children a better future by coming to the United States. To my brother, Isaiah—you have always had my back and been my best friend. To my mentor and friend, Steve Ivester—thank you for giving someone like me a chance; without your support, I would not be in student affairs. To my son, Ezra—may you find fulfillment in your work in the same way you have enriched mine. And finally, to my wife, Christina—it is always a joy to do life with you.

Britney—I dedicate this book to my Baylor colleagues. You all challenged me to think more deeply about how my faith intersects with my higher education practice, and I am better for it. Thanks for journeying through the PhD experience with me and for all the Torchy's Tacos, Korean BBQ, Starbucks, and (attempted) Magnolia Table runs for food and fellowship. I am truly thankful for your friendship.

INTRODUCTION

· ·

Student affairs functions in a rather pragmatic way here. Theory is seldom used to frame our work, and theology is also neglected.

—David, fourth-year student affairs staff member

S tudent affairs started largely as a "secular" discipline.[1] The field's founders gave only minor attention to religion and spirituality, and theological language or reasoning played no role in the development of early statements and theories that guided the field.[2] Instead, its leaders drew on other narratives to inspire and guide their outlook—particularly the secular psychological story of human development and the national political goal of educating citizens. For example, the American Council on Education's revised 1949 statement "The Student Personnel Point of View" articulated its end as "education for a fuller realization of democracy in every phase of living." For these leaders, democracy served not merely as the country's political philosophy but as a guiding philosophy for education and life. Thus, the student affairs movement claimed, "Our way of life depends upon a renewed faith in, and extensive use of, democratic methods, upon the development of more citizens to assume responsibilities in matters of social concern, and upon the active participation of millions of men and women in the enterprise of social improvement." Colleges and universities, therefore, needed to inculcate in students "a firm and enlightened belief in democracy."[3] In an increasingly religiously pluralistic higher education system, promoting democracy was an end on which all Americans could potentially agree.

For Christians, the problem with this approach is not necessarily the emphasis on supporting democracy but the fact that Christians in student affairs have a different focus. We interviewed Deborah (note that all interviewee names throughout this book will be pseudonyms), who is a vice president for student life and has worked in both state universities and Christian institutions; she shared the following with us: "The state university is forming people in a particular kind of public citizenry project. We're doing something really different. We're shaping people to be members of the body of Christ in a full mind, body, spirit holistic way. I think it's just a completely different project." Despite these different aims, Christian colleges and universities have gone about "professionalizing" their student affairs divisions by hiring professionals with newly minted master's degrees in student affairs who soaked up secular student affairs theories, frameworks, and categories intended to apply to the public citizenry project. The theorists behind these works often try to make metaphysically vacuous generalizations about the students the profession is intended to serve. They also downplay their metaphysical assumptions and usually avoid larger philosophical or theological questions about personhood, the good life, and more.[4]

But does the metaphysically barren nature of most student affairs ends, theory, and education truly matter? Of course, if "all truth is God's truth," it should be no surprise to find some professional training is often empirically factual, theoretically benign, generally "moral," and thus, helpful. As a result, one Christian student affairs professional recently told us that he fails to see any purpose or benefit to a theology of student affairs. This professional seemed to suggest that talking about Christian student affairs is as odd as talking about Christian baseball, Christian trumpet playing, or Christian fantasy writing. The fundamental practice, which in this case is caring holistically for students, is something grounded in God's good creation and therefore warrants no discussion of a distinctively Christian approach. Instead, the argument goes, we merely need Christians to pursue excellence within the student affairs field.

The problem with this outlook is that at the heart of student affairs is the student. Thus, whenever we talk about student success or caring for the whole person and fail to acknowledge that the student is made *Imago Dei*, in the image of God (Gen. 1:26–27), the whole of the discipline can become distorted. We simply cannot understand the whole student without understanding God and our relationship to God.

The Challenge

Not surprisingly, many Christian student affairs leaders (SALs) find young professionals, and their reductionistic and metaphysically meager theory base, ill prepared to work on Christian campuses.[5] In this regard, the professionalization of student affairs poses a unique challenge for Christian colleges and universities. For instance, in 1996 a study of senior student affairs officers (SSAO) at Catholic institutions produced an alarming finding for many Catholic administrators.[6] The researchers found that although the SSAOs recognized that integrating the Catholic identity and tradition into their work was an important element of their job, they struggled to accomplish this goal because "they did not have sufficient knowledge and formation to assist them in their role of interpreter of the Catholic identity of the institution in the realm of student life . . . nor did they have somewhere to go to learn."[7] To address this problem, some key faculty and SALs helped bring about a crucial initiative. In 1999 they started the Association for Student Affairs at Catholic Colleges and Universities (ASACCU), which hosted an annual conference. A follow-up study of Catholic SSAOs in 2005 discovered that, as a whole, their comfort with being interpreters of the Catholic identity of the institution had changed both significantly and positively as a result of these efforts.[8]

The study also found that "the specific approaches and strategies for mission interpretation were idiosyncratic to the resources and collaborative leadership between SSAOs and their presidents."[9] Additional critiques of student affairs at Catholic institutions also made it clear that there was a greater need for a more widely agreed upon framework for Catholic student affairs work.[10] Although frameworks from professional groups existed at that time, they never addressed the unique theological perspective and context of Catholic colleges and universities. Consequently, a group of educational leaders helped produce the *Principles of Good Practice for Student Affairs at Catholic Colleges and Universities*.[11] This resource has proved immensely successful and has garnered significant use among many Catholic campuses by both SALs as well as presidents.[12] These efforts have been further bolstered by the publication of an edited volume based on the principles of good practice.[13]

Although Protestant SALs birthed their own organization much earlier than their Catholic counterparts (i.e., the Association for Christians in Student Development started in 1980), to this day a common statement of best practices for Protestant Christian student affairs professionals does not exist. Student affairs professionals at Christian colleges have published several edited books about unique Christian approaches to student affairs,[14] but these volumes were not meant to offer a comprehensive theological vision. Our project, therefore, seeks to address this void. The specific purpose of our overall study is to determine how Christianity animates the practice of student affairs professionals at Christian colleges and universities.

Part of this task involved examining the literature Christian scholar-practitioners authored over the past three decades that sets forth what might be different or unique about a distinctively Christian approach to student affairs. Chapter Three is an overview of our findings from this literature. The ambitious purpose of the study behind this book is to try to join these redemptive efforts to redeem student affairs from its metaphysically vapid roots.

The bulk of our effort involved the use of mixed methods research to explore and analyze the best thinking and practice within the field of Christian student affairs. We undertook two different surveys with close to four hundred total participants from seventy-one institutions and interviewed more than seventy student affairs staff from forty-three different institutions to discover answers to our major questions (see Appendix B). We then analyzed the responses from a biblical and theological framework to find the strengths and possible limits of our findings. Then, compiling the various pieces, we constructed collective visions for the many facets of Christian student affairs. In addition to representing the best of the field, these collective visions allowed us to see if there was anything missing.

Finally, we formulated a set of principles based on our findings that can help guide Christian student affairs practice. We then distributed these principles to various leaders in Christian student affairs to obtain their feedback. After their input, we refined the principles for this publication (see Appendix A).

In the end, we hope that this effort will help student affairs practitioners imagine and live in light of the overall biblical vision. David I. Smith and James K. A. Smith highlight the importance of theological imagination for the work of teachers, and we think their insight also applies to the work of Christian student affairs. They quote an illustration from Etienne Wenger:

> Two stonecutters . . . are asked what they are doing. One responds: "I am cutting the stone in a perfectly square shape." The other responds: "I am building a cathedral." Both answers are correct and meaningful, in that they reflect different relations to the world. The difference between these answers does not imply that one is a better stonecutter than the other, as far as holding the chisel is concerned. At the level of engagement, they may well be doing exactly the same thing, but it does suggest that their experiences of what they are doing and their sense of self and doing it are rather different. The difference is a function of the imagination. As a result, they may be learning very different things from the same activity.[15]

In a similar manner, we think theological vision is vitally important for the way student affairs professionals imagine their craft. Are we primarily helping students become autonomous self-authors, or are we helping students who image and represent God to glorify him by seeking to build his kingdom? How we imagine our task makes all the difference in the world.

The Task at Hand

So why imagine our task as "Christ-enlivening student affairs?" I (Perry) have argued elsewhere that we need to abandon the phrase "the integration of faith and learning" for three reasons.[16] First, we are made in God's image to join with God in his creative and redemptive work. Yet, theologically speaking, God does not go about integrating faith and learning. Our need to integrate faith and learning stems *not* from our imitation of God's actions in the world, but our human limitations—our lack of omniscience and our fallenness. Our highest calling as educators involves imitating Christ by creating and redeeming in our area of calling.

Second, the phrase "integration of faith and learning" downplays our need to focus on creating learners and learning. The phrase was developed when it was unclear how most of the learning being created in pluralistic universities related to a Christian worldview; therefore, Christians had to focus on integration. Yet this emphasis neglects the fact that we also need to create our own learners and learning, as well as create our own colleges and universities to do so.

Third, asking how one integrates faith into music or engineering sounds like a difficult question. For example, what is Christian jazz? Phrasing our task this way neglects the fact that creative excellence is just as important as redeeming image bearers of God. To create great jazz is to bear God's image. To create a residential life community of character where fun, fellowship, and deep learning occurs is to bear God's image.

To counter these deficiencies, I have offered other phrases such as "the creation and redemption of learners and learning"[17] and "faith animating learning."[18] Regarding the former, I have come to agree with one reviewer who simply said that the phrase is just too clunky. Plus, I think the phrase ignores the important role of God's ultimate restoration in the Christian story. Finally, I concluded that the most important reason for the problem with both "the integration of faith and learning" and "faith animating learning" is that the phrase leaves out Christ. Christ is the one who makes all wisdom that humans learn come alive, whether through creation (John 1:1–3; Col. 1:15–17), redemption (Col. 1:18–22), or in the final restoration of God's kingdom where all knowledge will be revealed (1 Cor. 13:12; Rev. 19–21). This side of heaven, we know most fully through Christ, and even once we gain wisdom, we need Christ's Spirit to give us the strength to live into and out of what Christ has made alive, which includes our own thinking, affections, will, and behavior.

That's why we think we need to start talking about "Christ enlivening" or "Christ animating" (we will use the two phrases interchangeably) when we talk about whatever aspect of the academic world needs to be enriched or improved. Even the best of all our integration efforts are dead without the enlivening work of Christ, who brings them to life. Christ is behind the creation of great jazz (no matter who composes or plays it), the redemption of fallen residential communities, and our ultimate hope that God and not science or some new political arrangement will be our coming savior when it comes to creation, justice, or eternal love. Thus, we need to explore what it means for Christ to animate student affairs.

The Audience and Scope of the Book

This book is meant for three audiences. First, we are writing for current Christian student affairs professionals throughout higher education. This audience includes both those working in Christian institutions and those in pluralistic institutions. Second, we are writing for students in student affairs programs who wish to learn about a Christian vision for student affairs. Finally, we are writing for those curious about what this unique vision might look like.

The book is organized into five parts. Part One draws upon our surveys to examine who we are as student affairs staff and how we develop and care for one another. One of our findings is that the development of staff in the area of what has traditionally been called "integration of faith and learning" is vital. Hiring Christian staff members does not ensure that they are competent in this skill. Part Two then provides an overview of the literature regarding what it means for Christ to animate student affairs. We undertake this overview in order to obtain the building blocks for a richer theology of student affairs.

Part Three then draws on our surveys and interviews to address the whole Christian student affairs field and examine the answers participants gave regarding the fundamental questions that any approach to education must answer: (1) *Who* are we trying to help students become? (2) *Why* are we doing this? In other words, what are our ends? (3) *What* is the curriculum and the substantive wisdom regarding the truth, goodness, and beauty we hope to teach students? (4) *How* are we doing it? Part Four moves to specific operational areas within student affairs, such as residence life and student conduct. Part Five then addresses important topics within student affairs, such as race and sexuality. We will close with a conclusion that draws out the themes—both strengths and opportunities for the field—we saw throughout our research. Our proposed "Principles of Good Practice" (Appendix A) draws on these themes and attempts to summarize our findings in a way that makes them readily accessible and practically applicable for practitioners.

PART ONE

Christ-Enlivened Student Affairs Staff

"What makes your student affairs practice *Christian*?" This was one of the questions that we asked our seventy interviewees. Here are the first lines of some responses:

- That's a great question. [**pause**] Yeah, that's a good question . . .
- That's a tricky question.
- Your question is so good, because what makes it Christian [**pause**] I think [**pause**] is what [**pause**] . . .
- That's a good question. I think [**pause**] it's telling that I'm pausing here. [**pause**] I think it says a lot . . .

As is often the case, there is much said in the unsaid; we think the pauses of these interviewees speak volumes. These opening lines, the likes of which were surprisingly common, seemed to suggest that many Christian student affairs leaders (SALs) had not given much thought about how their faith identity might animate, inform, or shape their professional identity.

Fortunately, a host of additional riches lie in the previously unstudied thinking and practice of the professionals themselves. The collection of experiences, thoughts, and expertise we have the privilege of sharing has been honed by years of practice—countless conversations with students, conduct hearings, staff meetings, and certainly more than a few lessons learned the hard way.

To organize what we found, we rely on a framework we use throughout the book that helps us classify the various responses we received and, ultimately, construct an appropriately complex picture of how Christ enlivens student affairs (see Figure I.1).

Figure I.1. The Christian Student Affairs Imagination

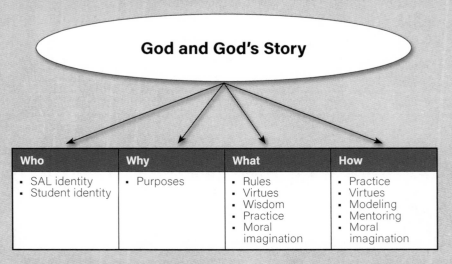

The model is structured around the basic questions included in any educational philosophy. Under an overarching animating narrative (the narrative of God and God's story), we want to know *who* is doing the teaching and *who* SALs want their students to become, *why* SALs are doing what they do, *what* is the nature of the content that SALs attempt to impart, and *how* do SALs go about imparting it? Under each of these questions, we have included sub-elements that help construct the larger categories. For example, to better understand *what* SALs seek to impart, we need to know not only the rules and restrictions they impose, but also the virtues, wisdom, and moral imagination they seek to cultivate in their students and in themselves. This book explores this model at length because we believe it is not enough to merely know the means of carrying out student affairs practice. As SALs, we must also understand the who, why, and what that informs those means.

1

WHO ARE WE?

Understanding Our Christian and Professional Identities

If we don't have a concept of who we are,
it's really hard for us to care for others.

—Aubree

All that we do centers on first being the people
of God in order to do the work of God.

—Cindy

One of the most curious things about the New Testament epistles is how they begin. Paul and the other writers consistently seek to help early Christians understand who they are "in Christ" before they can realize how to act as Christians. Thus, the first parts of most epistles, such as Romans, Galatians, Ephesians, Philippians, Colossians, 1 and 2 Thessalonians, do not contain commands. Instead, the opening chapters discuss the identity and work of God through Christ and our identity in light of this reality. Only later do the authors instruct us how to live in light of that identity. This approach is like what the Christian student affairs leaders (SALs) quoted above say. Before talking about the practical ways Christ animates student affairs, we want to take a similar approach in this chapter by first exploring who we are as both professionals and Christians.

Routes into the Profession

If we *really* want to get to know someone, we ask the person about their story. When my wife and I (Perry) were dating long-distance (she's

Canadian and we met in Russia), to get to know each other we shared cassette tapes on which we recounted to each other our life story up to that point. Narratives reveal an important core of who we are.

It helps to start at the beginning, so in order to understand the professional identity of our SAL interviewees, we asked them about how they became professionals. We heard a lot of stories like this one:

> Growing up, people asked me what I wanted to do, and I would just say, "I want to help people." I always kind of felt a little bit foolish that that was my answer, because it just wasn't a profession, right? It was like, "I want to be a doctor. I want to be a teacher." Whatever. But even as I got to college, my undergrad is in family psychology, and realized I didn't want to go necessarily into counseling, per se, but I liked investing in the lives of people, supporting them, challenging them, pushing them to be better, walking with them in the highs and lows of life. Always have had a little bit of a pastoral bent toward me and so, yeah, somebody said to me, as a freshman, "I think you'd make a good RA." I'm like, "You really think so?" So, I did that for three years and after . . . didn't really have a certain job I wanted to do, so I applied to work as an admissions counselor at my alma mater. So, I did that for about a year and a half, almost two. Transitioned into residence life, was an RD, for five years.

Like the story above, more than half of our participants described their route as "unusual," "circuitous," or a "winding road." Andrew, a vice president of student affairs, theorized about the route into Christian student affairs further: "It's a funny path. I was just telling somebody yesterday, because I teach in our higher ed program at [institution]. And I often will tell our young professionals, 'Everyone has a different path [into] this calling.' I really do think it's a calling to embrace. And so, I didn't graduate from my undergrad with a student affairs degree. Nobody does." To Andrew, the diverse routes into the field reflect the uniqueness of the calling. This calling, as Andrew noted, is not one that has a home during undergraduate education.

As a result, it is no wonder student affairs professionals come from a variety of different disciplinary backgrounds. As professionals described their training in our interviews, they referenced eleven different disciplines, ranging from "higher education" or "student affairs" to less related disciplines like a "master's degree in exercise science" or "architecture." Most interview participants had degrees related to student affairs/higher education (41 percent) or Christian education/ministry (34 percent).

The diversity of educational backgrounds is revealed in our larger survey. Though we did not ask survey participants to indicate the field of their degree, the degrees themselves and the institutions at which they were earned indicate a diversity of training. Most survey participants were working in Christian student affairs with either a bachelor's degree (30 percent) or a master's degree (49 percent). Seventy percent of these participants (working with a bachelor's or master's degree) received their degree from a faith-based institution. The next largest block of degrees were participants who were working with some form of a doctorate (13 percent). Of those with a doctorate, just under half (49 percent) were earned at a faith-based institution. A final point worth noting is the number of professionals with non-higher-education professional degrees—5 percent were trained in a seminary or divinity school and 2 percent were trained in a business school.

Motivations for Entry

Without a single pathway into student affairs, what *does* lead people to the field? Analysis of the interviews and survey responses revealed professionals were motivated to become SALs for a variety of altruistic, personal, and faith-based reasons. It should be noted that the categories are not mutually exclusive—many professionals mentioned reasons that fell into multiple categories.

First, when asked about what motivated them, the majority of SALs indicated they were motivated by the opportunity to develop students. One survey participant described Christian student affairs as "almost entirely focused on developing people." Mary, a director of student engagement, articulated a similar purpose: "This is what it's all about. It's all about the students for me . . . to see them grow. . . . It's very fulfilling." For Mary, it was the opportunity to develop students that brought her role a sense of significance. Participants did not always use the word "development."

Others described Christian student affairs in the following ways: "bringing out the potential in people," "for transformation," "trying to mold . . . young men and women," "identity formation," or "cognitive development." Matthew summed up these sentiments well: "I just find that to be a really ripe time to do some fun work with them about growth and identity and other stuff." Regardless of the language used, a significant percentage of SALs were motivated by a desire to develop students.

Others focused less on the development of students and emphasized that it was a general desire to help others that motivated their work. Participants made statements like, "I knew I wanted to help others" or "I like helping people." Others talked about a desire to work in the "helping professions," a desire to "give back" or to "serve" subpopulations within higher education. Lisa fleshed out the motivation to help or serve others a bit more fully:

> Within six months [of working in Christian student affairs], I realized, "Oh my goodness, this is my home. This is my profession. This is what I want to have as my career." . . . In my undergrad, I was a communications major, public relations, advertising, and then business minor. I thought I was going into HR—something definitely serving people—but I thought I was going into human resources or a hospital or something. What I found is that I could use the desire to serve people, but I could serve college students. It's a great mix to feel like I can be in the ministry but yet be in a profession that's not traditionally in the church walls.

Here Lisa references her varied undergraduate degrees, her desire to work with people, and her desire to work in ministry. Her quote reflects many of the stories we heard in our interviews. Participants shared that they saw Christian student affairs as an opportunity to draw together the seemingly disparate strands of their backgrounds and beliefs into a single role.

Second, most participants indicated at least some of their motivation came from experiences during their own undergraduate lives. When asked what motivated her to work in student affairs, Natalie said her involvement with "orientation programs" led to "some of the most formative

experiences in [her] collegiate career." Robert, a chief student affairs officer, recounted his transformative undergrad experience in greater depth:

> I did not like my first year of college at [institution] . . . a small
> school. I was not a huge fan of campus life at the time, and I was
> just struggling with my transition. I had a director of residence
> life pull me aside during the spring semester and say, "Listen,
> I know you were involved in peer education in high school.
> Have you thought about applying for our peer education group
> here?" I had not considered it, but with that invitation, I took
> her advice. I applied for it and ended up being on the steering
> committee my sophomore year, and my student affairs expe-
> rience just kind of blew up from there. So, it was really that
> conversation, that care, that she knew who I was, and that she
> understood, probably saw that I had not gotten involved yet, and
> made that outreach to me when she really didn't have to. So, that
> moment kind of sparked me, because I think it really shaped
> a lot of who I was in college. I wanted to serve in that way for
> other college students.

Even those who had a negative interaction with student affairs were, in
turn, drawn to the field. Melissa, who now serves as a dean, described the
process of losing her leadership position as an RA:

> [The] process of being held accountable for my mistakes and how
> the staff at my institution, my RD, and the upper administration
> walked me through that process with incredible love and care,
> but also that firm hand of justice was there, and that account-
> ability—it radically transformed my own view on what it meant
> to be a person of integrity. My view on the balance of justice and
> grace and how they're needed hand in hand . . . that was really
> the impetus after I graduated. I just said I want to be able to have
> the kind of impact on college students that they had on me.

In numerous stories like these, the implication was just as Melissa and
Robert shared—because of the significance of their student experience,

the professionals hoped to take part in offering transformative experiences to future students.

Third, several participants also shared that their motivation stemmed from a realization that their personal gifting aligned with the nature of the work. Thus, they viewed their work as a "calling" or as an avenue to "steward" their "giftings." Rose, a vice president for student affairs, shared how her spiritual gifting aligned with her roles: "When I was [a residence director], I did a lot of shepherding. As a VP, I did a lot of administration. Always leadership. So, it's really a gift-match." Such an articulation infers a specific understanding of the nature of Christian student affairs. When describing how student affairs allowed him to use his pastoral gifts, Jaxon claimed that SALs are the "pastoral staff for campus." In addition to an avenue to utilize pastoral giftings, Michael, a director of student activities, suggested that student affairs also allowed him to utilize his "passion for diversity and inclusion . . . [and] developing leaders."

Finally, most participants indicated that their practice was in some way motivated by their faith, but only a few highlighted it as the primary motivation for entering the field. Those who did list faith as a primary motivation did so in two main ways. The first group described Christian student affairs as a place to enact faith-informed practice. For example, Mark, a dean of student affairs, suggested it was the idea of "relational based ministry" that drew him to the field. Emma, a residence director, described how she was drawn to the field because of the opportunity to integrate "student care and spiritual formation." The integrative nature of Christian student affairs was also reflected in Ryan's comments, who suggested he was motivated to enter the field because it gave him the opportunity "to work with college students in that crucible of faith and life and learning. [It] helped them to wrestle with where they're at and what they feel, and how they're going to respond to that in the world that we live in. And how to do that in a Christ-honoring and Christ-centered way."

A second group saw Christian student affairs as an avenue to serve God. George, a senior director, saw his practice as an opportunity to "serve Jesus with [his] whole heart." A survey participant stated as much and more when he shared his motivation this way: "I desire to do my work excellently as unto Christ. It impacts the way I see students and my role in their lives and the overall community of the institution." In general, faith provided motivation for entry by way of opening opportunities to see students in increasingly integrated ways and providing a sense that the work was done in the service of God.

Overall, for a field that lacks a singular pathway, there was a surprising amount of overlap in the described motivations for entering the field. Our participants revealed a collective belief that the Christian student affairs identity involves the opportunity to serve God by using personal giftings to cultivate significant experiences for students in order to develop students in Christian ways.

Describing Ourselves

In addition to storytelling, another way to get to know someone is by listening to how they describe themselves. In our surveys, we sought to listen to how SALs characterized their Christian and professional identities.

Christian Identity

Those of us who identify as Christian are not simply Christians. We often describe our Christian identities in more specific ways, such as an association with a particular tradition or denomination. Thus, we asked survey participants to identify which of these associations they would choose for themselves (see Table 1.1). We found that participants tended to choose terms that were more generic in nature—such as "Evangelical," "born again," or "Bible-believing"—rather than a specific denominational label. In fact, only a sixth (17 percent) chose a specific denominational label.

Table 1.1. Self-description of survey participants ($N = 219$)

Description	%
Evangelical	24
Born again	24
Other—denominational identity	17
Bible-believing	14
Theologically liberal	10
Mainline Protestant	6

Description	%
Theologically conservative	4
Charismatic	1

When we asked SALs to identify a more specific theological affiliation, they demonstrated significant diversity (see Table 1.2). The largest groups of SALs in our sample shared that they came from a Baptist (19 percent) or generically "Evangelical" background (19 percent). This breakdown largely reflects the breakdown of institutional denominational affiliation within the Council for Christian Colleges and Universities (CCCU).[1]

Table 1.2. Theological traditions of survey participants (*N* = 234)

Tradition	%
Baptist	19
Evangelical	19
Other	15
Reformed	13
Wesleyan	11
Anabaptist	8
Churches of Christ	5
Pentecostal/Charismatic	5
Anglican	3
Catholic	2
Lutheran	2

Statistical analyses revealed a few significant differences between those who identified with certain intellectual traditions, specifically regarding views about the role Christian student affairs should play in helping students learn citizenship by cultivating justice and righteousness in society. Those in the Anabaptist tradition rated this distinctive of student affairs practices significantly higher than others—especially over and above the Evangelical, Baptist, Reformed, and Wesleyan traditions. Though less statistically significant, we saw other ways that professionals choose distinctives reflecting their faith traditions as well. For example, those from the Baptist and Church of Christ traditions had the highest church involvement (an aggregate score comprising church attendance, small groups, etc.). Those from Catholic and Lutheran traditions had the lowest involvement by these metrics.

Despite identifying with a variety of theological traditions, the SALs we examined also indicated a high degree of association with what scholars label *orthodox* Christianity—someone who adheres to certain basic beliefs associated with what C. S. Lewis called "mere Christianity."[2] In our quantitative survey, virtually all SALs indicated theological beliefs consistent with historic Christian teaching. Nearly 90 percent of our survey participants affirmed the Bible as the inspired Word of God. Similarly, more than 90 percent of participants indicated they believed in at least the probable existence of heaven (99 percent), hell (93 percent), Satan (95 percent), and angels (98 percent). Finally, more than 95 percent of participants indicated that Christ is the only source of salvation.

We also asked about our most fundamental theological identity as humans—being made in God's image (Gen. 1:26–27). All participants agreed (and 97 percent strongly agreed) that "all human beings, regardless of their race or ethnicity, are made in the image of God." Although this affirmation of bearing God's image is not surprising, it tended to have a rather narrow use. Throughout our interviews and surveys, the *Imago Dei* was most frequently used with reference to two issues. First, some SALs drew upon it when discussing diversity on campus, such as in these two cases:

- *Interviewer:* "OK, and how do you think faith and a Christian worldview inform your institution's approach to diversity? Specifically, with racial and ethnic diversity."
  Interviewee: "Oh, well, I mean, our biblical worldview is that we are all created in the image of God, and that's all there is to it. That's how I understand it."
- "If you say you and I are both created in the image of God and you really mean that, and you take the time to think, 'What's the impact of that? If my African American sister really is the image of God, I can't look at her the way this group of people would say you've got to look at her.' Yeah. You just can't. You know?"

Second, this theological reference also came up when asked, "How does your faith inform your response to issues related to sexuality on campus?" Numerous participants mentioned answers such as the following:

- "I believe we were all created in the image of God, and God created us male or female."
- "We attempt to proactively communicate a biblical view of being created in the image of God, which includes sexuality. *Many* things are a departure from that ideal, not simply X or Y trending social issue."
- "We have the obligation to see the image of God in all his people and not focus exclusively on any one aspect of identity in determining our worth, our sinfulness, our ability to be part of God's body or part of his plan."
- "I believe that all people are made in the image of God and are loved by God. I use this overarching narrative to inform my approach and grace the language I use."

Interestingly, only one participant in our interviews or surveys mentioned this identity when answering the question "What makes your student affairs practice Christian?" We believe this indicates an underutilization of this foundational understanding of the human person.

To summarize, when it comes to one's faith-based identity, although there is a wide variety of Christian identity diversity regarding general labels or specific faith traditions, Christian SALs clearly identify as orthodox Christians who view everyone as made in God's image.

Professional Identity

In our survey, we asked Christian SALs to choose from a variety of words to identify themselves (e.g., administrator, advocate, coach, counselor, educator, friend, lawyer, mentor, pastor, other). Participants could choose two different identities. Considering the various ways that participants entered the field, we thought it would help to clarify how they thought about their role. Table 1.3 provides the percentages of individuals who chose a particular identity.

Table 1.3. What identity best approximates the nature of your job? (*N* = 247)

Identity	%
Administrator	53
Mentor	33
Educator	21
Counselor	13
Advocate	12
Coach	12
Pastor	10
Other (e.g., advisor, shepherd)	6
Friend	5
Lawyer	0

Clearly, Christian SALs see themselves as functioning less in a pastoral role—a more traditional approach to early Christian student affairs—and more as an administrator, mentor, and educator.

These answers reveal the difficulty of answering the question, "What do you do for a living?" or "What are you studying?" Perhaps you have an answer you feel good about—I (Ted) never did. I knew the importance of our work, but I did not have a succinct way to describe the range of work that we do, nor how our faith might make it *distinctive.* My replies, and those of my colleagues, generally resembled a rambling mess about how we are administrators, but we do not just enforce policy; we help oversee student events, but we are not just party planners; and we mentor students, but we are not counselors or pastors. The lack of coherence in my responses reflected a crisis of identity—perhaps yours does too. I knew what I was supposed to *do* as a SAL, but I did not know who I was supposed to *be.* I did not have an identity big enough to encompass the entirety of my work. Moreover, there were times where it seemed that my Christian convictions seemed to conflict with stated "best practices" of the field. Thus, before we can answer the question of *who* we are, we must discern how to merge and prioritize our Christian and professional identities.

Merging and Prioritizing Identities

To merge and prioritize identities, we must first clarify how we are using the term. Identity is one of those concepts that feels easy enough to grasp but evades complete understanding. Part of the confusion stems from the multiple ways the word "identity" is used (e.g., psychological identity is distinct from sociological identity, which overlaps with but is also distinct from moral identity). For the purposes of this book, we will focus on moral identity. In this understanding, to have an identity means one inherits a moral narrative, an end, and the whole tradition of thought about reaching that end.[3] For example, when a person identifies with the moral identity of "administrator," they inherit the whole tradition regarding beliefs about what constitutes a "good" administrator. The same could be said about identities like Christian, parent, neighbor, student, spouse, or citizen.

The tough work of moral formation happens in two ways regarding these moral identities. First, one must learn what it means to be good in a specific identity (e.g., a good student affairs professional, a good parent, a good spouse). Second, we must learn to merge different identities and prioritize specific identities in places where they come into conflict (e.g., one could simultaneously be a daughter and a wife, and have to choose at times between being a good daughter or good wife).

The task of merging identities is something that takes the kind of theological and moral imagination described in our Introduction. One way we think that merging can be done is to take basic professional identities and reframe them using theological identities. For example, if more than half of the SALs we surveyed think of themselves as "administrators," we would suggest that they be taught to see themselves as how God views us in Genesis 1:26–30, as *stewards* of creation. SALs are charged by God with stewarding higher education students, money, facilities, ideas, and more. We found two SALs who already drew upon this identity in these two areas:

- *Students*: "We're entrusted with the responsibility of stewarding what has been given to us by the student, by the family, by the parents. We have the responsibility to use our best gifts to be a conduit for the Holy Spirit to do work."

- *Resources*: "You can find it hard to find resources allocated to you. But what that does—and I've done this intentionally over the last five years with student affairs—is to say, 'What do we need?' And sometimes it is pizza parties. I mean, we do need those things. So it wasn't that we just cut out fun. But what do we need? And how do we take the resources that we're charged with stewarding and use those to the best of our ability? And so, if I'm sitting here with ten chief student development officers, I'm wanting us to be honest with our budgets and say, 'What are you all doing, and can we do this better?' Because I'm figuring things out, but I'm sure I could probably reallocate and do things better."

We contend that the identity of a steward needs to be one of the foremost identities for Christian SALs who are made in God's image. In fact, both identities (steward and image bearer) come from the very beginning of the Christian story in Genesis 1.

We also think that Christian SALs should think of themselves less as educators and mentors, and more of disciples of Christ who educate and mentor students as part of the discipleship process. Doing so situates these important but lesser identities within the context and story of our greatest identity as disciples of Christ. This identity comes from the Great Commission (Matt. 28:18–20) and helps reorient us to Christ's life, work, and story.

Does being oriented to this identity sound too theological or unrelatable? In a focus group with student affairs vice presidents, we heard a related conversation about whether student affairs work is discipleship. We found that a few wanted to use words that would be more acceptable in a pluralistic context instead of "discipleship," although they still understood their task theologically. One noted they use "whole purpose formation," although theologically it just means "sanctification. We're fellow partners with the Holy Spirit in the sanctification of our student's lives—in our lives." Still another chimed in that although they might talk about discipleship ten years ago, today they talk about "human flourishing." One also noted they use

> Christian identity formation. . . . I think that makes Christian
> student development distinctly different from the church. My
> concern is if we use discipleship, it further confuses students
> about "You said you're not the church, but you're kind of doing
> all the same stuff, and you use the same language." I think, to
> me, we do draw on more than just Scripture, we do draw on
> research, and the church isn't necessarily doing that. My pastor
> quotes research once in a while from the pulpit, but I think what
> we're drawing on is more than just discipleship.

Yet there was also a defender of discipleship language, who mentioned, "We've doubled down on this language. We're getting ready to launch our next strategic plan, and it's all under the heading of discipleship. So that's academic affairs, student development, that's athletics. We do see discipleship as that core thing we're doing. That it would encompass flourishing. It would encompass those sanctifying kinds of things. . . . I don't think discipleship, in my current understanding of it, is exclusive to the church." In our own view, we believe that Christian identity formation should be part of discipleship, because discipleship for Christians encompasses all of life. Whether it is a Christian chemist encouraging a PhD student entering the same field or a college minister talking with a student about anxiety, we contend that it all involves a form of mentorship we think Christian SALs should label *discipleship*. Importantly, SALs should also see themselves and identify as disciples of Christ.

Why Identity Matters

What is the benefit of understanding our Christian and professional identities and how they might be merged? We believe this understanding is important to share for three reasons. First, it helps us clarify what identities related to "Christian" and "student affairs professional" unite and divide us. It is important to remember that although our student affairs work and certain orthodox Christian beliefs unite us, our unique backgrounds and beliefs lead to a variety of approaches within our field. These approaches cannot be separated from the identities and backgrounds associated with each professional. We found that these distinctions are often shared among professionals at the same institutions, but—as Erin notes—this is not always the case: "My university is not denominationally set in some things, so it's very fluid. So, we have people from all different denominations coming in, which is great because it makes it eclectic and it really helps us serve our students well. But when we really don't know where the university falls, we all kind of are coming at it from different practices and different assumptions about God and ethics, and what students should be doing and what they shouldn't be doing and so it does create confusion." Erin's comment highlights an important point we want to affirm. Every SAL is a unique person made in the image of God who brings with him or her a unique set of identities, beliefs, and life experiences that will affect the core assumptions they bring to their student affairs practice. Thus, a value we find in understanding this data is to remind each other that we each have our own assumptions about the nature and function of our role. Although it is tempting to avoid conflict in pursuit of homogeneity, a homogeneity at the level of practices only is a shallow unity. Instead, we believe further development of our field will require and benefit from continued (sometimes contentious) dialogue about these foundational identities and how to merge them.

Second, regarding professional identity, over half of SALs have received degrees in higher education and/or student affairs, usually at faith-based institutions. Our data indicates that many of these professionally trained staff see themselves as administrators, mentors, and educators and not as pastors or friends. It is possible that this self-perception might reflect a disconnect between a faith identity and a professional identity if the professional identities are not placed in the Christian story. Therefore, our field would benefit from thinking about how Christ might enliven student affairs by discussing what Christian administrating, educating, and mentoring involve. We have suggested that this discussion might entail relabeling these identities as "stewarding" and "discipling" to connect more overtly with the biblical narrative.

Finally, this information bears reporting because, to our knowledge, it is the first time our field has been the focus of extensive scholarly research. As such, these metrics serve as an initial baseline measurement of the makeup of our field. We hope future research can continue to clarify the demographics, beliefs, and identities—as well as their implications—with increasing precision.

Conclusion

This chapter has provided some of the context of the individuals who comprise the Christian SAL community, but a moral identity is composed of more than "who"; it also includes the why, what, and how of Christian student affairs practice. How does our Christian identity interact with our identity as Christian student affairs professionals in *practice*? These are the questions we take up in the remaining chapters. Our hope is that by the end of this book, you will have not only a more thoughtful response to the question of what makes your student affairs practice *Christian* but also a better understanding of how Christianity forms your professional identity. When we take the time to renovate our mental models, we expand our imagination for what a good Christian SAL looks like and are thereby better equipped to respond in the heat of the moment.[4] We believe this to be truth whether the heated moment is a student crisis, a defense of your work to a senior administrator, or the question "What do you do for a living?"

2

DEVELOPING THE DEVELOPERS
Caring for the Souls of Student Affairs Leaders

*To me, the care of the staff is pivotal. If my staff is not well,
they're not in a good place. If they don't have what they
need to be effective and impactful, then we can open the
doors to damage all day. You can do that—it happens.*

—Wesley

One thing that helps or hinders our development is how those around us tend to our souls. Any great institution cares for its employees and seeks to develop them. One would hope that Christian student affairs leaders (SALs) would care deeply about the souls of their colleagues (like Wesley) and that their institutions would dominate the *Chronicle of Higher Education's* list of "Great Colleges to Work For." Yet we also know that Christian institutions emphasizing sacrificial love and care for students may neglect and fail to develop those staff or faculty who are doing the caring and loving. For instance, we experienced this exchange with Paige:

> *How would you say your institution supports the Christian for-
> mation of employees in general?* I don't think they do. *Would you
> care to elaborate on that at all?* The demands on us are so signif-
> icant that even taking time to go to chapel is almost impossible.
> When I visit classrooms, I'm always overjoyed that professors

almost universally pray at the beginning of class, and yet that rarely happens in meetings. I think my boss has prayed for me twice in the three years I've reported to her. If we have a meal, sometimes. No one ever asks me where my faith journey is. And I, honestly, am not great about asking my team that—probably because it's not ever really been modeled for me. So, I haven't done that well.

This response is a travesty within the context of Christian higher education.

So, what is the current state of care and professional development among Christians in student affairs? This chapter answers this question, discusses some of the care practices SALs have found helpful, and then engages in some critical theological reflections about both the lack of care and the kinds of care being offered.

We should start by saying excellent professional practice, such as quality annual reviews, consistent challenge and support, clear communication regarding expectations or failures, and more, are all important elements of Christian soul care and professional development. However, this chapter does not focus on the best practices of professional development one might find on any pluralistic campus. Instead, we sought to identify the unique forms of professional development at Christian institutions that enlarge the scope of care beyond purely professional competence. We focus on four things: (1) the "two-spheres" model that some SALs experience, (2) the soul care of student affairs staff—the tending to their inner spiritual life, (3) the development of a Christian vision for how Christ animates student learning, and (4) the areas SALs highlighted for improvement.

The Two-Spheres Model of Student Affairs

On the curricular side of Christian higher education, scholars have written about what some have called the "two-spheres" model of Christian higher education.[1] In this model, faith and learning are kept separate. Thus, while Christian piety may be encouraged through chapel, prayer, devotions before class, and other symbolic actions, the classroom content remains similar to what one finds at a state school. One of the greatest surprises found in our results was that a different kind of two-spheres model exists in student affairs. When we asked the question "How would you say your institution supports the Christian formation of employees in general?," *one-third* of our interviewees gave answers such as the following:

- "Hmm. Pass. [pause] It's not really built into the culture where I'm at. It could be; it's just they have not done it."
- "Honestly, I don't know. I don't know that I've really seen [my institution] doing anything specifically for the spiritual development of their employees. I can't think of . . . [pause] Honestly, nothing comes to mind."
- "It doesn't really. [pause] [Our institution] kind of leaves people up to do things on their own. So, there's no intentional work, or there are no intentional initiatives to support people with spiritual formation."
- "Not as much as I would expect from an institution so closely tied with the church . . ."
- "So, besides our HR interview when we first came in, where they asked your statement of faith, I have never been asked about my church commitment or my involvement or any of that."
- "I don't feel they do. [pause] There seems like there's no intentionality of helping and faith-building, and there are no resources really. [pause] I think even, in that, if you were to question your faith or to go through a period of lack of faith, I think that would be looked at pretty poorly."

We found it noteworthy that participants from institutions with higher academic reputations more commonly thought their institutions failed to give attention to soul care. Overall, this group received the impression from their bosses that matters of soul care should be left to the church and that SALs at Christian institutions should be busy with the professional work of caring for students.

These findings made us wonder: Is the professionalization of Christian student affairs staff undermining the pastoral nature of professional development that involves soul care practices like listening to each other and speaking theologically into each other's lives? Emma, a SAL at a strong academic institution, thought so: "I actually feel there's a fear about the faith within professional settings in some ways . . . so I think we used to be really ministerial, really relational, and it's like we need to become more educational, more professional, which means less sharing, less praying together." Ultimately, Emma felt like the message communicated was the "two-spheres" message: "We are not the ministry or spiritual formation department, and so we need to isolate that." In other words, leave the ministry and soul care to the ministry professionals, whether it is the church or the campus pastor or chaplain.

Of course, not all participants had this experience. Two-thirds of our participants talked about various ways they or their institutions care for the souls of SALs. For those wanting to improve in this area, what could we learn from these institutions or SALs? We found a wide range of answers.

A Christian Vision for Soul Care

Motivation makes all the difference in the world when caring for and finding strength to care for students. A central motivation for Christian SALs was their echoing of the main theme in 2 Corinthians 5:14–15: "Christ's love compels us." Richard related, "As I think about the individuals in my department, same at [my institution], every one of them, faith backgrounds are different but every one of them loves Jesus at the core of their being. He is their reason for doing what they're doing." In addition, SALs also found motivation in knowing that they are not alone in their work. They are joining with God. We found some SALs asked questions of their staff that revealed this central motivation for caring for students. Emily, who works in residence life, described this kind of conversation:

> We love the girls, but why do we love the girls? It's because we love the Lord and we love people. So, just kind of always centering it back to what we're actually doing here, we love Jesus, and because we love Jesus we then can love other people—not just the people being the focus but Jesus. Jesus is the focus. That's where our worship lies. Because of that, everything else will flow from that—when you're in a healthy place. I've found myself in nonhealthy situations where it's like people-focused, you know? I can get off track.

Part of caring for Christian SALs involves healthy and transparent conversations like these, which serve to reorient and reorder our work from a focus on ourselves or our students to a focus on the character and work of the Triune God.

In our analysis, we also found a range of key practices that foster this refocusing. Resisting the two-spheres temptation often came about through taking time to implement various spiritual practices or liturgies.[2]

Spiritual Formation Reading Groups

Cali talked about how her staff sought to get to know each other in ways that stretched beyond the professional context:

> If we aren't able to know each other's families, if we aren't able to really know the real you outside of work, it's really hard to have those honest conversations when we're mandated to. I can speak from experience to know when I speak to my boss, it's harder for me to open up about something if she is unaware or if I don't feel comfortable. So, I think that's something that really plays in both for professional and student staff; if we don't have opportunities to live alongside one another, or just to experience the real person, then the opportunities for us to really challenge one another theologically are much narrower.

How did SALs foster that type of authentic communication that reached beyond their professional selves? She pointed to one important practice: "I think something that helps us is when we do both separate and together Bible studies, book studies, something biblically based, so that we have opportunities to really wrestle with it together." She was certainly not alone. In fact, numerous SALs pointed to this practice as enriching their professional and spiritual lives.

One common method SALs employed to foster spiritual conversations, and hopefully growth among staff, was to read a book every semester or at least once an academic year. Ryan mentioned how his reading group moved beyond mere intellectual discussion. They were reading *Making of an Ordinary Saint* by Nathan Foster as a staff and discussing various spiritual disciplines. Yet they would do more than discuss: "We'll talk about it a week, we'll practice it for a week, and then we'll come back at our next staff meeting [and] talk about, 'What was that like for you? How did that work? Was it something that you really engaged with well? Did you wait until last night to do it to kind of practice that? But what's God teaching you through that practice? How is he showing up? What does that look like? What does that mean for you?'" These kinds of reading groups nurtured conversations and deeper practices that went beyond developing specific professional competencies.

Prayer and Devotions

Not surprisingly, SALs incorporated devotions and prayer with staff and not just students. Ryan even responded, "This is going to sound too Jesus answer-ish maybe, but we start every one of our staff meetings out with prayer and with devotions. As we care for each other and one another as a part of that . . . I believe that's a way to model that for each of my staff. I know that they do that with their own staff as well. Even for student activities, they start out all their meetings with prayer, and then one of them will lead a devotion as a part of that." There was a bit of variance in the structure of the devotions or prayers. Sometimes the supervising SAL led the devotions, but in most cases, the responsibility for devotions was rotated among staff. Melissa related, "We always start out team meetings with a short devotion and prayer that somebody from the staff brings. So, that's been really cool, just to even hear the different perspectives that each one brings to the table." The obvious advantage of this approach is that it gives everyone a chance to lead spiritual conversations.

Prayer also took different forms. Ashley shared how prayer is a weekly practice: "We meet every Tuesday for prayer. Everyone in campus ministry and student development, we get together and share each other's burdens and pray for each other." Another noted that they engage in a certain kind of "centering prayer every week." For others, prayer might be understood as a standard part of the office/university culture. Wesley, who works extensively with student discipline, noted, "There are days we'll walk into the office and it's just kind of standard culture for me. We'll say to each other, 'Hey, I haven't prayed enough today.' We know what that means. 'Give me some time. I've got to get right and get centered before I try to do this work.'

So, we definitely . . . we have those conversations." Sometimes, prayer just occurred in mentoring contexts. "I regularly pray with my [resident assistants] when we have our one-on-ones," James told us. "I mean, it's nothing super elaborate. I just pray for them briefly." Certainly, a pervasive sense that one must hear from God and talk to God was a sign of a healthy and spiritually nourishing culture.

One-on-One Mentoring

For many SALs, soul care is delivered to their staff through individual one-on-one mentoring meetings. In these meetings, they ask not only about professional development but also broad life matters. Ryan related, "I feel like that's my obligation, to really support and encourage my staff in their spiritual life individually and their development." Heather described her specific approach:

> I want us to start first on our own self-care. I want us to first
> start on our own [spiritual] disciplines. Are we going to church?
> Are we involved in church? Obviously, those are sensitive con-
> versations, so you have to do that strategically. But I think, really,
> I've tried to talk about "What is self-care?" Self-care is spend-
> ing time in prayer, being involved in your church. . . . Are you
> having time for yourself? I've done some creative things for my
> staff to kind of help inspire and encourage them. But I think
> I really want to develop a foundation where we, as a team, are
> really encouraging each other in that.

For Heather, self-care went beyond a cultural definition that involves pampering, "me time," or Netflix. Instead, she set a vision for self-care that was deeply rooted in the life and history of the church. She found that this type of self-care is what ultimately led to deeper conversations about life and work.

For Michael, these deeper conversations came about with his staff using a similar approach as with his students: "With them [staff], I ask the same questions that I do of my students about how they're doing spiritually and about what's going on in their personal lives that oftentimes lead to really rich conversations about our faith. Oftentimes, it's just more about their spiritual journey, what they're experiencing in their personal lives, their joys, their struggles."

Several times, student affairs staff talked about how they ask particular questions to approach those issues, such as:

- "What do you need from me?"
- "Do you need more challenge or support right now?"
- "What are ways that I can support and encourage you? Are there places I can challenge you right now as an individual?"
- "How are you doing in your walk with Christ right now?"
- "How is church going?"
- "How am I helping you grow? What do I need to do more of to help you?"

Out of these conversations come important substantive conversations that touch on the core of a person's life. Ryan described an incident that embodied this approach: "One of my staff members was dealing with a lot of stuff from his past and was needing some counseling, and we were able to connect him with a Christian counselor to continue to process that. So, then our conversation is not about the processing, the deep stuff he needed to do, but rather the outcome of 'How is the counseling going for you? What is that looking like? How are you growing? What's God doing in your life in your experience right now as a part of that?'"

Kaylee described how the answers to a question about what the staff person might need are more straightforward: "Sometimes it is a spiritual answer. Or sometimes it's like, 'I need a day off.' I say, 'OK, you have a day off and don't answer your phone. Turn your phone off. I'll take care of whatever comes up.'" In all these cases, the mentors moved beyond professional questions regarding competence and programming to matters of the heart and soul.

Chapel and "It Just Happens Organically"

We pair these two responses—chapel and "it just happens organically"—together, because they strike us as the two poles of how to approach the soul care of one's staff. On the one hand, chapel embodies the formal approach to soul care, while "it just happens organically" reflects soul care that happens serendipitously. Both have their strengths, as can be seen by the responses of some SALs. What SALs particularly appreciated about chapel is that it either involved the whole university community or was specially designed for employees to worship communally. The special chapels for just the employees were perhaps once a month or once a semester. As Melissa noted of these, "That's been a cool thing." For staff, these often became communal times (e.g., "My whole team goes to chapel every time"). Lucy even talked about how her team combined their prayer meeting with chapel attendance. She noted, "We in fact go early and pray before chapel together as a team, which has been really cool."

Other SALs discussed how they relied less upon structure and more upon organic conversations. These SALs give examples of this approach:

- "I think [soul care] happens organically. We connect on one-on-ones; we plan together; we collaborate; we challenge students together."
- "More organic. Yeah, [soul care] happens, definitely, organically."
- "Our student affairs staff consistently maintains and pursues active relationships with the Lord, which leads to meaningful and robust 'water cooler' types of conversations."
- "I don't have a catechism, so to speak—theological catechism that I intentionally weave in, but I feel like through my own devotional reading of Scripture, the Lord, I feel like, brings to my attention the things that he wants me to be weaving into my staff, both in individual meetings but also in the things that we specifically talk about when we meet together."

Although there is an authenticity to this organic approach, it may be difficult to sustain, and it may likely ebb and flow since there are no communal habits or practices in place that help support it.

Less Mentioned but Creative Ideas

The following examples were all creative practices that were mentioned by only a few participants, yet we think they deserve wider attention, consideration, and implementation.

Testimony sharing. Sometimes people at a Christian institution can work together and not know each other's story—particularly their personal story of how God has worked in their lives. One SAL talked about how he/she made it a practice every fall to have different SALs share their testimony of what God has done or is doing in their lives every week. This kind of testimony practice furthered intimate conversations about one's soul among coworkers.

Delegating soul care to others. One of the ways to avoid any awkwardness of having one's boss try to speak into one's spiritual life was for the institution to offer the chance to have spiritual care from others. A few institutions paid to make spiritual direction with a trained professional available to all staff. As one SAL related regarding the program, "Whether people choose that or not is totally up to them, but that's a resource that I think is pretty unique to our institution, which is great. And I use that. That's a gift. We get it for free, so that's huge."

Sabbath/rest time. One practice mentioned by a few SALs concerned a cultural emphasis upon rest, particularly Sabbath rest. One SAL mentioned their institution provides "a model for students of vibrant and healthy spiritual life—specifically asking our student affairs employees to live with healthy boundaries, space for relationship with God, rest, Sabbath, healthy families, and good boundaries" as an institutional best practice. Another SAL shared that their institution provided "Sabbath time for one month in the summer for personal renewal, study, and rest." We found these comments to be in striking contrast to those who felt inordinate professional demands, coupled with a lack of institutional support for their spiritual well-being.

Providing resources. One of the more unique ways to support the spiritual life of SALs pertained to the gift of resources. Of course, SALs talked about the funding available to attend professional development conferences such as the Association for Christians in Student Development (ACSD) conference, but a few also mentioned other unique forms of support. In some cases, this gift involved time off to attend spiritual retreats or to go on mission trips. Robert mentioned, "So, we have a three-day 'extending hands leave' that if you wanted to serve in the community, if you wanted to do a field trip with your kid's school, or if you're going on a mission trip with your church, that you could take three days that is not vacation, that is not personal time, to do that work." Another mentioned how there is time and space given for staff to lead service and mission trips as part of their work. In one case, it involved material sorts of gifts. Caroline shared, "The first thing that comes to mind, is actually as a Christmas gift, they sent us a Christian media outlet. So, it's a Netflix-like service where we can go in, and there are documentaries, there's short films, but really, it's just helping us to grow in terms of the spiritual area and our work with our students. So, definitely they hit the nail on the head with that one." Of course, resources at Christian institutions are often limited, but some of these creative ways of providing resources could be provided by institutions even with limited resources.

How Christ Animates Student Affairs Practice

Beyond caring for the souls of SALs, the second area of unique professional development involved helping SALs foster a Christian vision for how Christ animates student learning. In our broad survey, we specifically asked participants if they thought they were well-trained in this area. As Table 2.1 indicates, almost three-fourths (74 percent) thought they were well-trained or extremely well-trained.

Table 2.1. Do you think you are adequately educated to integrate your Christian faith into your student affairs practice? (*N* = 292)

Response	%
Extremely well-trained	26
Well-trained	48
Somewhat well-trained	20
Somewhat under-trained	3
Under-trained	2
Not at all trained	1

Still, almost a quarter of participants expressed much lower confidence regarding their education. Some of these participants wrote comments with their responses:

- "I have not received specific education or training on integrating faith into my work. I think it is assumed that practice happens naturally."
- "I'm a woman of personal faith, but I don't believe my institution continues education on faith development or how to integrate faith in our workplace."
- "I did not attend a graduate program at a Christian institution. I have received very little training on this since transitioning to a Christian employment context."
- "My department does not talk about how we are educating our students in the Christian faith through our work specifically."
- "The assumption is that we are Christian, so we must be integrating our faith."

We find these quotes to be good examples of the problem with assuming that we just need to hire Christians, and then they will "naturally" integrate Christianity into their work. As some of the best research on talent reminds us, people do not naturally become excellent at something.[3] They need coaches and teachers who can direct their practice, so that what they practice becomes second nature to them.

Specifically, SALs raised issues with the idea of soul care being synonymous with the integration of faith and practice. For instance, Caroline noted, "I think we're all inclined to say we integrate these things because we're praying before meetings and sending Bible verses out to help people and each other through our days." While we do believe soul care is an essential aspect of integration, it tends not to encompass learning how theological perspectives might reframe one's disciplinary imagination in the way that we mentioned in the Introduction.

One of the SALs we interviewed who recognized these problems pointed to a solution that he saw in the faculty. The faculty had a required faith and learning seminar in which they participated. John noted, "And many people in student development would like to participate or have something like that for staff. We currently don't have that." Actually, a number of SALs talked about this kind of formal community structure—one that allowed for discussion about how to think about one's Christian life as a whole and one's professional life in particular in light of the Gospel and God's story. Matthew discussed how he talks about how "we're all created and loved by God. We're made in the image of God. So, with that in mind, how do I then relate to myself and to others with that in mind as a reality?" The theologically based discussion led to thinking about practice in a certain way.

This discussion took many forms on different campuses. For instance, Carter shared how new student affairs staff get to join new faculty in a faith integration course at his institution. He observed, "Student development people are listening to different faculty members, and now you can get the juices flowing. The culminating part of that is that you have to write a faith integration paper based on your discipline." Valerie discussed how her institution has a yearlong course, which is a breakfast once a month, in which participants read, do homework, and write a paper on the integration of faith in their student affairs area. Still, Austin talked about how his institution set up a specific "institute" for training the different student affairs divisions:

> And in part of that institute, we talk about integrating your faith
> into everything that you do and making it a very real part of
> your life every day. I think that the vice presidents have different
> ways of doing it within their areas. A lot of times, it's "Read a
> book. Discuss it," you know, those kinds of things. But then also
> taking our staff away for a time just to focus in on your faith,
> and how is that growing and how do we live that out when we
> get back to campus?

As Austin mentioned, these kinds of meetings often involved either a book discussion or retreats. The discussions, as Nathan noted, "use a book that is clearly focused—not on student development theory—but on faith development for our staff development." Robert mentioned that it was important to provide this kind of discussion regularly:

> In my professional development that I provide for staff on a monthly basis, we look at higher ed topics and we put them through a Christian lens. We put them through a faith lens. Whether we're talking about Title IX, whether we're talking about race on campus. . . . We just had professional development on Gen Z, and so no matter what we're doing, we're always putting that through a faith lens in our conversations. What we have found is that if we are talking about it in a professional development context, it is going to trickle down.

For others, they focused less on topical discussions and instead chose an influential book that could begin a discussion about how Christianity informs student affairs. What all these demonstrate is the intentional and regular effort required to foster staff conversations around how Christianity animates the practice of student affairs.

Areas for Improvement

SALs offered three types of critique of practice regarding Christ-infused thinking. First, SALs talked about the need to combine soul care and practices that promote continual thinking about how a biblical perspective might change practice. For example, although addressing soul care is important, it is incomplete unless practices that foster Christ-animating discussions are added. As one survey participant told us, "Very few people talk about faith integration within student affairs, or we only talk about Christian behavior such as prayer, Bible studies, etc. We don't talk about how our Christian values might influence our budget practices or how it might influence a system of accountability." Without these conversations, one gains the view that the integration of faith and learning "is not a primary aspect of being the Housing Coordinator," as one survey participant told us. We certainly think that the strong emphasis upon traditional Christian activities such as chapel, Bible studies, and prayer is important, but there must be a recognition that Christ can and should animate how we creatively and wisely place students together in housing, to give just one example. We need to use the wisdom we have as Christians in student affairs to consider what faith has to say about critical race theory, student development theory, and spiritual formation of college students.

The second problem SALs acknowledged is one of spirit and will. For example, when asked about soul care, Melissa noted, "I mean, there's a weekly prayer time that any staff or faculty can go to. I think there's about ten people I've heard that go regularly. I've actually never gone. But it's one of those things; it's available." Emma admitted that she might not take kindly to supervisors asking about her church involvement or spiritual walk. "I don't know, because I think I would feel resistance if they did in some ways. Like, 'You are not the checkbox of my spiritual formation.'" Here we think that the default should consist of two things. First, SALs should seek to create a culture of expectation that their staff participate in some element of corporate soul care, whether it be leading devotions or participating in a prayer time. Second, we suggest that SAL supervisors should initiate a conversation with those under their care and ask them what kind of mentoring relationship they want. Do they want it to be strictly professional, or are they open to questions that probe into the person's walk with God as a means of growth and care? If they want the relationship to be strictly professional, supervisors should encourage their supervisees to seek soul care through other university avenues, such as the spiritual life staff.

Of course, there must be trust in this kind of relationship, as well as a common theological foundation for discussion. Emma spoke about a longing for authentic group discussions about difficult theological topics and spiritual struggles; she wanted "space for us to discuss." As a result, Emma longed for a type of soul care that would allow for honesty about struggles and doubt. Similarly, when it came to integration issues, she noted:

> We hold different stances on sexuality. But the university holds a stance, and so there's just this ignorance that they're different. We're all very aware, but it's never talked about, because you're afraid of losing your job. And I do think we need to represent our institution's views to our students, but I do think they need some space for us to discuss. And I think we discuss ideas, but we don't discuss our own personal reflections ever, because that's

> too scary, maybe. And I would say I align pretty much with [the institution], so I don't feel like it's threatening to me. But I know that there [are] . . . coworkers who are nervous . . .

Overall, care for the souls of one's staff, an atmosphere characterized by the virtues of trust and honesty, an affirmation of common Christian essentials, and intentional time for conversation are the important ingredients for fostering deep and rich forms of SALs' spiritual development.

To close, we want to emphasize that we think that a well-devised approach to integration of faith and learning discussions—whether in a monthly meeting or weekly book reading group—would be one solution to this concern *if* the group discussion is characterized by an acknowledgment of a common Christian narrative and the virtues of trust and authenticity. For instance, Melissa explained how this worked with her discussion about diversity. She started by referencing a book that provides a theological foundation for diversity work:

> Diversity matters to God. . . . So, we're starting there. Then getting into some diversity theory and different things, or identity theory. . . . My leadership team and I talked through that and really came to that place of recognizing because this is such a held value for each one of us and because we think it's important, everybody is going to view this a bit differently coming from their own backgrounds, but we all agree on the one thing, which is our faith in Christ and our commitment there. So, we start from a theological perspective as we dive into this big gnarly discussion of diversity training and all that's going to be in there. We really wanted to start it off with a foundation of looking at it theologically.

Here, we will also do the same. Chapter Three seeks to provide an overview of the past conversation regarding faith, learning, and student affairs from which we can build both our current conversation and a theology of student affairs.

PART TWO

Surveying the Landscape

Student affairs is a relatively young academic field. As a result, Christian practitioners and scholars only began putting together a Christian vision of the student affairs profession a few decades ago.[1] Since that time, numerous edited volumes and journal articles have been published on this topic. The chapter contained in this part specifically seeks to pinpoint the theological building blocks that can help build a more comprehensive Christian understanding of student affairs while also noting some missing materials. In the end, we hope that this effort will help student affairs practitioners think and live within the Christian narrative, so that "Christian" does not become a mere add-on to student affairs.[2]

3

DOES GOD MAKE A DIFFERENCE FOR STUDENT AFFAIRS?

The Christian Story in the Literature

A Christian anthropology for student development calls us to encounter Jesus in one another through love. As student affairs professionals . . . we are called to live a vocation that invites all members of the community to practice the "art of loving." . . . We ask ourselves, "What is the will of God in this moment, with this person?" The answer is simple: to love that person who is made in the image of God. We must initiate a love for the other right away without expecting anything in return.

—Michael James, *Student Life in Catholic Higher Education*

In this chapter, our "search for God" in Christian student affairs literature is really an effort to discover how leaders writing about student affairs overtly connect *theology* and the *biblical narrative* to their work. We organize our findings using the four basic questions any educational philosophy must answer: Who? Why? What? and How?

Who?

"Who are we?" is the most fundamental question facing student affairs practitioners. If you do not know your identity, you do not know who you can and should become. Identity orients us as Christian student affairs leaders (SALs) both metaphysically and morally.

Endowed Identities from Creation

We receive identity orientation from the creation story in four major ways. First, one of the most-often discussed theological connections made by authors concerns the belief that all humans are made *Imago Dei*, in the image of God. This fundamental uniqueness provides a meta-identity that establishes human worth. As Shirley Hoogstra and John Witte wrote, "The image of God doesn't mean we're all the same, but it means we all have value and worth—in spite of, and because of, our differences."[1] Seen from this perspective, various types of students are not problems to be solved, but are individuals made in God's image who deserve love.

A second theological conclusion that emerged from the creation narrative is that the gender binary of male and female is God-given, normative, and an integral part of our identity.[2] Sandra Estanek contends that each person, created in God's image and likeness, has inherent and absolute dignity. "This unity of body and soul," she adds, includes gender, noting that "the Church holds that binary heterosexuality is normative. 'Being man' or 'being woman' is a reality that is good and willed by God."[3] This theological outlook, which Evangelicals have historically shared, creates significant tension with current cultural norms and within these Christian educational institutions themselves.

Third, another creation-based identity that received emphasis from authors is that of being a steward (based on Gen. 1:28–30). We are called to take care of creation (which includes ourselves). Kirsten Riedel, Emilie Hoffman, and Jessica Martin observe, "In order to faithfully love God with our whole selves, we must practice good stewardship of our hearts, souls, and minds—essentially, our entire created being."[4] As part of this stewardship, like God, we ourselves create and demonstrate a certain amount of sovereignty over our creations. Part of this creative activity includes the ever-expanding variety of work vocations with which God calls us to engage. Furthermore, as Chapter One mentioned, it provides an important identity for administrators who are in charge of stewarding students and resources.

Finally, since God is Trinitarian and we are created *Imago Dei*, we are created for community. Recognizing the relational nature of the triune God, Kristin Keiffer, Amy Van der Werf, and Doug Wood suggest that "the importance of community stems from our creation. In Genesis it is a relational, Triune God who lovingly forms man from the dust and imprints the divine image within him out of a desire to create community."[5] In this view, our differences can be special gifts that God can use to enhance the community.

In summary, the Christian student affairs literature answers the question of "Who?" by declaring that God created us as valuable image bearers endowed with his dignity. We are also gendered and social beings who need community (such as family, friends, and neighbors), as well as a specific work vocation. Moreover, when we conduct these social relationships as image bearers who demonstrate God's virtues of love, hospitality, holiness, stewardship, and other virtues, we experience the flourishing for which we were designed.

Sinners

Interestingly, throughout our whole literature analysis, we found few extensive discussions about sin or the fact that we, as human beings, are sinners. Indeed, one could even argue that student affairs writers seem to have an aversion to the term. Of course, some authors acknowledged the fall by talking about dealing with students' brokenness. The most extensive discussion of the fall came from D. Terry Thomas and David S. Guthrie.[6] They noted that the fall means we develop areas of life without attention to God's purposes, which would imply that this issue is one of the core problems with fallen forms of student affairs. Their discussion, however, does not elaborate what sin does to the profession and practice of student affairs, how sin wounds the students in our care, or perhaps even how sin blinds student affairs professionals to the idea that students need salvation. Overall, this lack of overt attention to our identity as sinners demonstrates a strange neglect of an important theological truth.

Redeemed

Fortunately, through Christ, God provides the possibility of a new identity beyond that of a sinner or even someone who is a failure, mistake-prone, or broken. For instance, Stephen Beers discussed a model of faith development that differs in its Christian particularity from that of James Fowler's scheme.[7] Beers's model included recognition of one's selfishness, one's value as being made in God's image, and the need to understand how Christ provides a way of redemption to recapture God's image. Moreover, Beers and Skip Trudeau point out how further development occurs "where the redeemed person's actions and intentions join the work of God in redeeming his creation."[8] Through Christ's redemption, we are also part of Christ's body. The image of the body in 1 Corinthians is used as a reminder of what the best community looks like. Hoogstra and Witte noted, "knowing that God can look at your community as the body of Christ calls us to do the same, recognizing the part that each resident plays."[9] Again, the model for character in this Christian family is Christ.

Inheritors

Like our identity as sinners, our identity as inheritors of God's kingdom received little emphasis in this literature. For comparison's sake, consider what John Amos Comenius, one of the greatest Christian educators, wrote to teachers of young children:

> [I]f the little ones at present seem unimportant, regard them not as they now are, but as God intends they may and ought to be. You will see them not only as the future inhabitants of the world and possessors of the earth, and God's vicars amongst His creatures when we depart from this life, but also equal participants with us in the heritage of Christ: A royal priesthood, a chosen people, associates of angels, judges of devils, the delight of heaven, the terror of hell . . . heirs of eternity.[10]

Certainly, viewing students through the whole biblical narrative can radically transform our understanding of students' identity. Yet many SALs failed to draw upon two important parts of this narrative.

Why?

Theologically informed visions of Christian student affairs usually followed from this story-formed identity. The idea that God created us informs what exactly "whole purpose development" means, since, as Thomas and Guthrie suggested, "God desires the created order to develop in ways that conform to God's intentions for it."[11] If we are meant to bear God's image in a variety of ways, then the biblical story will provide the substance for those aims.

Interestingly, few authors mentioned anything about how the fall disorders God's creation and leaves humans to pursue other purposes besides God's. The exception to this finding proved to be the authors who wrote about disciplining students. In this case, understanding one's ultimate purpose and place in light of God's overall story transformed the student disciplinary process.[12] Andre Broquard suggested that "when your goal is to honor God through your confrontation and discipline, there ceases to be an 'us versus them' mentality. This removes barriers between you and the student. It communicates care, concern, and support, not judgment, condemnation, and resentment."[13]

Like discipline, much of the discussion about the purpose or purposes of student affairs at Christian institutions focused upon what we would call redemptive purposes accomplished through and with Christ for "transformation, not mere job preparation."[14] Beers observed that what differentiates Christian student affairs from more pluralistic forms "is that the Christian college developmental programs are attempting to partner with God to transform students into the image of Christ."[15] Mark L. Poorman described this redemptive transformation more specifically, writing, "As Christians, we are living to be the face of Christ for others; in this case, the students we serve. Various people are the presence of God to others in differing ways."[16] Considering these types of statements, what exactly does it mean to be the face of Christ? Usually, it meant to display Christ's virtues.

The ultimate of Christ's virtues was a certain kind of love, as Michael James described in our opening quote. Regarding the ends of Catholic higher education, James made clear, as do many other authors, that this end of loving God and loving others involves a kind of self-sacrificial love that is directed to all people, but especially the least of these.[17] One of the most engaging quotes, which was directed to resident assistants, declared:

> We must love our neighbors, especially our neighbors at the
> margins, those beyond the favorable light of power, outside
> the gate of privilege, beyond the pale of popularity, indeed

those that are distant [to us] and culturally different. Loving the neighbor requires a kind of active, sensitive, painstaking, time-consuming, self-giving appreciation, and attentiveness to loving the other—not others as I would like them to be or as I assume they are or as a means to my end or as a raw matter for my project or as "the lost" that need to be led by me, but as real others in all of their integrity, complexity, agency, agony, beauty, and intrinsic value as people.[18]

Other writers also discussed the goal of student affairs as teaching students to follow and model Christ as they described what they hope to convey to their students.

What?

The substance of the Christian life cannot be left to placards and mission statements. Thus, writers also shared a vision for student affairs that involved sharing and modeling a Trinitarian community of character where a whole range of virtues are taught and exemplified. The virtues they mentioned were not arbitrarily chosen. As humans made in God's image, God designed us to be most fully human when we imitate his character. Kristine Goodwin described one such connection regarding the virtues of hospitality and love: "We know through the readings of Genesis that God was the ultimate host, creating a world abundant with beauty and natural riches for our pleasure. He gave us one another for companionship and friendship and called us to love one another as He loves us. It is in this context theme that hospitality should be considered."[19] In this way, Christian community is unified around a common understanding of God, us, and God's purposes for us.

The virtue of servant leadership was one that received particular attention. Steve Ivester explained the virtue of student leadership: "Resident assistants can best serve students in their growth and capacity as servant leaders when they develop an intentional discourse that leads to a theological consideration of a theology of leadership that captures the example of Jesus Christ."[20] Similarly, James Maher called for a "spirituality of administration" that, at the core, considers administration to be "a labor of servant leadership." He claimed, "Such an approach recognizes that a spirituality of administration seeks not to make administration its end; rather, in the words of St. Paul in the letter of Timothy, to allow truth, beauty, and God's spirit to flourish."[21]

Writers also shared an ideal of the best community established and nurtured by the virtues of God's character. "For example, social relationships are part of God's created order and God has various intentions regarding how they best occur (e.g., with integrity; love neighbor as one's self)."[22] Catherine WoodBrooks wrote, "Perhaps the most important thing we can share during some of those heart-to-hearts with students is the beauty of God's grace, mercy, and forgiveness. His unconditional love is a difficult concept for people to accept. We strive to be our best possible selves, but God still loves us even at our worst."[23] In many cases, a certain amount of theological literacy seems to be assumed in that it is expected that students will understand the narrative and theological context for these virtues or what Christians would also call fruits of the Spirit.

How?

Since student affairs is a practical discipline, one of the most highly developed areas in this body of literature concerned how to impart certain content. Poorman pointed out that, for Catholics, the answer to the "How?" question is really "through everything."[24] The reason for the universality of his answer was that

> the Catholic vision perceives God working *through* persons, events, and material things. In all those discrete events and happenings of the day, or a week, or a year, the hand of God is at work in the life of the individual student. As we all know, there are certain predictable and perennial things that happen on a university campus: first-year orientation, job searches, volunteer opportunities, commencement. The Catholic vision sees these and all the points in our lives as "moments of grace," where God is working in what are sometimes the strangest and most difficult circumstances. Why is this principle of mediation important to residential life? As ministers, our hall staffs are doing more

than just counseling, policing, or hanging out. They live day-to-day with their senses tuned to the truth that God may be doing a new thing, a good thing, a *holy* thing in the lives of the students they serve and recognize that they may well be the agents for God's grace.[25]

Although most Protestants do not use this same sacramental language, we do share this outlook. Consequently, for almost every writer there were *no* "secular" methods.

As a result, the most important "how" involved learning to teach SALs and students to see everything in light of God's story set forth in creation and the Bible. For example, Susan Reese pointed out that successful spiritual formation practices "were based on noticing God's story in the midst of our story."[26] She went on to note, "Student development professionals also noticed that how they relied on the way God moved in their own personal stories had significant influence on who they ministered to and how they paid attention to the lives of their students."[27] Cara Cliburn Allen and Nathan F. Alleman also found that practitioners engaged in faith-integration developed a consciousness of God in every aspect of life and student affairs.[28]

Of course, other writers identified additional methods of importance that can be divided into (1) professional practices, (2) spiritual practices, and (3) virtue practices.

Professional Practices

Most of the professional practices were not unique to Christianity. That said, the practices were often transformed by distinctively Christian ends or content. One professional practice the writers mentioned was mentorship, a term commonly used in student affairs. In a biblical or spiritual context, it is known as discipleship. To find staff willing to disciple students, one of the obvious starting practices that scholars and practitioners often cited was hiring for the faith mission of their institution.[29] Administrators also pointed out the important staff development tools available once a professional has been hired for mission. These tools included retreats, monthly workshops, reading groups, or speaking series that discussed the integration of mission with one's practice.

Christian scholar-practitioners also talked about how Christianity shaped their approach to challenging students—a familiar student affairs concept that springs from Sanford's theory of challenge and support.[30] Steve Morley and Sarah Hightower described a Christian version of challenging students: "Offering challenge is about inviting someone to be her best self, to be who God has called her to be. It means being honest but not condemning. It means speaking truth and sometimes difficult words, but not out of a posture of superiority or authority. Rather, it means encouraging and inviting others to participate in the ways God is working in their lives."[31] In this account, a challenge should be clearly connected to our theological ideals.

In many cases, a regular professional practice was transformed by allowing and encouraging students to reflect upon what God was doing in a situation. For instance, reflection before and after participating in service learning is a common practice in student affairs. Yet, for the Christian, "reflection provides the opportunity for students to see how their faith can be strengthened through their work. The actor performing caring and compassionate service may allow students to see the work of God in others and themselves."[32]

Interestingly, authors mentioned both presence/fellowship and absence/solitude as helpful practices. Presence is something that God offers through Christ and his Holy Spirit—God Immanuel or God with us—and it is something we should offer especially to hurt students.[33] Indeed, a scholar found that one of the best support systems for students on the margins was the practice of fellowship.[34] Morley and Hightower also noted that absence can be a time when we make room for the Holy Spirit to work in a student's life: "When you withdraw from a situation or a person at appropriate times, this absence creates further room for the Holy Spirit to work in his life *and* your own. . . . Furthermore, your absence encourages your peers not to be dependent on you and empowers them in their relationship with God."[35] In addition, staff we interviewed suggested withdrawing from community allows God to work in both the staff person as well as in others. Morley and Hightower wrote that "in these times, we can lose sight of our humanness and often put less trust in God. We also lose sight of the larger picture and the promises of our Christian faith. The physical act of removing yourself from the location, people, and things attached to it allows the Lord to remind you of your capacity and how this seemingly overwhelming situation fits into his larger picture."[36] Absence without faith, however, becomes insensitive neglect. Presence without faith becomes destructive self-aggrandizing of one's saving power. Trusting absence or presence undertaken in faith recognizes that God will continue to work in others and ourselves amid the practice.

Spiritual Practices

Of course, more explicit spiritual practices were suggested in some of the articles we reviewed (e.g., prayer, monastic rules). Not surprisingly, prayer emerged as an important practice in multiple ways. Hoogstra and Witte wrote about white privilege to resident assistants: "Pray that God will open your ears to listen well, particularly when you recognize that someone is different than you."[37] Other authors talked about praying during a conflict or a crisis. Rev. Jay Fostner discussed how "once, we sent a simple email at 2:00 A.M. letting the campus know about a death and that there will be a prayer service at 3:00 A.M. The result was a church overflowing with community-members."[38]

As mentioned earlier, sin was rarely discussed in much of the literature except when practitioners referred to matters of student discipline. For instance, Andrew Shotnicki and Colette McCarrick Geary connected Catholic theology and practice with the student discipline process in a unique manner through the sacrament of penance, similar to what Protestants call restorative justice. They focused on helping students restore the damaged relationship through "acknowledgment of fault, contrition, and absolution." The theological context for this discipline was an understanding that penance is "the response of the penitent to the gratuitous and forgiving love of God, payments not imposed by God (when there are no conditions upon God's love) but ideally brought by the penitent on him or herself."[39] Shotnicki and Geary provided a powerful example of how SALs can help when the penitent may need some additional guidance about what to do:

> An example of this concerns a young man found responsible for misconduct revealed that his primary motivation for succumbing to peer pressure was his hope that, by joining in, "maybe these guys would call me when they are going to the gym." Recognizing his deep loneliness and resulting vulnerability, forgiveness is articulated through a sanction carefully planned to enable him the opportunity to access a welcoming and affirming peer group. In this case, assigning service hours on a popular campus ministry project enabled him to forge healthy friendships and become socially connected.[40]

Since the church has a long history of practices that deal with sinful behavior, these practices transfer quite directly to the student discipline process.

Writers also emphasized broader sets of practices. For example, Jay DeFruscio discussed using prayer, communal gatherings, testimony, and service to shape his athletic program, "We often began our school year with a prayer service for students, staff, and coaches in the chapel, with the coach and student sharing the benefits of leading an ethical, focused life grounded in a spiritual journey. Additionally, student athletes and coaches participated in department-wide community service projects and team retreats. Finally, all were strongly encouraged to participate with the entire student body and, where possible, become actively engaged in leading others on campus and in the local community."[41] Similarly, Keiffer et al. suggested that for RAs, "establishing a floor prayer chain, hosting open room dialogues, listening well to life-stories, and practicing hospitality"[42] are ways the RA can help to establish a caring community.

In another case, Haley Williamson argued that student leadership skills can be honed through the whole set of monastic practices and spiritual disciplines. She claimed, "These disciplines produce the inter- and intra-personal qualities educators desire to see cultivated in student leaders on their campuses (hope, strength, humility, trust, joy, compassion, gratitude, laughter, empathy; and the ability to see and interact with others in the ways God intends)."[43]

Overall, with God's help, these activities help produce the fruit of the Spirit as well as other positives (i.e., leadership potential; ability to collaborate; academic improvement; positive cognitive, emotional, and behavioral growth in students). In short, they made us wonder why we ever moved Christian education from the monasteries in the first place. Of course, there are other models that transformed the monastic context. For example, two Lutheran scholars pointed to this example: "Martin and Katie Luther housed up to thirty students at a time in their home, the Black Cloister, a refurbished monastery turned de facto dormitory complex."[44] This unique couple already modeled residential life with faculty.

Virtue Practices

Writers sought not only to teach Christian virtues but also to incorporate them into their practice; in fact, these virtues were cited as the most effective pedagogy. Some of the important pedagogical virtues included stewardship, hospitality, forgiveness, trust, and care. For instance, Robert Meyer and Laura Wankel discussed how they each conceptualized the concept of stewardship in a Christian way and then sought to practice this virtue. The unfortunate context for this practice was a fire at their institution that left 3 students dead, 58 injured, and 650 without a home. They described their application as they dealt with this horrific tragedy:

> In crisis situations, understanding and embracing stewardship is key to making proper decisions. It was very important on occasion for staff members to be sent home to rest, be with their own families, to replenish, pray, and refresh. To be good stewards of one's gifts at times means giving two hundred percent and at other times taking time off. The good steward finds the appropriate balance and is able to say and trust in prayer: "God I have given what I have for this day, the rest is up to you."[45]

This theologically informed understanding of stewardship brings a welcome understanding of human limitations within a profession that often keeps long and difficult hours.[46]

Hospitality and love were two other virtues emphasized as vital for cultivating a robust on-campus Christian community. Hospitality demands "that we work at being in right relationship with one another within the context of community, open to the encounter and exchange of guest and host, experiencing one another in an expression of God's love."[47] This approach to hospitality involves more than teaching its importance; it requires it being part of the very fabric of one's relationships.

Although we consider stewardship and hospitality as virtues rooted in God's creation, the virtues of inclusivity and forgiveness are clearly ones required due to sin and rupturing of relationships. As James 2:1–7 reminds us, inclusivity involves seeking to include those on the margins of society so that they have a seat at the table. "As an RA," Keiffer, Van Der Werf, and Wood suggested, "you should strive to be Christ-like and ensure that every person has a valued seat at your table."[48] Inclusivity could be said to be an extension of hospitality that seeks to overcome the relational alienation produced by the fall. Lisa L. Kirkpatrick incorporated inclusivity into hospitality, stating that "hospitality is one of the oldest and most critical Christian virtues and can be understood as welcoming, caring for, and engaging 'the other,' not just the powerful, but strangers and those at the margins as well."[49] She noted that the underlying theological reason for this practice is the view that all human beings are manifestations of God's love and representatives of Christ, including those with moral or theological differences:

> For example, an orientation leader once informed me that one of our new students had not eaten dinner because the dining hall closed before sunset. It was Ramadan, a Muslim holy time that we had not considered in our planning. Allowing the student to practice her faith while living on-campus is the very embodiment of hospitality, but we had somehow missed it. Whatever our students' faith practices may or may not be, we are called to welcome them with respect, for every person has value and is made in the image and likeness of God.[50]

For all, that belief that all humans are made in the image and likeness of God meant that they deserve hospitality.

The virtue of love for students was also mentioned and interpreted in light of the overall redemptive part of the Christian story. In other words, Christian student affairs practice requires the deep kind of sacrificial love God shows to us. Goodwin described this overall understanding:

> When student affairs professionals are asked why they choose the profession, they often respond, "because I love students." There is no denying that the work we do and the strong relationships we develop with the students are often filled with feelings of deep affection. However, the love referenced above is longer lasting and less conditional than affection. It is willful love. It is choosing to love as God commands us, demonstrating a commitment to each person equally in treating every person with respect and thoughtfulness, regardless of their beliefs or behaviors.[51]

Not surprisingly, the scholarship we reviewed also drew upon Christ as an example of how to demonstrate Christian virtue in a community. Goodwin claimed that Jesus is the ideal host that we are asked to follow—Jesus acts invitationally. Similarly, Beers wrote about how RAs need to practice the virtue of presence. He observed, "Scripture chronicles God's consistent story of being available and present in concrete ways, with the most spectacular example being the incarnation of Christ and his physical presence with us."[52]

In a study relating to racial justice, other administrators saw the vision of how—even though we are "flawed"—we are adopted into God's family, as inspiring the virtues of hospitality and inclusiveness: "We are supposed to take care of those who are on the outside and to bring them in, to treat them as family, as Christ did for us. He treats us as family. He treats us as children, when we're anything but that, you know? We are of Creation and we're flawed, but He has been so inclusive."[53] Overall, a variety of Christian virtues played an important pedagogical role in the development of students. This variety helps remind us that character development involves more than just a focus on one or two favorite virtues.

Conclusion

What difference does Christianity make for student affairs according to the literature? First, it defines practitioners and their students. God created us as valuable image bearers with dignity who are designed for a relationship with him and are asked to live in virtuous relationships with others in community. Although sin has broken those relationships, we can restore them through Christ and become adopted children of God who share a virtue-filled community with others.

At Christian universities, SALs in particular are charged with bearing God's image and imitating Christ by modeling individual and corporate virtues, such as God's sacrificial love and mentoring, and discipling students to do the same. Practitioners should practically promote this end through helping students live in light of God's story and looking to see how God is working through everything. Student affairs staff are also called to transform usual practices such as challenging students, being there for students, and listening to students by understanding and practicing these activities in light of the Christian narrative.

Clearly, we found several important themes with which to build an overall theological vision for Christian student affairs, but we also must point out crucial elements we found missing. The literature seemed to ignore our identities as sinners and inheritors. Furthermore, in the area of virtue development, other important Christian virtues did not appear, including humility, forgiveness, gratitude, and generosity. This last one is particularly important, considering findings that charitable giving appears vitally important to students' spiritual development.[54]

Of course, there are many additional Christian practices that are missing from this literature. James K. A. Smith's conversation about Christian higher education in general could also apply to student affairs:

> What we need is a kind of clearinghouse or digital commons in
> which different practitioners could share stories about exper-
> iments and initiatives in their contexts, being honest about
> both successes and failures. This in itself would be a Christian
> practice of *testimony*, bearing witness by sharing our stories,

and the result would be a growing catalogue of best practices as Christian universities try to cultivate environments that form not only Christian minds but Christian loves—indexing student desire to kingdom come so that they long for, and act for, *shalom*.[55]

Certainly, much more needs to be done to think imaginatively about how God's story relates to student affairs and to understand what Christ-enlivened student affairs might entail.

We believe the work presented here indicates a trajectory of hope. This trajectory sees the value of rooting the purposes of Christian student affairs in the broader vision of redemptive history. This trajectory sees Christian student affairs as cathedral-building, not mere stonecutting.[56] We are developing students made in God's image to be temples of the Holy Spirit and not merely instruments for institutional retention, a democratic society, or economic utility. Much work has been done, but much more remains as we look to establish a Christian theology of student affairs. The next three parts of this book gather together some of the best thinking about student affairs and suggest a more comprehensive vision for a variety of areas of student affairs.

PART THREE

Christ-Enlivened Student Affairs Practice

In Part Three, we shift our focus from the identity of the professional (Part One) and the literature of the field (Part Two) to the nature of student affairs in current practice. We continue to examine and expand our imagination for Christian student affairs by exploring *who* we imagine our students to be (Chapter Four), the ends (i.e., the *why*) that guide our practice (Chapter Five), *what* we convey through our practice (Chapter Six), and *how* we convey it (Chapter Seven). In combination, these chapters present our exploration and analysis of current beliefs about the key functionality of the Christian student affairs professional.

Figure III.1. The Christian Student Affairs Imagination

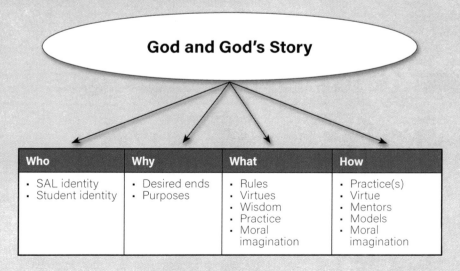

4

WHO ARE OUR STUDENTS?

How Christ Animates the Explicit and Implicit Views of Student Identity

I think the Christian environment is unique because we understand
that our students are created in the image of God and that drives
our interaction with them. . . . No matter what they're dealing with,
there's a deeper sense of commitment to helping that student grow.

—Jaxon

An excellent educator must first determine who their students are before they can provide a vision for who they intend their students to become. As Jaxon's comment above related, a robust construction of student identity and personhood is one of the defining features of a Christian vision for student affairs. The responses we received from student affairs leaders (SALs), when combined, reveal a distinctive imagination for student identity. Understanding these identities is crucial because our fundamental assumptions about students will change everything about our practice and how we view their development. In the coming pages, we will show that SALs generally imagined students in robust theological terms, though some pieces of the Christian vision were missing.

Image Bearers of God

Starting in Genesis, God defines who we are as humans. Or as Rose shared with us, "Every student is uniquely created in the image of God." Like Rose, well over half of the statements that associated faith with student identity referenced the reality and significance of the *Imago Dei*. Seeing students as bearers of God's image is a central and distinctive tenet of Christian student affairs. Yet, as previous chapters revealed, our understanding of this glorious truth is sometimes limited in scope—capturing only a sliver of the riches of meaning. In the following paragraphs, we borrow from particular SALs to expand our collective understanding of the richness of what it means to work with students who bear the image of God.

Imaging Relationship

If God made students in his image, we must know God better in order to help our students become more fully human. This journey can start with the recognition that God is Triune.[1] Ashley pointed out, "If we understand God as Trinity, as three in one, then being made in God's image means being made for relationship—being primarily relational beings first, rather than just rational beings or sort of brains-on-a-stick kind of thing." Michael rooted the human drive for relationship in image bearing as well before suggesting, "We really belong to one another." For Michael, understanding ourselves as image bearers not only helps us make sense of our fundamental drive for relationship; it also gives us a new way of seeing relationship. Just as scholar-practitioners wrote in the literature (Chapter Three), many participants specifically articulated the relational implications of being made in God's image when discussing diversity and sexuality, but a few also saw it as relating to the value of community and the importance of encouraging students to acquire "a vision of life that is bigger than themselves." Borrowing from these examples, Christian SALs can make this connection by helping students understand this dimension of the Triune God.

Divine Value

The relationality rooted in our image bearing is not limited to human relationships. If humans are made for relationship with the Triune God, then we also find our identity in the Triune God—God the Father, Jesus Christ the Son, and the Holy Spirit. So, understanding our identity means, as Alanna said, "being really grounded in our identity in Christ." Thus, being an image bearer is both an identity from the outset and an identity to be more fully realized through relationship with God.

Although students cannot gain more worth through understanding themselves as image bearers (because they already have that worth), students can more fully comprehend and reflect the reality of the image that they bear. Several SALs pointed to this reality when asked who they hope their students will be at graduation. For example, Barbara shared with us that at the end, she hopes students "know that they're image bearers of God and that they've seen that their worth and value is recognized. Those are things they don't have to earn." Similarly, John shared: "At a really fundamental level, I want students to know that God loves them, not because of what they do, but because they're created in his image. That's really significant. I find students really . . . struggling with that. 'I'm not really sure. Does God really love me?' If you don't feel accepted in that relationship . . . then it's going to be really hard." These SALs recognize that as students better understand that they are made in God's image and grow in their relationship with God, they discover the foundation for their worth, value, and love.

Divinely Defined Flourishing

The reality that students are made in God's image and loved by God also has implications for how we understand human flourishing. Rather than seeing flourishing as becoming who we as individuals want to be as self-authors, flourishing as an image bearer involves developing into who God created and calls us to be. Ethan told us that after four years, "I would want people who had a strong understanding of who they are [and] a firm and growing, expanding idea of who God has created them to be, called them to be." This fundamental understanding can impart to students a tremendous confidence they cannot find from their accomplishments, relationships, or other created sources. Gaining "a better sense of who they are, a real understanding of who God made them to be" then results in "confidence in that knowledge that will carry them, that will allow them to risk, that will allow them to be successful in life," as Nathan put it. In this way, the identity of image bearer provides a foundation for the learning, loving, and working we seek to model for students.

Called by a Divine Caller

Once students understand and rest in their fundamental identity, Christian SALs can help students acquire a second form of self-understanding— to know how to flourish by joining with God's work in the world. Miles described his objective simply as "guiding students to partner with the work God is doing in the world." Specifically, it involved students recognizing that God uniquely made them for a special *calling*, *vocation*, or *purpose*. As can be seen from the examples below, all three words might be used:

- "I hope that they have a deep sense of *vocation*. That they leave, maybe not having their ten-year plan perfectly figured out, but they have set faithful trajectories of *calling* in the areas that make up a good life, which includes work, but isn't limited to work, but it would also include family, it would include church, it would include community."
- "Students will develop a sense of *purpose*, explore the concept of *calling*, and recognize specific opportunities for contribution."

For students to develop this sense of calling, certain SALs wanted students to recognize that God is doing the calling, to listen closely to God's call, and to use their gifts and passions for this call to have a positive influence on society.

Several SALs understood recognizing one's vocation as far more than an intellectual process. It also required acquiring excellence in that vocation—another important subgoal of vocation development. James shared:

> I hope that they have a sense of expertise in whatever it is
> they studied. That they just go out and, whatever it is that they
> learned, do it well. I mean, not only does our world need skilled
> workers, but honestly that's also a witness to Christ. If you go
> out and you're all gung ho about Christ and Jesus, but you stink
> at your job in the workforce, people are going to tune you out.
> "This guy's a jokester. He's no good at what he does. Why am I
> going to listen to him over here?"

A helpful summary of the various visions articulated by several Christian SALs came from a leader who described her desire to "cultivate an academic community in which students flourish as they encounter the Triune God with their whole lives and discover the joy of their vocation."

God-Given Passions and Giftings

The final implication participants shared regarding image bearing was the way we reflect God's nature through our unique, individual passion and giftings. One way that some Christian SALs believed students gain a broader understanding of their calling is through a discovery of their giftings. Emma shared this progression regarding goals for students: "I want them to be confident in the skills that they have, because I think that somewhat comes from their identity but also this self-awareness of their giftings and their vocations and how they want to use those giftings for the kingdom . . . to see kingdom work to be bigger than just missions or things that we have seen in the past but have a broader understanding of vocation." As she observed, students' confidence came from the awareness of their identity, giftings, and clear sense of vocation. They could then use all those things for God's kingdom.

Image Bearing in Review

When combined to form a larger picture, Christian SALs sought (and, we would add, should seek) to make sure students know they are made in God's image; appreciate the love and worth they can experience from knowing they are made in God's image; grasp the true definition of flourishing as image bearers; recognize that God has given them unique passions, gifts, and a calling; and know they can feel confident in who they are in their gifts and their passions.

Therefore, the joy of being a *Christian* student affairs professional is that Christianity provides an agreed-upon narrative that serves as a touchstone for our view of students. Our narrative elevates students as image bearers of the most-high God. Thus,—whether they are intellectually developed, emotionally mature, socially aware, or not—all students have inherent, God-given value. Although this sentiment may seem familiar, it is a unique contribution Christianity has to offer that is never mentioned in student affairs literature or theories. Much of this theory cannot separate student value from student effort or achievement. Thus, the gift of Christian student affairs is that it recognizes students as not needing to act or achieve in order to justify or define their existence—they *are* because God made them to be and continues to sustain them in every passing moment.

This reality has two significant ramifications. First, it means that we have a narrative that can support seeing students in tension—simultaneously image bearers of God and yet still sinners in need of redemption and growth. This is the story that should motivate our student affairs practice—that God would so love sinners that he would die that we might live with abundant riches of the coming kingdom (Rom. 5:8). This leads us to the second ramification of the Christian approach to students—rather than placing students at the center of learning, we ought to place God and God's story at the center. This would mean our job, as many SALs have suggested, is to help students find their place in relationship to God and God's story. This also means SALs do not have to rely on their own wisdom to know who students are. Instead, they can rely on God's knowledge and wisdom to speak of the true nature of students—creatures created by, and in the image of, a holy God.

Sinners

The next identity we explore was noticeably absent in our conversations with SALs. Not once in all our research, surveys, or interviews did any of our participants use the identity words "sinner" or "sinners." Christian SALs appear to be averse to these identity words. In the few times that "sin" was mentioned in our interviews and surveys, more than half related to sex and alcohol. In fact, in one case, a participant in residence life noted that she avoids the word because it is "Christianese lingo." A few participants talked about student "brokenness," but much of it was attributed to broken systems, broken homes, or tough situations. Of course, sin does manifest itself in these systemic and environmental ways, but not to the exclusion of individual manifestations of sin and sinfulness. Yet a strong knowledge of the sinner identity is vitally important to impart on all college students. As Arthur Holmes stated, "The typical college student thinks of sin and righteousness as specific behaviors flagged by do's and don'ts, rather than as a pervasive condition of the heart, a question of moral identity."[2] Perhaps the identity is assumed by SALs, but its absence is striking because to do so is to neglect an important element of the Christian story (Rom. 3:23, 6:23). Why did Christ need to come to earth if not to save sinners? (Matt. 1:21).

In Christ

Of course, Christian SALs talked about what it means to be a Christ follower in terms of identity. Three specific types of references were made during this conversation. First, many SALs shared that being a Christ follower provided a fundamental sense of belonging that no college campus could ever provide. Michael reflected on how an identity firmly rooted in Christ is the real key to the good life:

> We do not find peace by rearranging the circumstances of our lives; instead, we find peace by realizing who we are at our deepest self. And so, it's really getting [students] to understand who they are, their identity, and their identity should be grounded in Christ, not in their discipline or field of study, not in their accomplishments, not in their relationships—although that all of those things could inform their identity in Christ—but that first and foremost their identity is found in Christ and in belonging to something much greater than themselves, belonging to and in Christ and in his kingdom, and thereby belonging to this notion of this communion of saints, throughout time and history and place.

This sense of fundamental identity provided a foundation for intellectual confidence and exploration for Erin: "I definitely think just knowing who they are in Christ can create a major self-awareness because when they have a major confidence there, I don't think we necessarily need to worry about [struggling with] seeing things from other people's lenses as well because it's not like we're going to be shaken. If we have that firm foundation, it helps us really understand others and also maintain our own self-awareness." In this regard, helping students find their identity in Christ reinforced aspects also provided by understanding that we are made in God's image.

Some SALs also shared that strengthening students' identity in Christ provided a source of commonality in a community that can enable students to break down walls that may be built by other stereotypes. Alana shared her experience fostering an academic community centered around Christ, encouraging students to join the "team":

> I want our students to be able to identify false dichotomies in the world and be able to say, "I don't have to live into either one of those stereotypes. I don't have to identify with this team or the other." And that the kingdom isn't really about being on a team; or if we're on a team, it's not about winning. Like, Jesus's team is about getting other people onto the team—living a life that can bridge things that seem like they should be opposite. I think that's what I want for students. . . . You have to be grounded in your identity in Christ to be able to do that.

For these SALs, finding one's identity in Christ involved reconnecting with our original identity as image bearers of God but also understanding our identity in a more holistic way through God's ultimate representation on earth—Christ. Being a Christian, a brother or sister of Christ in God's family, changes one's whole identity, which then has multiple implications for one's whole learning experience.

Truly Whole

In addition to seeing students as image bearers or "in Christ," several participants discussed how Christianity enabled student affairs professionals to see students as "truly whole." Nolan suggested that whole-person education is "one of the unifying best practices" of Christian student affairs. It may be a unifying best practice, but is it a *Christian* best practice?

Since its founding, the broad field of student affairs has attempted to impose upon educational institutions "the obligation to consider the student as a whole."[3] In this regard, the core problem for the field of student affairs has been understood as fragmentation and not sin. More than sixty years after the initial drafting of "The Student Personnel Point of View," scholars still contend that the philosophy of the "whole person" has remained "the most prevalent and foundational concept found in all of the [field's guiding documents]."[4] Such a contention begs the question: What is there left for faith to add if the field has already focused on developing the whole person for more than half a century? Some of our participants suggested their faith merely added another element to the whole; others suggested their faith redefined the whole entirely.

Free to Add Spirituality

Several of our participants suggested or implied that faith bolsters the professional commitment to student wholeness through the incorporation of spirituality. Steven, a dean of student affairs, articulated this distinct addition quite clearly: "Really the way I think we do student development in a Christian way is to constantly acknowledge that there's a spiritual component to the way that we live and move and learn. . . . Everything is spiritual." Anthony made a similar point by juxtaposing his Christian approach to secular practice: "I think when the secular world looks at student affairs, you know, you look at things like the wellness wheel and it might have spirituality in there. I think that [spirituality] is loosely done, because everyone is afraid in the secular world. We don't have to be loose about it. We can talk very clearly and directly to that spirituality." Anthony felt the Christian environment provided a certain degree of freedom to address students as spiritual beings. This was a freedom many of our participants expressed as they discussed feeling "free" to "pray with a student," "to talk about being a Christian," as well as a freedom to establish programs like chapel, Bible studies, and other activities resembling the life in the church (as discussed further in Chapter Seven).

But, as Steven mentioned previously, "Everything is spiritual." Therefore, he continued to argue, "more so than adding the spiritual components to campus life . . . it's really more [about] how we bring the spiritual into all the other aspects [of the student's life]." Steven offers a helpful insight here. He is suggesting that although SALs should celebrate the freedom to discuss student spirituality on Christian campuses, only doing so through "spiritual" outlets can perpetuate the assumption that spirituality is merely a part of who our students are, rather than something at the core that informs the whole. To keep spiritual matters in neatly defined areas of our campus ignores the greater freedom Christian SALs have to transform the entirety of their practice. If our practice should reflect how we view students, then our practice ought to reflect the reality that spirituality permeates all aspects of a Christian's life. Unfortunately, the fragmentation of spirituality is but one instance of a larger pattern of reducing student personhood through segmentation.

Fragmented Wholes

An overarching tendency to see students as segmented beings was a common theme in the data. For example, when asked what he hoped to see in students at graduation, Christopher shared a vision of wholeness in Christ, with "students that are whole in every way. Students that not only have individual skills, or personal skills, in being able to navigate the world, a sense of equanimity, resiliency, a sense of self, identity in Christ, but also cross-cultural skills, ability to interact with others, them living out the fruit of the Spirit. How to handle and navigate through, in a diverse world." Statements like this were common. Although Christopher's vision acknowledged his desire to see the student as whole, the only way he could do so was as a list of parts. In other responses like this one, the cross sections of whole students varied (e.g., skills/worldview/identity/culture; academic/social/spiritual; or emotional/intellectual/spiritual), but when discussing students as "whole," SALs tended to segment students into various fragments rather than discussing the "whole" itself.

In response to the prevalence of this kind of fragmentation of students, Steven claimed, "we don't necessarily know how to be whole people." Steven's issue was not with the emphasis on developing or discussing our various identities. Nor was it his intention to suggest that SALs should only focus on what makes us all the same. It is, of course, appropriate to emphasize various segments of our identity (e.g., gender, ethnicity, profession, class, etc.)—especially when certain identities have been historically underemphasized and marginalized. Steven and others readily acknowledged that our different identities need to be acknowledged, discussed, and—for God-ordained differences—celebrated. Yet Steven believed a failure to connect these conversations to the universal claim of the *Imago Dei* had an unintended consequence—a tendency to fragment. In this way, the *Imago Dei* is both a universal and particular claim.[5] We each reflect the image of God (universal), but we all do so in different ways (particular). We each hold particular identities that are varied and beautiful, even as we are all image bearers who are united through Christ—unity yet not uniformity. However, as we emphasize segments of our identity using secular theory, we worry that some in the discipline have failed to recognize that students are unique not only because of the segments that comprise their identity, but also how these segments are situated within the whole. In light of Steven's comment, the critical task for SALs is to help students see the beauty in diversity as well as to (1) help students situate various parts within the whole and (2) encourage students to reflect on how the parts might be related to each other.

Perry L. Glanzer, Nathan F. Alleman, and Todd C. Ream discussed the pattern of segmentation we are concerned with when they claimed that "in most cases, cocurricular educators define the whole student only in reference to the intersection of parts with no overall sense of what a flourishing human being is."[6] Rather than merely adding spirituality back into the highly defined borders between segments on the wellness wheel, allowing Christ to enliven the whole person can help SALs envision students in a way that is less fragmented. Again, we are not arguing for SALs to gain the whole at the expense of the parts (i.e., we disagree with any argument that claims our identity is in God and all our other identities are irrelevant); instead, we suggest we need a vision for how to situate the parts within the whole. A handful of our participants offered exemplary statements about what it might look like to allow the Christian faith to fully animate and thereby redefine what it means to see a student as truly whole.

Faith-Animated Wholeness

Being distinctively Christian requires an exploration of what it means to be a whole person, beyond just a sum of identity parts. Nolan provided an argument for why SALs should allow spirituality to enliven how we see student identity development, suggesting:

> We can't just divide, chop up the mind, the heart, and the body
> and have a thoroughly Christian approach to these things. . . . I
> think all of the other theories we've talked about are really help-
> ful, but they are in essence incomplete. They get at one aspect
> of our development, which is good. And that's not to say that

a Christian [theory] has to fully cover everything, but I think
there is room for one that is a little bit more whole-person
focused and expansive, which would integrate well with
Christian worldview and faith.

It is our belief that the Christian faith has the capacity to provide a vision
for students as "truly whole" that goes beyond a comprehensive list of the
fragments. In reality, no list of student identities, capacities, dispositions, or
motivations could adequately account for the complexity of what it means
to be a whole person. Conversations about student wholeness should not
focus on fragmented parts but on what binds the whole *person*. Sociologist
Christian Smith suggests that in reflecting on what comprises a whole
person, we seek answers to the wrong question. He contends that "the personhood of persons cannot be disaggregated in a reductionistic operation
to some lesser or simpler collection of parts, without a loss of ontological
essentials. The personhood of persons is irreducible." Rather than using the
parts to build toward the whole, he suggests we ought to see the parts as
proceeding from the whole he calls "persons," or "centers with purpose."[7]
The whole person precedes—and thereby contextualizes—the parts. Yet
much of student affairs theory and practice works under the assumption
that the parts combine to determine the whole.

Although Smith does not directly reference Christian theology in his
argument, we think he touches on a truth central to the Christian narrative. We are made in the image of God first; *then* we develop our particular
capacities as creations made to reflect the image of God. Ellie does not
use Smith's technical language, but her comments reflect his arguments
about personhood:

I think lately it's become apparent to me how a Christian faith
is incorporated into my practice by how I view students, or how
I view people I work with. That's been huge, to know that when
they're being a challenging student, there's some level of brokenness, or some issue there that's deeper and connected to a lot of
things. . . . They might have an issue here, it's showing up in this
way, but it's connected to so much more. . . . Just knowing that,
there's something deeper behind everything and how I view my

students, trying to love on them. Knowing that love that Christ has shown for me when I continue to be challenging or to not do the right thing . . . I can have that love for my students.

The Christian faith motivated Ellie to describe the wholeness of her students—including their "brokenness"—in a way unlike the fragmented view of students presented above. Instead of focusing on the parts, she emphasized the connection and interaction between the parts. It may seem like we are splitting hairs, but this subtle shift toward wholeness has significant implications.

When we fail to see the student as a whole, we have a limited imagination for how we might actually serve them. In our increasingly specialized departments, it can be easy to spend our time focused on a particular segment of a student's life (e.g., vocation, leadership, roommate relationship, misconduct, etc.) to the neglect of others. When we do, we lose the opportunity to see how our area of focus might influence or relate to other areas of a student's life. For example, in our excitement to provide students an opportunity to lead on campus, it can be easy to give them responsibilities that will build their leadership skills but significantly detract from their studies, their relationships, their health, or their church involvement. Similarly, we can spend so much time helping students find a vocation that aligns with their passions that we neglect the pragmatic realities of socioeconomic status or student debt. Rather than these reductionistic approaches, when we help students grow, we should treat them as truly whole by helping them situate that growth within the context of their whole life and selves.

Conclusion

At the outset of this chapter, we sought to explore the ways the Christian faith enlivens how SALs viewed their students. In sum, their faith enabled SALs to see students as image bearers of a holy God and as "truly whole." These are gifts that help us see students in beneficial ways beyond what the secular field as a profession has to offer. But these two concepts are somewhat abstract and can be challenging to apply in practice. When asked about how their faith informs how they see students, SALs tended to focus on the more abstract theological concepts mentioned above, and only traced the concepts down to the level of practice. As such, there is still work to be done in exploring the unique ways the fundamental student identities discussed in this chapter might connect to the specifics of our Christian student affairs practice.

5

THE END OF THE STUDENT AFFAIRS PROFESSION

*Why are we really here? Why are we here? We love the
[students], but why do we love the [students]?*

—Emily

*Public education wants to do no harm. Whereas we want to add . . .
we know the person we're trying to create. There's a formational
vision—a unifying vision toward which we are moving.*

—Carter

What is the goal of your student affairs work? To answer this question, you cannot simply recite a platitude such as "to educate the whole student," a phrase used by several participants that tells us nothing about what a whole student looks like. In fact, one famous college president said of this phrase, "of all the meaningless phrases in educational discussion, this is the prize."[1] If one seeks to develop someone or something, one needs some *specific* idea about the final ideal to which one's development aims. For instance, a good viola teacher has some idea about what an excellent viola player looks like, a good baseball coach must have some idea of an excellent baseball player, and a good professor in biology must have some idea of what constitutes an excellent biologist. For any student affairs professional, their objectives should relate to some vision of the well-developed graduate.

Yet one of the most surprising findings from our study was the luke-warm way in which Christian student affairs leaders (SALs) indicated that their Christianity influenced their overall objectives. When we asked the degree to which Christianity influenced various areas of their student affairs practice, survey participants indicated that their faith had the smallest influence on their objectives (see Table 5.1). This finding struck us as astounding.

Table 5.1 Level of influence Christianity has on the following areas of work (*N* = 300)

	Motivations for engaging in the work	Worldview or narrative guiding your outlook	Overall objectives	Ethical approach	Methods and practices
High	75%	83%	57%	90%	59%
Medium	21%	13%	36%	8%	35%
Low	2%	2%	5%	1%	5%
None	2%	2%	1%	1%	1%
Don't know	0%	0%	1%	0%	0%

Thus, this chapter focuses on those Christian student affairs professionals who did say Christianity transforms their ends for students and how, perhaps, we need to envision even more radical transformation. In particular, this chapter will look at objectives that clarify and expand upon the student-identity-related ends mentioned in Chapter Four.

Help Students Become Faithful Lovers of God and God's Creation

When you get to know God and God's creation, God's view of you as his creation, God's love for you through creation and Christ, and God's special design for you, you learn to depend upon God. That's when you experience the strength and vitality of God's Holy Spirit in your life in a way that allows you to love God, others, and yourself. Not surprisingly, SALs saw this end as fundamental their vision of a developed student. As Kaylee shared, "I hope for [students] to walk across the [graduation] stage being a lover of God, deeper than they were, and for them to love people well and engage people well." Like the Psalmist who talks repeatedly about God's steadfast love and faithfulness, Christian SALs want to strengthen both students' love for and faith in God. They mentioned hoping for "faith development," "a mature faith," and "faith integration." Or, they wanted "to connect our students to their faith journey" and "to restore/strengthen a student's faith."

SALs also understood that this faithful love is something each student must personally develop. Although students might have experienced a sort of arranged marriage with their faith as their parents directed them to God's love, college became an important time for students to take ownership of their faith. As Richard said, "I want our students to come to a place where it goes from Mom and Dad's faith, the church's faith, youth pastor's faith, youth group's faith, to owned faith . . . to get started toward a faith that becomes truly theirs. . . . That's my goal." In some cases, SALs understood their role as helping students move toward a new faith in Christ. Natalie related this story:

> I have a student, an international student, who came to our institution from a country that had no exposure to faith. . . . This student wrestled a lot, or was really resistant at first, to any talk of God or faith or anything like that in a classroom. And really struggled. The student worked a lot with our campus ministry, got to know our campus pastor, really had some good conversations, and actually just last semester was baptized, which is amazing. This student isn't perfect. This student still struggles in certain areas, but the fact that he was able to be baptized at our chapel service in front of his peers and the community is a huge testament, I think, to what God can do. And that's exactly what we hope for.

Simply said, Christian SALs want students to become deeper and more faithful lovers of God.

Develop Christian Critical Thinkers

If you look at assessment guides for any college in the United States or Canada, you will find that all academic institutions want to produce critical thinkers, which one SAL defined as students "who can speak really well to all different sides of issues." Yet SALs at Christian colleges hoped for something even more. They wanted Christian critical thinkers. What did they mean by this?

First, they wanted students to understand the foundational Christian worldview and how it influences all learning. For non-Christians at a Christian institution, this may involve what Andrew told us he hopes students say: "'I've come face-to-face, at least, with the claims of Christ in my life.' Because we're a Christian institution, but not all our students are Christian. And many of them leave having experiences but not deciding that they want to pursue Christianity at that point. But at least they've come to terms with . . . or we've presented those truths to them." Andrew's understanding of students' relationships with Christ involved all areas of their lives and not merely personal piety. Developing this Christian world-view does not simply help them think. It supports them in practical areas of their lives. As Emma, a residence director, shared, "I also want them to be a really good choosers . . . so they have a theology that helps them not figure out the one path, but to realize that God has made them to be good choosers, to know that life is full of lots of options, and that they get to be good discerners of what that actually is—like what good discipleship is. That it's not trying to figure out the one way, but it's knowing that God has given you skills and tools to make good choices." Overall, one clear task for Christian SALs who wish to steward the students gifted to them is to help students gain a cognitive understanding of the gospel and its implications for every area of their lives, especially their cognitive-thinking abilities and decision-making skills.

Second, Christian critical-thinking skills require that one not merely tear something down with intellectual wit. Instead, one must combine thinking with Christian virtues. Kathy noted, "I think one of the things that's important to me is that they can think critically, read critically, and communicate those thoughts. Particularly for coming out of a Christian college, I hope that they have learned to do that with compassion and extending grace, understanding that I think the Christian faith calls us to excellence and to be our best at what we do." Critical thinking by itself can be an incredibly dangerous weapon without God's virtues to guide it. In this case, Kathy hoped students would combine their intellectual skills with the moral virtues of grace and love, but the list of virtues SALs mentioned could be expanded to include faith, hope, humility, forgiveness, kindness, joy, and more.

Finally, SALs understood Christian critical thinking as the willingness to ask deep questions of God and of themselves. For SALs, it involved asking students to confront their doubts and questions. Hannah strived for students

> to be critical thinkers who don't shy away from doubt and questions but are able to deeply think through the doubt that springs up in all of us at some point or another, and not the bad kind of doubt but the good kind. That means you're actually thinking and wrestling. So, rather than just skirting through college with kind of ignoring our problems or whatever, digging into those so that they can [spend] the rest of their lives feeling equipped for struggles and feeling ready to be resilient, knowing that their faith is a part of being resilient versus something that will protect them from all problems.

Overall, SALs sought to develop their students into Christian critical thinkers who know how to analyze a topic from a Christian worldview, who do so with Christian virtue, and who are not afraid to explore deep doubts, questions, and wounds in their life.

Develop Christian Character and Community to Renew the World

Virtues are what psychologists call character strengths, what Christians often label the fruits of the Spirit, or as one SAL articulated, "the characteristics of Christ." They include things "such as humility and compassion and charity, hospitality." In order to truly become virtues, they must be deliberately practiced under the tutoring of mentors until they become habits. SALs at pluralistic institutions usually aim to help students acquire certain types of virtues, such as respect, responsibility, hospitality, and tolerance. In contrast, Christian SALs prioritized an additional set of virtues using different language. As one SAL mentioned, "We shift from a least [common] denominator, tolerance-based programming and move into what 1 Corinthians 13 talks about—love. We can move in a new and fuller direction."

SALs also wanted students to be more than loving. As John of Salisbury once said, "Charity [love] is never meaningless and apart; it conducts honor, self-control, sobriety, modesty, and the whole army of venerable virtues to man as to the temple of the Lord."[2] Not surprisingly, SALs wanted students to learn how to "live out of the fruit of the Spirit" and other forms of Christian character. SALs like Hailey wanted students to be grateful, hopeful, compassionate, humble, caring, servant-leaders, and more, "that they would be kind of courageous and brave people not only to stand up for truth but to be able to advocate for themselves, to be able to advocate for those that don't necessarily have a voice, to be considerate and thoughtful of the other." Moreover, SALs wanted students to develop these virtues, because they are the virtues of Christ. As Rose explained, "So, for the advancement of the kingdom . . . reconciliation, mercy, justice, evidencing the character of Christ all throughout—that's why we do what we do. Whether a student comes to us as a Christian or not as a believer, at whatever stage that they are—for them to be what God fully created them to be. That's what we're shooting for—for the glory of Christ." Behind all of these quotes lies a vision for moral and academic excellence in every realm of life.

SALs like Kathy recognized that developing one's intellect or vocational skills means nothing without a similar passion for moral excellence: "I hope that at graduation they take some pride in whatever it is that they're going to do, that their future employer will say, 'Hey, that's the best whatever employee,' versus 'Hey, they're not trustworthy, or they're not consistent.' . . . I hope that they've learned that their character matters." Some would add that they hope students not only learn that character matters but also acquire Christ-like character in college.

This envisioned character development was not an individualistic pursuit. Character development, SALs believed, must be combined with the goal of creating a community—one that was "true," "loving," and "peaceful." SALs also wanted students to learn how to "participate," "serve," and "engage" in this community. In these responses, the aim of SALs took the focus off of the individual and shifted it to "communal faith development."

In these responses, "Christian community," "living as the community of Jesus," and "modeling life together based on biblical principles" were held as the ultimate aims. They wanted students to discover "that when they leave a university and community isn't handed to them via the RA or student programs," they can find or build a community of character.

Of course, building Christian community requires some special knowledge and skills—one of which is learning how to deal with differences. SALs saw three important components of this goal. First, they wanted to develop in students the ability to have hard conversations with their roommates or friends. They craved for students "to see conflict as a healthy, good part of a relationship that can usher you into more intimate, real, authentic relationships." A second part of dealing with differences pertained to the Christian and non-Christian divide. They hoped to teach Christian students how to "articulate what you believe in and why you believe in it, and yet do that in a way that's not demeaning or rude to people who see things differently." Finally, they sought to teach students to be multiculturally competent, or interculturally competent, and demonstrate cultural humility. As Brantley stated, "My goal is for students—whether they be White, Black, Asian, or Hispanic—to understand some of the cultural dynamics of places outside of where they come from. Now, of course, they can't know everything about everybody, but I would hope that after they graduate that they know what it is to do ministry in a place that's different than the place they came from." As the last part of this quote recognizes, SALs aimed for students to look beyond building their own loving Christian community to building a loving community beyond the church.

Consequently, SALs discussed broader goals of "meaningful service," "community service," "community engagement," and "global service." These responses implied a goal beyond the campus grounds, as espoused by Paige: "We are helping students understand who they are, how God created them, and what they're good at, what they love, so that they can go out and build the church and benefit society worldwide. My hope is that everything we're doing is toward that end." One vice president for student life shared how her division's commitment to discipleship flows out of her institution's Christian mission and extended beyond the confines of the campus: "The mission of [the institution] is to equip students to think deeply, act justly, and live wholeheartedly as Christ's agents of renewal in the world. This mission undergirds all that we do in Student Life. In fact, our divisional mission statements map onto the larger college mission and reads: 'Student Life cultivates cocurricular learning experiences that disciple, develop, and equip students to thrive as Christ's agents of renewal in the world.'" As in this case, the responses that fell under this theme saw discipleship as extending beyond a Christian community. For instance, Fiona discussed this transformation in a student from Asia. Like many students from less wealthy countries, he had a dream about coming to the West, learning English, and living in the United States: "This student, he came and had this idea, he's 'going to get a degree and he's never going to come back to [name of country],' because it's underdeveloped and there's no way you can make changes. . . . So, the experience [at our institution] was so transformative for him that he actually did go back to his home country. He started a learning center for kids from an orphanage, where they could get their first skills." Fiona concluded that SALs "don't want [students] to just think about themselves . . . but think about the countries and the communities that they come from and what legacy they can leave."

Summary

What participants told us in their interviews reflected their ideals of what they hoped they could accomplish with their students during their four years of undergraduate studies. A summary list of the top ideals for Christian SALs included:

1. Help students understand what it means to bear God's image.
2. Guide students to partner with God's work in a specific vocation.
3. Guide students to identify their individual passions and giftings.
4. Help students become faithful lovers of God and God's creation.
5. Develop Christian critical thinkers.
6. Develop Christian character and community for human flourishing and renewal of the world.

These ends were sometimes articulated alone, and at other times they were combined in some form. For instance, Miles described the cornerstones of his institution that captured many of these distinctives:

> Our four cornerstones are faith in Jesus, God-honoring relation-
> ships, God-honoring excellence, and service. We have license to
> ask and to challenge every single one of our colleagues or peers
> in the office when they're doing something, "What cornerstones
> are you driving?" . . . It's not quite the same as defining learning
> outcomes, but it's a very, very similar process of saying, "When
> I'm inviting students out to Chili's and we're having dinner, it's
> really important for me to be able to say, 'The purpose of this is
> to create God-honoring relationships.'" I want to demonstrate
> to students that they could get together with people, and for an
> hour and a half they can a have a conversation that is completely
> free of vulgar language, that is completely free of negativity. It's
> completely free of the types of behavior and comments that are
> easily found at other dinner tables other places, [which] don't
> yield God-honoring relationships. And so, you're going to model
> through that.

We found the ends that Christian SALs seek to set forth to be inspiring, comprehensive, and theologically rich. Just accomplishing these ends certainly would take much of a SAL's time.

The Realities of Current Practice

Of course, the degree to which these ideals are implemented in practice varies. Table 5.2 reveals the quantitative survey responses of SALs to the question "Please indicate the degree to which each of the following are a distinctive element of your institution's student affairs practice." The survey included a larger range of ideals, some of which we think that SALs need to consider including in their overall objectives.

Table 5.2. Distinctive elements of institutional student affairs practice (n=243)

	Objective	Score*
1.	Approaches crisis management with Christian care, sensitivity, and perspective	5.57
2.	Models and encourages students to develop Christian virtue (e.g., love, faith, hope, forgiveness, humility, peace)	5.38
3.	Develops students' sense of purpose and identity in Christ	5.35
4.	Grounds institutional policies in a biblical worldview	5.24
5.	Assists students in discerning and responding to their calling and vocations	5.21
6.	Provides service opportunities with a Christian mission	5.09
7.	Helps students develop a Christian worldview about learning and the vocation of a student	5.09
8.	Overtly helps all students find their identity in being beloved image bearers of God	5.06
9.	Invites and models participation in spiritual disciplines (e.g., prayer, reading Scripture)	5.01
10.	Helps students create a healthy student culture and learn how to redeem its brokenness	4.95
11.	Equips students for discipleship locally and globally	4.86
12.	Builds community in distinctively Christian ways with special attention to "the least of these"	4.79
13.	Helps students learn citizenship by cultivating justice and righteousness in society	4.64
14.	Invites students into the life of the local church	4.59
15.	Provides staff development that equips staff to live out the Christian mission	4.41
16.	Teaches students to steward and delight in God's creation locally and globally	4.41
17.	Encourages a Christian view of time (e.g., Sabbath rest, times of denial, thanksgiving, celebration)	4.23
18.	Educates students about stewardship of the body as God's temple	4.02

*__Note:__ The score was derived from averaging the a number values assigned to the following responses: (6) One of the most important distinctives; (5) An important distinctive; (4) A somewhat important distinctive; (3) Less distinctive; (2) Not distinctive; and (1) Not student affairs responsibility.

The top response indicates that student affairs staff perceive that they are quite effective at responding to crises in a Christian way—an end that was not articulated overtly in the qualitative research. In addition, when it comes to helping students recognize their identity in the Triune God, their sense of purpose and vocation, developing Christlike character, and providing students with service opportunities with a Christian mission, their campuses truly shine. In this regard, one could argue that SALs are giving attention to almost all the goals we found articulated in our qualitative research.

Yet some of the additional goals that we include in a statement of best practices (see Appendix A) are not given as much attention. For example, when it comes to discipleship, the encouragement of certain spiritual disciplines (e.g., prayer, rest), stewardship of students' bodies or God's creation, and helping students transform society are viewed as less distinctive aspects of their student affairs practice.

Areas in Need of Growth

From our interviews and the survey that mentioned campus distinctives, it appears that the major weakness with contemporary Christian student affairs has to do with the biblical theme of stewardship. We rarely found this theme in our research, except as something that is absent but needed. For instance, the three lowest distinctive ends that SALs reported in our quantitative survey pertained to teaching students stewardship of their body, time, and God's creation. One would think that a Christian approach to student affairs would make these three things important priorities. Instead, when discussing weaknesses with Christian student affairs, one participant gave this answer: "When I asked that question [about how they integrate faith and learning] of our director of the wellness center or the rec center, he said, 'Well, you know, we have these classes, you know, "Run hard the race that's before you"' or something like that. And I'm like 'That's not it.' That's checking the 'We're a Christian school' box. I think it's more about stewardship of your body and stewardship of your time and how we might do the most good through being healthy people."

Patricia replied to this same question by identifying stewardship of the body as a neglected theme. She noted that what she needed was "a clearly articulated sexual ethic that's a high level. . . . I actually do like steward-ship of the body, because I think it relates to women struggling with body image, I think it relates to pornography, I think it relates to sexual addic-tions. I think it relates to relationships. I think that we could build on that." Andrew identified this question as an area that needs work: "How do we take the resources that we're charged with stewarding and use those to the best of our ability?" Based on our findings, there is little question that the stewardship of one's body, a person or institution's resources, or God's creation are all areas where goals need to be established and improve-ments made.

We believe that stewardship of time and teaching students how to rest is a core building block to a Christian approach to student affairs. We wonder if Christian SALs have taken all of the literature about the impor-tance of student involvement to heart but failed to realize that *involvement is different than stewardship*. A vision for stewardship helps prevent one's involvement from becoming an idol that leads to burnout. Interestingly, only one of seventy interviewees, and less than 5 percent of our quantita-tive interviewees, mentioned Sabbath practices. One mentioned starting to incorporate the practice: "I have recently implemented Sabbath prac-tices within my student affairs work because it seems like I constantly see exhausted students." Most others who mentioned Sabbath practices talked about it as an element in their own lives (i.e., "Prayer and other spiritual disciplines such as Sabbath are really helpful for me to manage stress").

A vision for stewardship would also encompass staff development (the fourth least-emphasized distinctive and a clear deficiency already discussed in Chapter Two). This emphasis might involve developing staff in numer-ous areas. For instance, when asked what they think are the most important opportunities for growth in student affairs at Christian colleges and univer-sities, Andrew mentioned, "Budgets. I say that tongue-in-cheek. . . . How do we take the resources that we're charged with stewarding and use those to the best of our ability?" Stewardship certainly involves understanding the university and students themselves as gifts to be stewarded.

Another underdeveloped theological principle has to do with the stewardship of our minds and creativity. The one SAL who mentioned this point noted that if students understand themselves as made in God's image, "they begin to live out this idea of seeing themselves as a creation, a creation of the Creator, and in a sense a subcreator as well." If we bear the image of the ultimate Creator, we can help students understand and take joy in being subcreators. For instance, creating and building a student group, starting a unique ministry, or sustaining a loving Christian community is part of being made in God's image. What are creative ways that our graduates learned to join with Christ in reversing the effects of the fall in the world?

Speaking of the fall, we want to point out once again that both in the Christian student affairs literature and our interviews that SALs avoided talking directly about sin. Admittedly, this focus can be difficult, as expressed by Nicole:

> I think the hardest part is that brokenness is everywhere. So, I think that's where it can get tricky. . . . I think about some of the harder parent or student conversations I've had to have this year and it's kind of like, "Well, I sent my child there so this shouldn't be an issue." You know? Yeah. Whatever it might be, that is evidence of brokenness. So, I think the hardest challenge is that while it should feel different because of who people are and what their purpose of life is and why they care about people, . . . you're not escaped from the brokenness of the world and the ways in which relationships and people are fractured from the fall.

We think that having goals to speak more forthrightly about sin and the effects it has on even the Christian world would help prepare graduates who are clear-eyed about the spiritual battle that Jesus undertook for us and our need to join in the fight that Christ has won for us.

Related to this topic, we also noticed that Christian SALs placed more emphasis upon themes that emanated from the theological doctrine of creation (e.g., we are made in God's image and created for a unique purpose) than they did on themes related to redemption. Redemption was discussed more when it came to discipline (see Chapter Nine). Yet there are other important aspects of redemption that need emphasis. For example, when it comes to students' identity, what it means to be "in Christ" has important implications. As Robert McGee highlights in *The Search for*

Significance, particular redemptive doctrines such as reconciliation and propitiation have significant ramifications for grounding our fundamental worth and identity.[3]

Finally, we think Christian student affairs needs a clearer understanding of the particular virtues and practices students need to develop. Sometimes the virtues mentioned that SALs hoped to develop in students resembled what Kohlberg called a random "bag of virtues" instead of virtues rooted in our understanding of God's character.[4] We did not garner a sense that some virtues—what one of us calls "redemptive virtues"—are more important.[5] These virtues include faith, hope, and love, as well as the clear virtues of God/Christ we are told to imitate. For instance, holiness was mentioned in only two of our interviews, but it is a virtue God calls us to imitate (1 Pet. 1:16). Other specific virtues of Christ we are told to imitate are humility, servant leadership, forgiveness, and acceptance (Phil. 2:1–7; John 13:14–16; Col. 3:13; Rom. 15:7). Our Christian virtues are not the same virtues as those emphasized by other communities, and we should make that clear.[6] If we are created in God's image, children of God, resident aliens of the world, and citizens of God's kingdom, then we understand that true identity fulfillment comes not from creating one's own self and showing tolerance for others; it comes from dying to ourselves as Christ did for us, so that we may truly live, bear God's image, and demonstrate God's virtues. Rose gave a nice summary that included some of these neglected themes:

> Every student is uniquely created in the image of God. We're entrusted with the responsibility of stewarding what has been given to us by the student, by the family, by the parents. We have the responsibility to use our best gifts to be a conduit for the Holy Spirit to do work . . . for the advancement of the kingdom . . . [through] impactful engagement with the world. Reconciliation, mercy, justice, evidencing the character of Christ all throughout—that's why we do what we do. Whether a student comes to us as a Christian or not as a believer, at whatever stage that they are—for them to be what God fully created them to be. That's what we're shooting for—for the glory of Christ.

Christian SALs should be seeking to help students learn to bear the image of God in society. Self-authorship or autonomy is not the end goal. State universities want students to learn how to be autonomous decision makers within a liberal democracy who design their own lives. Instead, Christians believe we are designed to be coauthors and not self-authors. Transformative Christian SALs want students to learn how to depend on and join with God in advancing God's love and kingdom for God's glory.

6

WHAT ARE WE TRYING TO TEACH STUDENTS?

Student Affairs with Substance

Then Jesus declared, "I am the bread of life. Whoever comes to me will never go hungry, and whoever believes in me will never be thirsty."

—John 6:35

I was in student ministries with a student, and because she was in student ministries, we'd meet every week and talk about what she was supposed to be doing. And she came in and we established kind of a discipleship time, a mentoring time, in my office. Her challenge was her identity was not in Christ. . . . She came into my office one day and she told me that she had a 3.9 that semester. I said, "Hey, that's awesome." But what she meant was for the first time in her life she hadn't gotten a 4.0. She said, "You know through the Scriptures we've been looking at, this is really freeing. I had a 3.9 and I'm the happiest person I've been in a long time."

—Nicholas

Being an educator in the deepest sense of the word means teaching students how to live in light of Christ's story. As James K. A. Smith reminds us, "It is not enough to convince our intellects; our imaginations need to be caught by—and caught up into—the story of God's restorative, reconciling grace for all of creation."[1] Nicholas helped a student caught up in perfectionism experience freedom in finding her worth in Christ. According to other student affairs leaders (SALs) from which we heard, this restorative, reconciling biblical story provided a basis for the content or substance of Christian student affairs. SALs believed their role was to communicate the biblical story and challenge students to imagine their lives within it. Thus, not surprisingly, more than four-fifths of SALs (83 percent) saw their Christian identity as having a high degree of influence on their overall worldview or guiding narrative.

Placing Life in the Christian Narrative

Some participants shared that they nurtured this process by making sure students and staff continually kept a knowledge of God and his story at the center of their work. Andrew used career services as an example: "You walk into our career office, and you're not just getting a résumé review or just a, 'Here's how to look for a job.' But you're having a fuller conversation about how Christ calls us to certain places and things and how do we discern that in our lives? And there's a richness in those conversations that you wouldn't find at non-faith-based institutions." The examples we provide in this chapter proceed through the biblical story using the common themes identified by theologians to summarize the overarching narrative—creation, fall, redemption, and restoration—to give some idea of the substance SALs intend to impart to students. In comparison to our literature review in Chapter Three, you will notice some overlap but also some differences.

Created and Loved by God

Teaching students to live in the Christian story started with their core identity. Who do students think they are? Thus, from the start, Christian SALs understood their task as very different from SALs at secular campuses. Mark observed that because "40 percent of [his institution's] students are not active Christians," they wanted to focus on a distinctive emanating from Genesis 1:26–27 and Genesis 9:6—students are valued image bearers of God. Alana shared her moving experience of communicating to a student that she is made in God's image and loved by God:

> I have a particular student. She had to leave school for a semester, because of finances. . . . Her home life was pretty rough. She had also struggled with some suicidality. So, during that time I had already connected with her, and she was really struggling

financially, even to get groceries and that sort of thing. So, there were some folks who were able to help her with basic needs, even though she wasn't still a student with us. She was able to come back and finish out her degree, and this student, [who also] identifies as a lesbian, said, "For me, this experience has been deeply transformative." And it's really settled her. To me, that's I think when we do things at our best. Just a community that loved her well and didn't love with an agenda that had to be completed by the time she left in four years. I mean, I do think that if God designed us, he's given us good ways to live, and that's how we experience our greatest human flourishing. That doesn't change the way that I feel about those things, but . . . I would rather her leave knowing who she is. She is most deeply valued, and her identity as a child of God is the most important significant factor about who she is.

Overall, Christian SALs had a set of clear concepts that they wanted students to know—they are made in God's image and they are deeply loved by God.

Suffering and Sin

One of the essential components of the scriptural story is that we live in a fallen world, we ourselves are sinful and fallen, and, consequently, we will experience sin and suffering in this life. For SALs, this recognition included being honest with God, ourselves, *and* students about the suffering in our own and others' lives. Wesley confessed, "We sometimes have to suffer, and we have to live with those thorns in our side that we wish we could change and not have. So, for me, it's bringing all of those things to the table and recognizing that in myself, being open for students to see that in me, and at the same time not making excuses for those things in my life— and helping them understand that being a Christian isn't being perfect."

In light of this imperfection, SALs recognized that part of their job involved making sure students have a knowledge of the rules that are used to maintain a certain kind of Christian community. Interestingly, few SALs talked about their community rules extensively unless we directly asked about a particular area (e.g., student conduct; see Chapter Nine). We found this refreshing since we believe it is more biblical and healthier to focus on positive creation ideals—a focus set forth by Jesus (e.g., Mark 10:1–19)—instead of rules that act as what we call "fall control." As Jesus said about a particular Jewish law when talking to the Pharisees about divorce and marriage, "It was because your hearts were hard that Moses wrote you this law" (Mark 10:5). What is more, the law cannot redeem; it can only convict one of sin (as detailed in Gal. 3:11, 21–26). From those we interviewed, Miles, who did talk about rules, discussed them in a similar manner:

> So, we talk a tremendous amount—when it comes to sin, when it comes to our student handbook, and what our policies are leading students to do. What kind of decision-making processes do our policies encourage them to adopt? What kind of [methods is] Satan notoriously successful with on our campus, on college campuses in general, and [what is] our role in protecting students from that? In many, many situations, we don't want to be paternalistic. We want students to be exercising increased responsibility, and we want to have policies that incentivize that. In many, many other arenas, we want students to understand that even though they may not like it, we know more than they do. . . . I think integrity and care demands that we leverage the experience and expertise that we have to bless and benefit those people that are around us. And so that means we will have policies that are absolutely justified, because we believe that without it you would make decisions that harm you. And some of those decisions are not just incidental harm. They are sinful harm. They involve soul harm, and they involve spiritual warfare. And we don't want you to become a victim of that.

As Miles understood, sin is not simply a bad choice. It harms your inner being in twisted and demonic ways.

What many SALs sought to focus on, and what Jesus directed the Pharisees to focus upon, are creation ideals. In the passage mentioned earlier, Jesus redirected the Pharisees from concerns about the laws governing divorce to God's creation ideal: "But at the beginning of creation

God 'made them male and female.' 'For this reason a man will leave his father and mother and be united to his wife, and the two will become one flesh.' So they are no longer two, but one flesh. Therefore, what God has joined together, let no one separate" (Mark 10:7–9). Interestingly, to make sure that students focus on more substantive Christian ends and virtues instead of moral rules, Patricia talked about a distinction her institution makes in its different documents: "We moved away from our community covenant being a document that outlines conduct. We've pulled out behavior from the community covenant and put that in a student code of conduct. Here's your behavioral expectations. The covenant is simply a document that describes our life together, which I really like. We'll tap into that when we're talking about, 'You broke code of conduct things, but that inhibits the community that you agreed you wanted to be a part of.' So, that's a nuance, but I like that nuance." According to this distinction, the community covenant sets forth the highest ideals of Christian community, such as the fruit of the Spirit, and the student conduct code contains the rules associated with "fall control."

Joining with Jesus in Reversing the Fall

For SALs, joining with Jesus in reversing the fall involved three concepts: (1) understanding one's identity in Christ; (2) mistakes and failure do not have to define you; and (3) Christ reversed the fall for us, and we can join Christ's work by following Christ's example of sacrificial love and living.

First, SALs tended to talk about helping students understand their identity based on two parts of the biblical story. As we have already noted, they drew upon the beginning of the biblical story to converse with students about finding worth and value in being image bearers of God. In addition, as the opening quote indicated, they also talked about an identity that is shared by Christians in particular—that of being in Christ. As George noted, our identity in Christ "provides a unifying rallying point that I think a lot of other types of institutions lack." Of course, this emphasis on being in Christ had more salience among SALs at institutions where the student body is completely Christian.

Second, in light of one's new identity in Christ, the message that many SALs then sought to communicate to students who made conduct mistakes was that mistakes and failure do not have to define you. Nicole discussed how this worldview influenced her approach to talking with RAs who needed to be dismissed:

> I think about how I interact with students, even if I'm having a hard conversation . . . [like] some of my conversations with RAs—telling them they're not going to be able to have this job anymore because of X, Y, or Z. Even in those conversations, my hope is that they walk out of the conversation knowing that what happened doesn't decide who they are in my eyes and certainly not in Christ's eyes. So, I think . . . I would hope, at least, people are feeling some hope even in that hard situation. That they would not feel like they are a screw-up and can never recover from what happened.

Quite often, SALs shared stories of students who made a mistake that cost them dearly but did not, in the end, define their lives. Nicholas talked about a student planning to enter the army as a paratrooper who made a fateful choice:

> He and a group of rugby players get drunk, steal our ID machine, because they wanted to make IDs so they can be 21 and get into bars. They get caught. The police get involved. They get felony charges. As we walked through this experience with [name omitted], in particular, he was willing to work with us. And it cost him a lot. In fact, he got kicked out of the army. He was on track to be a Ranger. I mean, what it cost him was enormous—in fact, just this last year I wrote to the governor of the state of [local state] to pardon him, so it would be removed/expunged from his record. He gets kicked out of [our institution] for a while, he comes back, we do a mentoring thing for a while, he finishes, goes on and gets a master's in business ethics, and he's a leader in the fire department in the Southwest. So, when I think about students struggling and making mistakes, whether it's big or small, and being willing to be shaped by the

experiences, . . . that in a sense propels the student to become a better human, a better Christian.

Here's a student who willingly paid a dear price for a mistake that would change the course of his life. Yet he flourished as a result. As these stories attest, what does define students for Christian SALs is that their primary identity comes from God and God's story. They are not defined by one incident. They can be forgiven and redeemed. It's also that story that then motivates them.

Relatedly, one of the final ways Christian SALs substantively engaged in Christian student affairs concerned living out their faith. In this respect, they embodied James's admonition that all the thinking and speaking in the world makes little difference if one does not actually put the substance of what one thinks, believes, and says into practice (James 2:14–26). They discussed this approach in two ways: (1) the language of virtues or fruits of the Spirit and (2) practices common to the body of Christ.

Much of the substance that SALs sought to teach and emulate to their students involved a particular set of virtues, many of which we discussed in the last chapter. For example, when our survey asked them about some of the best aspects of their student affairs programs, many pointed to the virtues that the staff model to students. The virtues that received the most mention included the following:

- *Accepting* (e.g., "Christian students, as well as other students, *all* feel accepted and able to express and obtain their needs.")
- *Caring* (e.g., "Caring for the souls of our students. Not just enforcing 'good behavior.'")
- *Discernment* (e.g., "I try to model and demonstrate a prayerful life, a thoughtful life, a discerning life, that when decisions come, you know, I try not to make any hasty quick decisions or responses, which I certainly do at times, but I try to model some of that contemplation.")
- *Grace* (e.g., "Teaching and implementing grace.")
- *Hospitality* (e.g., "Residence Life is launching a cohort program for RAs this fall to practice hospitality from a Christian perspective. Students will spend time in each RD apartment learning

about hospitality and a Christian understanding of land and space while also observing and participating in how each RD practices hospitality.")

- *Humility* (e.g., "Humility and willingness to learn . . . to learn from mistakes and from one another.")
- *Love* (e.g., "Going above and beyond the 'job' to show Christ's love in tangible ways.")
- *Presence* (e.g., "Practicing a faithful presence with each student.")

We would suggest that although these virtues can be prized by those outside the Christian tradition, the biblical mandates to practice these virtues play a key role in their emphasis. For instance, we are specifically told to imitate Christ's acceptance (Rom. 15:7), humility (Phil. 2:1–11), love (John 13:34), and servanthood (John 13:12–17), and to show hospitality to strangers (Heb. 13:2), confess our sins to each other (James 5:16), and be present with the sick (Matt. 25:36). Christian SALs undoubtedly had absorbed this teaching and sought to pass it along to their students and staff.

In our interviews, SALs told us a variety of stories that illustrated what they meant by demonstrating some of these virtues. John shared with us about his time working at a pluralistic university. At that university, he replaced a residence director who, in his words, "was there to enforce the rules but didn't care about the students." In contrast, John took a different approach:

When I got there, I'm knocking on doors, and I have food in my hand, and I'm asking them, "Hey, this is who I am, and I just want to get to know you." They're like, "Are you kidding me? What are you really here for? Do you think I did something wrong?" It's like, "No, I had some chips and salsa, and I just thought it would be fun to knock on doors and just greet people." We'd invite floors down to our apartment and students over, and they just, the idea of hospitality, they just hadn't seen it before, and so I mean, to me, a real pinnacle was after my first year at [institution], the student government, every year, gave an award to a faculty or staff member. They call it the Student Government Service Award. No one in student affairs had ever gotten it. I was the first. The people I worked with were like, "Oh my gosh, how did you do [it]? No one in student affairs has ever gotten that kind of recognition from student government." I said, "I'm just building friendships with people. I'm just getting to know people." I was enforcing the rules, but they knew that it was because I cared about them.

John's fruit of the Spirit also led to some deeper conversations: "People would say, 'I notice the joy that you have. I notice the respect that you have for people, for your wife, and I want to know more about what makes you tick. Why do you care about me as a person?'"

This Christ-like care extended to modeling how to be aware of the suffering and woundedness in others' lives. Helen articulated how living in the Christian story entailed being sensitive to this kind of woundedness: "I think that the student affairs professional's approach to their work is that if they know Jesus and they know Scripture and they're operating with those values, then at the forefront of their mind are those on the margins, those in pain. Not thinking about power, but thinking about supporting and loving and kind of opening the gates in the way that Jesus would. Having eyes to see those who are most in need and serving those."

The stories provided here show us some examples of positive hospitality and love at work on campus. Another response captures the influence of the practice of virtue in a difficult situation. Andrew had a fifth-year commuter student, mere credits away from graduating, who showed up the last day of class and told him, "I need a medical withdraw." Andrew responded to the student's difficult situation from a Christ-centered perspective:

> From the details I knew at the time, I said, "OK, we're not going to grant it. This should have been done months ago. I don't have the documentation." So, there's also a balance and liability, and these things that we have to stick to compliance wise. That's all going on in my head. Well, what ends up happening is he's upset. Mom comes in upset. And I agreed to sit down. . . . We ended up having this very lengthy conversation that gave me context that I didn't have, and [o]nce I understood the context and we talked through it, I didn't totally reverse the decision, but I worked

with them [on] something that was very reasonable on our end but that had them walking away saying, "I feel cared for." To my knowledge, the mom is not a believer. I believe the student is, but I don't know if the mom is. And in that moment, my prayer was that this is, in some way, a manifestation of Christ's love, of hospitality, of grace that she reflects on . . . and it makes a difference. Was I thinking of that at the moment? I may have, but as I reflect, I hope that's what was happening. And that's what we do.

Andrew sought to communicate God's love, hospitality, and grace. He did not just choose any virtue. He chose to emulate these particular virtues demonstrated in the Christian story.

SALs also mentioned that the substance they shared with students contained a set of practices that they would not teach in a pluralistic setting. These practices included things such as prayer, Bible study, worship, testimony, Sabbath rest, and so forth. James K. A. Smith has called these kinds of practices "liturgies."[2] They are not character qualities or virtues that imitate God's actions to others as much as specific actions we should take to sustain and foster a right relationship with God. These disciplines iterated by participants included the following:

- *Prayer*: "Feeling free to pray with a student if I need to, or praying for students, feeling like I can be really open about that is such a freeing kind of experience."
- *Worship*: "Making sure that I go to chapel, because I want my students to know that's important to me, just like I expect for it to be important to them. Making sure that I'm involved in my local church . . . modeling that."
- *Scripture reading*: "You know, I think on one level, there are just Christian spiritual disciplines I incorporate into staff development with my RAs . . . focusing on Scripture once a week during staff meetings or even simply praying with them."
- *Sabbath rest*: "Providing a model for students of vibrant and healthy spiritual life—specifically asking our student life employees to live with healthy boundaries, space for relationship with God, rest, Sabbath, healthy families, and good boundaries."

SALs were quick to point out that these practices could not be formulaic. They needed to be understood as practices that help develop a deep relationship with God and emanate from a heartfelt desire for that relationship.

If there was a meta-virtue or meta-practice that Christian SALs shared as undergirding both virtues and practices, it was that of dependence. This dependence was necessary just to demonstrate virtue. After all, that is why Christians call virtues the fruit of the Spirit (Gal. 5:22–23). Unlike past moral philosophers (e.g., Aristotle) or contemporary virtue theorists and positive psychologists (e.g., Peterson and Seligman),[3] Christian SALs recognized that more than good habits or following some sort of system were necessary to produce virtue. They needed the Holy Spirit. As Matthew observed, "It's more of an art than a science. . . . There's a lot of messiness to it. Maybe we could do a better job teaching our students that the messiness is OK, that we all just do the best that we can and try to follow the Holy Spirit. And we're not always going to know whether that was helpful or not or the absolute right thing to do." This kind of ambiguity meant that one continually needed the wisdom of God. One could not just obtain all of the necessary knowledge from a master's degree and become a great professional. As Eden articulated, she constantly needed God's wisdom: "If I'm not constantly seeking the Lord, it doesn't mean I'm on my knees every twenty minutes; it's the conversation I'm having with him and me staying with what God has called me to, and me continually asking, 'How do I do this? How do I do that? How do I connect with this student?'" Thus, dependence needs to be modeled to students. Without this meta-virtue and practice, everything else becomes problematic. Emily confessed her battle to remain Christ-focused in her work:

> For me, personally, if I'm not modeling it for my students, then I'm doing it out of my own strength, my own education, my own will, [and] my own purpose. I miss the agenda that God has written. So, it matters. It matters when I challenge students on what they believe. It matters when I talk to them about diversity and give them perspective. It matters when I say, "Hey, how about listening to this other student?" when they're talking about conflict. There are all these lessons, but if I'm not filtering

it through the lens of my faith in Christ, then the answers are going to be different. . . . I begin to react and not respond. I don't love them well into what God's called them to be.

When one models the dependence on the Father that Jesus modeled, one comes closer to living out of the Christian story. Emily went on to share:

Doing student affairs through the lens of a Christian perspective means that my relationship with the Lord and my growth will be evident in my job and in the ways that I treat people and the ways that I handle situations, and the ways that I view students, and the ways that I interact with them or my boss or my RAs. I guess it means that through not just my own life but everything that I'm also promoting out from my building, and my girls, and my RA team, that what I'm promoting is a likeness to Jesus and a Christian worldview and not that that's a cookie-cutter thing.

All in all, this process involves teaching students to think, speak, and live theologically with a focus that relies upon God and not the ability to articulate the latest academic theory or cultural movement in higher education.

Is There Anything Missing?

Christian SALs clearly have rich and extensive visions of what they wanted to teach students. In fact, there was little that we thought was missing. Still, throughout our research, both in the literature and in our interviews, we noticed a few important themes that were not discussed in detail.

Most importantly, what we noticed was the absence of the need to educate students more explicitly about how to deal with sin and evil. For some reason, SALs do not like to use the word "sin." We saw this absence in numerous ways. For example, although SALs tended to focus on dealing with suffering in light of the Christian story, they did not talk about sin and evil in the same way. Furthermore, they did not talk about one of the central motifs in the Gospels (a major theme of Mark) or one of Paul's central messages (Eph. 6:1–20; Col. 2:8–15), that life is lived in spiritual conflict with Satan and demonic forces, and that Christ has triumphed not only over sin but also demonic and spiritual powers. Although SALs talked about student discipline related to the responsible use of alcohol and sexual temptation, there was no sense that students needed to be prepared to engage with the spiritual forces of evil in the world through Christ and Christ's authority. We also saw this absence in the virtues and practices discussed. For instance, we did not hear discussions about loving your enemy, nor did SALs discuss the practices of repentance and confession to God (outside of student discipline).

Second, we found that discussions about institutional evils or issues of "social justice" were difficult for most institutions. Some of the SALs' responses below give some sense of the conversation on Christian campuses:

- "The social justice piece—we're still kind of sorting through a little bit."
- "Social justice—I'll talk about how I think we're struggling with some of that."
- "But as far as social justice, that's definitely an area of growth for us."
- "I would say I've been surprised, coming from two other institutions where social justice is at the forefront, especially my undergrad in Minnesota. It's very different. This isn't talked about as much."

From our interviews, it would appear that Christian campuses need to provide forums for conversation about—and Christian perspectives on—the contemporary use of social justice language, as well as a positive vision of Christian approaches to social injustices. Moreover, Christian SALs likely need to provide greater attention to the unique way Christians must confront evil and reverse the fall (through and with Christ).

Finally, beyond the missing redemptive virtues discussed in the last chapter, we noted that one of the key ways we are called to imitate God was not listed among the character qualities SALs talked about conveying to students. The missing virtue was holiness (mentioned only twice in all our interviews and twice in all our surveys). As 1 Peter 1:15 commands, "But just as he who called you is holy, so be holy in all you do." We are not sure why this virtue is neglected, although holiness is certainly not a virtue one finds in positive psychology or lists of character qualities found in state laws mandating character education.[4] Perhaps Christian student affairs has been secularized in ways it does not realize. Perhaps it also relates to a desire to be relevant to the world, and holiness calls one to be "set apart" for God. We are not sure. We do know that we think Christian SALs may need to think again about what it means to call students to holiness.

7

THE HOW(S) OF CHRIST-ENLIVENED STUDENT AFFAIRS

There is a rich, interesting, and important conversation to be had about faith and pedagogy. It goes beyond questions of the worldview or perspective expressed in course content, and it is not reducible to questions of character or treating students kindly.

—David I. Smith, *On Christian Teaching*

Does Christian student affairs have a unique pedagogy or method of teaching? There are two dangers when it comes to answering this question. One danger is to think of the "how" of enlivened Christian student affairs as primarily chapel, Bible studies, and prayer groups. This is the Christ-added approach to student affairs pedagogy that mimics a similar approach to faculty pedagogy in the classroom.[1] For instance, Jacob shared, "There are just Christian spiritual disciplines I incorporate into staff development with my RAs, focusing on Scripture once a week during staff meetings or even simply praying with them—even offering not just counseling but counseling from more of a biblical perspective." Although disciplines such as communal Bible reading, Bible studies, and prayer groups certainly remain central to cocurricular spiritual learning and formation, merely adding them to otherwise secular practice does relatively little to make our approach distinctively Christian. It should be remembered that even the methods more typical of cocurricular learning can be incredibly formative.

The other extreme would be to claim, as our participants did: "All things are spiritual no matter what you are doing," or "I don't think that there's anything I'd layer on top of [my practice] and say, 'This is what makes it Christian or not.' I think it's Christian because I am Christian. So, for me, it's because that guides my own practice and that's going to guide my intersections, hopefully." This is what we call the "Christ-assumed approach." It assumes little reflection upon practice is needed, when, in reality, creating effective programming that successfully integrates the Christian faith takes a significant amount of work. It is work worth pursuing but work nonetheless.

We suggest a third approach is needed. We need a Christ-animating approach that asks: What are the *full* range of specific pedagogical practices student affairs leaders (SALs) believe help students flourish in Christian higher education? Moreover, what might it mean for student affairs practice to be Christ enlivened? In this chapter, we will explore Christian SALs who embody the Christ-animated approach before offering a few suggestions of our own.

Distinctive but Not Unique

Before we explore robust Christ-animated approaches to Christian student affairs, it is worth acknowledging that, at times, a distinctive approach may not result in a unique pedagogical method. For example, Nolan shared, "So, a lot of the programming that we do, especially in my area, is leadership development. So, it is how do we steward these opportunities for students to lead their peers, whether it's through student government, student activities, intercultural programs, calling and career interns, whatever it might be. How do we leverage that opportunity to develop them into servant leaders?" In this case, otherwise indistinct methods (e.g., student government, activities, programs) are animated for Christian purposes through a Christ-animated objective—developing Christ-like servant leaders. Many of our participants shared comments like Nolan's, indicating that the who, why, and whats of the SAL profession are perhaps their most distinctive element.

This reality may be why 40 percent of our survey participants reported that the degree of influence of Christianity on their methods and practices was medium or lower—the second lowest among the five categories we surveyed. The only lower category was *objectives*.

Table 7.1. Level of influence Christianity has on the following areas of work (*N* = 300)

	Motivations for engaging in the work	Worldview or narrative guiding your outlook	Overall objectives	Ethical approach	Methods and practices
High	75%	83%	57%	90%	59%
Medium	21%	13%	36%	8%	35%
Low	2%	2%	5%	1%	5%
None	2%	2%	1%	1%	1%
Don't know	0%	0%	1%	0%	0%

As is often the case though, our qualitative findings provide numerous examples of those who did perceive a significant influence.

The Meta-Practice: Dependence on God

One of the reasons our Christian student affairs pedagogy may not seem different from student affairs pedagogy on pluralistic campuses is that the most important practice is often hard to see or discern. For example, a number of SALs, such as Andrew, highlighted the role of the Holy Spirit in ultimate student flourishing: "We can only do so much. We can program. We can provide services. We care for them, provide a level of safety, feed them. But we can't do the work that only Christ can do in their hearts and minds. So, if I can say, yes, they got to graduation, and we provided those things at least for them to experience that somewhat, then we've done our work. And I trust that the Holy Spirit is going to do his work in their lives."

For many SALs, although their efforts are necessary and important, their confidence did not come through their own efforts but ultimately the Holy Spirit. Miles said, "I've got total confidence that the Holy Spirit can do what our university can't." This was not an excuse to neglect the "best practices." Instead, it was a theological proclamation that student flourishing does not ultimately come from our own efforts but through God's grace and wisdom. We found the following pedagogical practice shared by Hannah particularly inspiring:

> One really practical thing that I remember them training us in is just how to do one-on-ones—where you're sitting with a student and you picture there being a third chair and that's for the Holy Spirit. Versus "I'm thinking off the top of my head to say anything I can to help this student and advise this student," you're like, "The Holy Spirit is present with us, and so that is going to inform how I speak to you, how I listen to you, and hopefully get that power from the Holy Spirit versus just my own brain."

Hopefully, we can help prepare the soil for growth through practices of dependence such as these.

The Pedagogy of Community Building

We found SALs loved talking about "community." Various SALs, for example, when answering a question about their best practices, iterated comments such as "[the greatest strength] at our institution is the strength of community" or "fellowship and community." As Eden told us, her focus is "How do I teach them [students] how to build community? And that when they leave a university and community isn't handed to them via the RA or student programs . . . [they] take responsibility for who they surround themselves with, and who they pour themselves into." SALs viewed the pedagogy of Christian community building as involving numerous elements.

The Physical Setting

A few SALs noted that how Christ animates a setting can be quite overt. Miles shared, "We try to keep our Christianity very, very publicly facing, and so we try really, really hard to keep as much Scripture or Christian iconography visible in our campus experience." Yet there are more subtle ways for Christ to animate a learning environment as well. In his book *On Christian Teaching*, David I. Smith discusses how he intentionally organizes the classroom for the first day of his German class.[2] Instead of having the chairs in a row, he places the chairs in groups of four in order to facilitate relationships and discussion.

The cocurricular learning environment has a much greater variety of learning environments than a classroom. For example, Jennifer talked about creating a separate space for graduate students "because most of them are living off-campus and when they come to campus they tend to gravitate just towards the building where their classes are, or maybe where they're teaching. So, this space has helped create more community. I think that's a big chunk of what we do—is helping them create community so they're not so siloed in their own departments." Another SAL's vision for Christ-animated practice included community bathrooms: "Right now, our residence halls are set up to where you never have to know your neighbor, which is really unfortunate. So, if I could change anything, no money aside, it would be that I would actually build a traditional residence hall, with hall-style dorms and sharing bathrooms. . . . Students hate it, but it fosters community." Certainly, what turns a "space" into a "place" or community makes a tremendous difference.[3] Creating loving social interaction first requires creating the architecture and design that fosters social interaction. After all, the ultimate kingdom of God is something fashioned by Christ ahead of time for us ("I go to prepare a place for you," John 14:3). Fostering the kingdom of God on earth requires this kind of design as well.

Corporate Worship

Unsurprisingly, "chapel" was named by our participants as one of the main uniquely Christian corporate practices. This name is a bit odd since in most every case, "chapel" is not even held in a chapel.[4] Furthermore, we usually call classes by the subject being studied (e.g., cell biology, constitutional law, etc.). It would make more sense to call chapel "God" (that would certainly also keep it from being used for simply talking about good morals apart from God).[5] In this regard, "chapel" is not exactly a pedagogical practice, although certain corporate practices happen in the context of chapel. Anthony supplied the most extensive description of the pedagogical practices that occur in chapel that make it exceptional: "I think chapel is the clear distinctive and it's because it is so unique. No non-faith-based school has everybody in the community get together one or two or three times a week. That bringing together the community, being of one mind, to worship, to pray, to seek petition, to learn together, I think, is the most distinct."

Like Anthony, some SALs saw chapel as one of the most important spiritual formation practices of Christian higher education, because it was the place where the whole institution can "celebrate together, worship together, express our faith together in community." In most Protestant institutions, the actual pedagogy of chapel includes a time of singing and lectures or panel discussions. In our interviews, though, worship singing was never mentioned by itself as a unique pedagogy of Christian student affairs. Perhaps this is because singing songs of worship together, a practice in which all can participate, usually gets short shrift when it comes to writing about pedagogical or spiritual practices, even though singing is commanded hundreds of times in Scripture.[6] For example, James K. A. Smith left it out of his description of practices or liturgies in *Desiring the Kingdom*.[7] In general, chapel was often mentioned largely as a different type of teaching context that involved everyone (or most everyone).

The Pedagogy of Covenants, Modeling, and Mentoring

SALs wanted students to build "deeply intentional, deeply formative, not perfect, but healthy Christian communities" within college so that they could "begin to then develop the skills to transfer it to other environments when they leave our campuses." Specifically, this community building involved three major things: (1) community covenants, (2) modeling particular virtues or fruits of the Spirit, and (3) mentoring in certain relational skills or spiritual practices.

Community covenants. One unique and distinct form of pedagogy in Christian student affairs is the community covenant. The community covenant functions somewhat like a syllabus for student affairs, although the degree to which it lays out aspirations, rules, or both, varied by campus. In our overview of these policies, the best approaches focus on aspirations and use biblical, theological, and virtue language to provide reasons for the aspirations instead of simply listing rules for fall control (see Galatians 5 about this dynamic). In addition, these policies apply to the whole community. The rules, or "fall control policies," are then placed in student and faculty handbooks. Students, staff, and faculty all need a compelling vision of the good life for their community. A great example of how this vision can work was provided by Carter:

> We had a student who, unfortunately, kind of fell through our cracks in a lot of ways. This was a kid, it comes to Thanksgiving break, and [he] hasn't been to very many classes. He's about to fail out, and I have the very awkward difficult conversation with Mom and Dad. . . . They're frustrated with their son, as we all are. But then they're pretty frustrated with me, as the representative of the university that said, "We're going to take care of your kid. We're going to provide all these kinds of support and things like that." . . . They were really mad. They should have been. The result though is that this student is going to be expelled from the campus immediately. Then the next day, I come to my office and there are thirty kids, guys from his floor, waiting for me. I'm early to the office. So, for them to get there, they've got to be there by 7:30. They bring out this [community] covenant. They show me all of these things where they had broken the covenant to this kid. . . . "We didn't do this. We didn't bear his burdens. We didn't hold him accountable." So, they asked for a second chance with this kid. . . . They were saying, "We should be in more trouble than him."

Carter ended up calling the parents and student: "They were cleaning out his room when I got a hold of him. I said, 'I've got to tell you this.' I brought him back up, and he stayed. And he went to every class for the rest of the semester. Still didn't pass anything, 'cause he just couldn't. He was so far behind." Still, the student persisted with the help from his community in the residence hall. He passed the winter term and eventually went on to graduate. As Carter said, "So, to me, that sense of where the community is built so intentionally that the people in the community, the students in the community, take responsibility for it—that's great." Any pedagogy, such as this community covenant, that inspires students to care for each other and carry each other's burdens certainly is Christ animated.

Modeling virtues. The second ingredient to community building involved not merely substantive teaching about virtues (covered in Chapter Six and usually listed in a community covenant) but also the actual pedagogical practice of modeling virtues.

- *Forgiveness* and *grace*: "Working closely with other staff and faculty on our campus and showing how to disagree in love, ask for forgiveness when wrong, and show grace to others."
- *Honesty*: "I think the other part that makes it Christian is I believe in the opportunity to have faults . . . for me it's bringing all of those things to the table and recognizing that in myself, being open for students to see that in me, and at the same time not making excuses for those things in my life—and helping them understand that being a Christian isn't being perfect; being Christ-like means our lives are constantly being made more like his."
- *Hospitality*: "Hospitality, welcoming students into our lives, not just hosting events or acting as administrators."
- *Love and service*: "Loving and serving God, loving and serving people, and not forcing Christianity on students, but to model it and show them Jesus through your work."
- *Patience* and *self-control*: "Because our student population is so diverse (faith-wise), we have students who do not necessarily know the Lord, so it is critical that our meetings, especially conduct based meetings, are grounded in the fruit of the Spirit. We try to demonstrate patience and self-control in how we choose our words and our attitudes going into those meetings."
- *Presence*: "Being incarnational. Student development professionals are frequently present and available to students. This physical presence often translates into mentorship relationships or simply accompanying students on their spiritual/educational journey."
- *Wisdom*: "I try to model and demonstrate a prayerful life, a thoughtful life, a discerning life, that when decisions come, I try not to make any hasty quick decisions or responses, which I

certainly do at times, but I try to model some of that contemplation and all of that. Which to me is all a very spiritual process."

We think all of these virtues can be found in any community, but certain redemptive virtues, such as forgiveness, humility, and agape love, require giving up power. They are and should be particularly modeled as part of the pedagogy of the Christian body.

Of course, even churches can be fallen. Thus, SALs recognized that Christian communities from which the students have come may have taught them a different, distorted pedagogy that only issues support or challenge, and not both. Valerie shared her experience with this level of confusion:

> I think that sometimes I see students a little bit confused about when they come and either their Christianity provides a model of relationship that is condemning or kind of critical, or just kind of points out all your flaws and makes you feel less than. Or, we're going to have a community that just says, "We're going to just love everybody and not ask anything of anybody. We're not going to call anybody out. We're not going to expect more. We're not going to have standards." And I think both sides of those sort of exist sometimes. So, I think it gives us a model of the biblical Christianity, which says, "You are completely unable to do this on your own." You know? "We know you're a mess. We expect you to be a mess. However, God's grace covers all of this. But we're not going to let you stay in the mess. . . . It's not flourishing, and so because of our faith we want to call you to a higher standard, and we think that God can do that in your life."

As Valerie communicated, a healthy body of Christ at a university prioritizes God's grace and both challenges and supports students in light of the Christian story and its particular ethic.

Mentoring. The third pedagogical emphasis involved one-on-one or communal mentoring of certain relational skills or spiritual practices that involves the merging of Christianity and our other identities (e.g., what it means to be a Christian friend, Christian neighbor, etc.). Collectively, SALs identified Christian mentorship as one of their best practices in helping students flourish in college. For example, Caroline noted, "I think the greatest strength is the mentor[ship] component because you're really helping these students, not only flourish while they're on your campus, but also helping them develop skills that they can take with them and carry throughout their lives." What exactly is cocurricular mentorship, though? Once again, SALs largely identified three components of mentorship: commitment, expertise, and wisdom.

The first thing that is needed to undertake this mentoring role is a particular type of commitment—not just to help students' safety or retention but also their discipleship. SALs described Christian mentorship as the "steady pursuit of the student," as being "really driven to know students," and as having a "deeper sense of commitment to help students grow." For some, this intentionality and commitment was embodied by SALs' desire to "walk life and live life" together, particularly by "walking with people outside of just the weekly meeting." This intentionality and commitment were exemplified by a mentorship story shared by Austin:

> I had a situation where [a student] made some bad decisions and was struggling. And I was asked if that student could come and stay on our campus for the summer and work and just allow me to mentor that student one-on-one for the summer. And so, we did that. And that was just a great experience, because we had that one-on-one time. He actually lived with me in the house . . . Through that, he ended up transferring to [our institution] and then graduating from [our institution] and is now flourishing in his faith and in his professional life.

This story beautifully symbolizes the embodiment of intentionality and commitment. Although Austin's willingness to allow the student to live with him over the summer was outside the boundaries of his professional duties, he understood the power of "living life together" and the power of Christian mentorship to change the life of a student.

Beyond commitment, to be a mentor, one needs to be an expert in certain kinds of practices, including how to teach them. For Christians, it means teaching students to integrate their Christian identity and practices with their other identities, such as friend, leader, neighbor, or steward, through deliberate practice. For example, Lucas told us, "I think our greatest strength is our capacity or ability to mentor students. . . . The skills [our SALs] possess are in listening and empathizing . . . and meeting a student where they're at." As mentioned in the quote, one skill is a virtue (empathy), but the other skill is what we would call a practice (listening)—"Active listening, engaging with the student to connect and understand." In other words, even when discussing seemingly nonspiritual matters such as careers, relationships, and various life choices, SALs help students make "God to be the center of it."

Of course, SALs' mentorship involved demonstrating or helping students with a range of deliberate relationship-strengthening practices that involved general things such as knowing students' names (e.g., "We are very relationship driven. Nearly all employees in our division know nearly all students by name") or learning how to ask deeper, spiritual questions (e.g., "asking 'How are you doing spiritually?' And then that could lead to . . . a very deep, rich, sometimes challenging conversation").

The most important deliberate practice mentioned by SALs involved teaching students to interpret life in light of God's story. Caroline highlighted this focus on interpreting life circumstances in light of God's story as she described how a student she mentored experienced failure:

> I had a student that was set to transition to our nursing school. She had made all the plans, and then truly by surprise, she actually failed a course. So she was not able to make that transition to nursing school. Of course, that's very difficult. She's a very motivated student; she graduated from high school early and had enough credit to transition to the nursing school early, so she saw this as a completely devastating roadblock. But just helping her understand that maybe it really was a God thing, and that maybe there was a reason for the delay, and just helping her seek out and just kind of think, "Why have I come to this obstacle?" I think mentoring and talking through those things

> with her—that's what really integrates the faith into Christian
> practices and to working with those students.

Students are faced with varying and unexpected occurrences in life, and
Caroline, along with others, wanted students not just to focus on their
desires but to seek to understand "Where is God in this?" Part of Christian
mentorship is helping students view circumstances of their life through a
theological lens and to understand God's presence—even in the midst of
struggles and failures.

This practical expertise leads to the third component of mentorship:
wisdom. Wisdom typically comes from learning from those who have
"gone before us." Due to this reality, SALs desired to connect students to
those who are a "couple of steps ahead of them in life that can give wisdom
and support, helping them with a reality check." Ruth reiterated the benefit
of having mentors as "having somebody to be an outside perspective to
bring some clarity and wisdom and even just to process through these big
formational questions that we have during the college years." Moreover,
growing in wisdom involved helping students navigate questions many
college students ask through a Christian lens, such as "What major should
I have?" and "What is that job going to mean for me finally?," in the proper
context. Although these are pressing and important questions, wisdom
cultivated the students' desire to see God's will within one's vocational discernment and ask, "Who [am I] called to be?" and "How [can I] use [my]
giftings for the kingdom?"

Areas for Future Growth

In closing, we would like to offer some reflections about possible areas for
future growth and creativity for Christian SALs regarding their pedagogy.

First, we suggest departments of student affairs undertake a liturgy
audit. Our use of *liturgy* here is a reference to the works of James K. A.
Smith, who traces the ways various practices, or liturgies, can shape the
desires of our heart.[8] Thus, a comprehensive liturgy audit would include
looking at current methods your office employs, and how those practices
might be shaping the desires of your students' hearts. Do your practices actually align with the espoused missions and objectives of your

department and institution? Do your practices help students see beyond themselves? Are your practices forming students into faithful followers of God and instilling Christian character, or are you merely adding experiences to a student's résumé? Have you articulated these differences to your students? A sample of this kind of alignment of practices with mission was articulated by Miles: "We have what we call 'four cornerstones' that all of our programing is driven through. . . . Our mantra is, 'When we're planning anything, if it doesn't involve two of these cornerstones, then we don't do it.' And so, our four cornerstones are faith in Jesus, God-honoring relationships, God-honoring excellence, and service. We have license to ask and to challenge every single one of our colleagues or peers in the office when they're doing something: 'What cornerstones are you driving?'" This kind of exercise helps ensure that objectives and pedagogy work together.

Second, Christian SALs should increasingly view their role within the context of the larger campus and church community. One of the greatest benefits student affairs has to offer is to provide an environment for students to synthesize their learning. Thus, an important "how" of Christian student affairs is to provide an avenue for students to reflect on and act in light of learning they have garnered from class, church, family, and social life. Christian SALs are uniquely positioned to enact this "how" because Christian theology maintains that a unified vision of knowledge finds its source in God.[9] Secular higher education has long since turned away from this unified vision for knowledge.[10]

Third, Christian SALs should think creatively about how to incorporate "other spiritual disciplines" (i.e., disciplines that are not often practiced but biblically prescribed) in their practice. Specifically, throughout our interviews, although SALs were quick to mention Bible reading, prayer, and solitude, other spiritual disciplines such as fasting, memorizing Scripture, simplicity, and giving (tithing) were not mentioned.

Does Christian student affairs have a unique pedagogy? We think it does—sometimes overtly so; other times not. But we hope that current and future SALs will continue the work of those presented here who have sought to imagine not just unique ways of thinking about Christian student affairs but unique ways of enacting it as well.

PART FOUR

Operational Forms

Having explored Christian student affairs practice in more abstract terms, we asked our participants to discuss central and significant operational forms of Christian student affairs. By *operational forms*, we mean core practical functions that resemble the most basic description of what student affairs does on campus. We recognize student affairs is much more than these two functions, but for the participants from which we heard, residence life (Chapter Eight) and managing student conduct (Chapter Nine) were the main ways the more abstract vision of student affairs was made incarnate.

Figure IV.1. The Christian Student Affairs Imagination

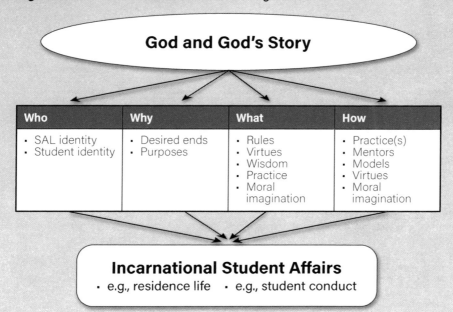

8

HOW CHRIST ENLIVENS RESIDENCE LIFE

Before school starts, in training sessions . . . we try to talk about
even the little logistical pieces, like putting in a work order.
Why do that? How does that show care for someone else? How
is that hospitable? And so how are both of those things part
of who we're called to be as Christians? You're living out your
theology when you're putting in work orders. You're living
out your faith when you're doing that consistently well.

—Alana, Residence Hall Director

Good residential communities, like good neighborhoods, churches, or families, do not simply come about by chance; it takes extensive and intentional work to make a character-forming community of virtue. This chapter describes how Christian residence life leaders envision their creative work and considers how they can more forthrightly imagine and live out their work within the whole of the Christian story.

Beyond Professional Identity to Theological Identity

What are the purposes that animate residence life student affairs leaders (SALs)? In our survey, forty-five residence hall directors shared what they thought was their professional purpose. They reported these top six functions:

1. Creators of safe spaces
2. Mentors

3. Community builders and administrative supporters
4. Teachers, educators, or trainers
5. Rule enforcers
6. Crisis managers

Residence life SALs understood themselves as creators of a certain kind of safe community with boundaries in which they can teach and mentor students.

Interestingly, only a few outliers understood their role in overtly theological terms (e.g., "To facilitate growth of the residents of my building in their relationships with each other, with the university, and most of all with God"). Still, these top six functions are not simply secular. Thinking within the Christian story, the first four purposes mentioned above and even part of the sixth could be said to derive from our creative ability as humans made in God's image. All of us create homes, look for mentors and teachers, and build communities. In many ways, residence life SALs hoped to embody the creation-stewarding role that God has bestowed on us.

The Creation of Community and a Quality Learning Environment

One of the ways that SALs talked about creating a healthy and robust learning environment involved what several of our participants called "the ministry of presence." In fact, some of our survey participants identified this ministry as their "best practice." One SAL described it in this way: "We value our RDs [residence directors] being in the buildings, eating with students, doing life with them. We believe that allows the relationship between RD and student to deepen, which allows us to serve them better in all aspects of their personhood."

Beyond being present, many SALs talked about the importance of their resident assistants (RAs) demonstrating active hospitality for their students. Anthony described the priority of hospitality and care in the little things when it comes to supervising his RAs:

> I think I have to start, first, by saying you have to be good student affairs practitioners. . . . What I say to my RDs is, "Yes, you are here to do ministry, but we have to be given permission from the students to do that ministry." So, if a student comes to you

and says, "My toilet is broken," and you never get it fixed, then when you want to say, "Let me speak into your life spiritually," they're going to go, "You don't care about me." So, we've got to show that we care and can do our jobs effectively and efficiently, first. Then they give us permission to speak into their lives. When that permission is given, then that's when I think we start doing the things in a Christian way that can't often occur in other institutions.

Excellence in hospitality meant paying attention to the humanly created physical environment and fixing physical brokenness—and not just relational brokenness.

As one makes sure the physical environment is welcoming and hospitable, then one could move to the creation of intentional relationships. This required what one SAL called the unique practice of "mission-centered conversations" with students. They also sought to make sure older students had those same conversations with younger students. Avery, who is the RD for a women's residence hall, gave a programming example: "We had this event . . . where [older] students were talking about Sabbath [to first-year students] and talking about how they've struggled with it . . . being vulnerable to say how they do it well and how they've struggled with it, or how they haven't done it well." Here we see an example of women seeking to create an atmosphere of hospitality and mentoring that is real, authentic, and vulnerable—a beautiful picture of the body of Christ.

Overall, for Christian SALs, creating a Christian community of learning and character involved a combination of certain virtues (e.g., presence, hospitality) and practices (e.g., mission-centered conversations, creative programming incorporating Christian practice).

The Front Lines of Fall Control

Of course, these beautiful moments are also punctuated by times of chaos, disorder, and discord. Consequently, every healthy community in a fallen world still must have rules and referees (the fifth purpose mentioned earlier). RAs are on the front lines of this work, and it often takes a unique personality to do it. As one who educates student affairs professionals, I

(Perry) can attest to seeing graduates take RD positions and quit within a year or two because of the challenges that come with being the one who must enforce specific rules. Many aspiring RDs love the positive joys of creating community and mentoring students but find it difficult to referee community life.

Christian colleges and universities are not exempt from fallenness and brokenness. We can, however, handle it differently. We noticed that many SALs followed Jesus's admonition not to focus on the rules that seek to limit the consequences of the fall, but to focus on the positive ideals God established for us (Mark 10:1–11). For example, as mentioned in Chapter Six, to make sure that students focus on more substantive Christian ends and virtues instead of moral rules, one vice president of student life shared how her division shifted the emphasis of their community covenant from a conduct document to a vision of the positive moral virtues and character qualities that they hope students acquire. According to this distinction, the community covenant sets forth the highest ideals of Christian community, whereas the student conduct code contains the rules associated with "fall control."

In addition, the veteran SALs saw their role regarding fallen behavior as more than simply rule enforcement. They usually saw themselves as mentoring students about how to deal with processing conflict and finding redemption in the thick of it. Nicole provided a helpful example of this type of incarnational redemption in her story of an RA mistake that resulted in termination:

> We had a situation this past year where we had an RA who encountered a student violation and didn't report it. And it ended up being a significant enough lack of reporting that we did need to let the RA go. And I remember in conversations with my boss just feeling really conflicted because up to that point the RA had been a really strong RA. And so, it was difficult to let the person go off of one decision, but the decision was significant enough that it did need to happen.

These are the tough decisions that drive SALs without the ability to reinforce standards out of the field. Yet, instead of seeing this enforcement as a tragic disciplinary action, Nicole's boss helped her place it in a larger story: "My boss encouraged me to think about a way that the RA could continue to still feel poured into and developed in the position . . . developed as a person, even without being in the position." Her boss's suggestion resulted in a creative solution:

> So, when I met with this individual to let her know that she was no longer going to be an RA, I made sure that the RD was there with me having the conversation, so that the support was being felt by not just me but also by the RD there. And the RD shared that she would like to continue doing one-on-ones with that student weekly for the rest of the semester. I also asked the student if they would be willing to meet with me on an every other week basis.

Consequently, Nicole met with the student for the rest of the semester. At the end, she shared:

> In my last one-on-one, I asked the former RA how she grew from that situation, and she said that she realized that she was trying to play God. When she was thinking through a scenario, there was never any room for failure. So, if she couldn't make sense of something in her head for how it might play out, and if it was going to play out in a way that seemed like failure would happen, then she would avoid it to avoid failure. She shared that through this learning and growth of being let go, she came to realize that failure is a necessary part of our dependence on God and of our growth and trust. And that if we try to prevent mistakes or prevent failures, that we're ultimately impeding growth that we could have with our relationship with God. It was just really powerful and really self-aware of that student to process that and realize that.

This story provides a wonderful example of how to envision and enact redemptive discipline within the larger Christian story. It also reveals how discipline can end up becoming one of the greatest joys (often in the long-term) of the job in the discipleship process.

The Redemptive Nature of Residence Life

Intriguingly, only a few SALs described their role in specifically redemptive or New Testament terms, such as being "pastors" or "shepherds" or discipling students. One of these exceptions shared how his institution reframes their profession as an RD into a specific theological role: "We are called dorm pastors, or DPs, and assume more of a guidance role for students and a mentor role for RAs. We are to exemplify the fruits of the Spirit and extend them to those around us. We help students explore and deepen their faith journey. We do all this all the while making sure the culture and environment of the dorms are enjoyable yet safe. That is done by making sure RAs are trained, rules are respected, and things are kept in order."

This SAL was one of the few to articulate the purpose of residence life as involving both basic stewardship issues of safety, community, and order-keeping, as well as what we call the redemptive portion of the larger Christian story. The absence of this theme in most responses surprised us.

This theme was a bit more pervasive in our interviews than it was in the qualitative survey responses we analyzed in the previous paragraph. Mark compared the mentality on his campus to the nature of the work at a nearby state school. He observed, "They've got one RA on a whole floor of a hundred students. And the RDs are just administrators, not relational. Our campus pastor says it best: 'Yes, I have the title of campus pastor, but I dare you to find someone, a staff on our campus, who isn't acting in a pastoral role.'" Alana was also very clear she did not want to be seen simply as a mentor:

> Part of my practice has been changing more, and I'm trying to move students less from seeing me as a mentor and more to seeing me as just a spiritual director . . . so, I'm connecting them straight with God, rather than giving them all my thoughts and opinions about the issues that are going on in their life, because I don't want them to be feeling like they need somebody like me in their life all the time when they graduate. I mean, we all need mentors, but when they graduate, obviously, I'm not going with them. So, [I'm] trying to do a better job of connecting them with the Lord.

Like Alana, a minority of residence life SALs conceived themselves as Christian teachers, disciples leading disciples, or spiritual directors.

Furthermore, for these SALs, evangelism and discipleship required the entire student affairs staff. Natalie shared about this holistic evangelistic process in a particular case: "We had a Muslim student we baptized, which is amazing. And she is a formally Muslim student from a Muslim country, and . . . we had to be very careful about not posting anything because it's dangerous. But it was a testament to, again, what God does when you are open to Muslims. So that was just a group effort from our global program practice and our living learning community that she lived in and [their] mentoring, and God was able to bring about faith. It was pretty cool."

The same long-term investment also took place regarding discipleship. Emily told us, "I guess I really see this job as disciple-making and that's probably one of my favorite parts of the job is that it's so set up to be easy for discipleship. We have RAs, they have girls, I pour into them, they pour into them. You know? It's like a trickle-down effect." This outlook proved to be a distinctive for several other SALs.

The Substance of Residential Discipleship

What does the substance of this discipleship or spiritual direction look like in a residential context? For SALs, it involved two things: teaching students particular spiritual practices and moral virtues. First, we should note that the spiritual practices we will mention in this section go beyond the normal emphasis on chapel, Bible study, and prayer. Of course, one we have already mentioned is the ministry of presence. As Kaylee emphasized, "Sometimes it's not even talking about these Christianese things, right? But it's I'm present with them. I'm available to them." Another practice already discussed involved learning how to have deeper conversations with students in their halls about things that matter. Emily talked about her process in this area. It all started with hiring: "I feel like I just try and really hire people who aren't just 'spiritually mature,' but really do love the Lord and have a desire to know him more." Then, Emily teaches RAs how to do various levels of conversations. They learn how to start with talking about basics, but then she teaches her RAs how to get to the deeper level issues with students and models that practice in her own work. She says that she helps them talk about front porch conversations, living room, and kitchen conversations. The front porch conversation is like, "Hi, I'm [name], and this is what I do. I'm mowing the lawn today." Then she discusses moving to more kitchen conversations, "OK, why did you choose your degree?" The living room conversations are usually where the challenge and support are. Questions about "Why did you do that?" also are involved in these conversations.

Another practice folded into these levels of conversations was teaching students how to listen in a uniquely Christian manner. This practice was described by Alana: "In my own practice, we've been doing more prayer together. So, sitting before the Lord and just inviting him to speak. With students I've been sitting and saying, 'OK, let's take that problem to the Lord and ask what he has to say about it.' Then just sitting and praying and listening together and letting them kind of hear from God directly." Although this practice was only mentioned by one SAL, we think it provides a helpful example of bringing God into the discipleship process that can help cut dependence on a human mentor.

The second part of the discipleship or teaching conversation with residence life SALs focused on how to demonstrate and pass along moral virtues to student leaders and students themselves. The same virtues mentioned in Chapters Six and Seven were also emphasized among those engaged in residence life. These included acceptance, caring, grace, honesty, hospitality, humility, love, presence, and service. Miles shared how this teaching works: "When we look at our expense reports and we say, 'Hey, this res[idence] hall just bought forty hammocks, right? Why did they do that?' They're trained to be able to answer that in light of one of [our] four cornerstones. They say, 'Hey, look, we bought forty hammocks because we took twenty inner-city kids out to the park and spent the day with them. And this is part of the service that we're teaching our students to embody.'"

Additionally, Christian SALs understood that virtue development might also involve discussions about the virtue of integrity, as related by James:

A lot of the stuff they do, 95 percent of it, is with nobody watching. Like, they're supposed to address situations when they come across them. How do we know they do that? Well, we just trust they do it. . . . So, because of that, we do a lot of training with them on just, "Yeah, no one is going to know. You could fool us, but it's not the right thing to do. There's something called integrity. When you say you're going to do something, you do it. If you don't want to do it, that's fine, but just tell us. Tell us, 'No, this isn't for me. I don't want to do this stuff.'"

James observed that at the state university where he used to work, the leaders would check in with the RAs more often than where he currently works due to the lack of trust. Yet his Christian worldview also made him realistic about the need for accountability: "I still do check in a lot, and I'm not naïve. We still have issues with it here. We still have issues with people not conducting themselves with integrity, not keeping their word. Because we're all human; we're all fallen. And they're learning how to develop that integrity." The key for James is that virtue development or fruit of the Spirit does not come through heavy-handed drills. Instead, a Christian approach requires something else.

Someone's like, "Who cares? Why are we doing this?" Well, we're doing it because of faith. Faith is absolutely a part of being a man or a woman of integrity. That's something that God wants in us. I think the faith that we have as a foundation allows us to have those discussions and allows us to have some backing. I'm not sure our students are better at it. I hope they are, but I know that we are at least trying to develop in them, and it's something that we regularly talk about.

In other words, accountability for a Christian RA is different than accountability for a non-Christian RA. Christians live in light of God's presence.

Furthermore, a few SALs also pointed out that ultimate virtue development requires God's Spirit for wisdom and strength. Kaylee shared, "What does it mean to not just [do] self-care, but . . . to be filled with the Holy Spirit in order to pour out? If we're not doing that well . . . we can't do our jobs the best that we can." This ultimate practice of dependence on God was often considered the most important virtue to practice.

We want to share a final story that Ashley related to us about the kind of sacrificial and Spirit-filled love demonstrated by an RD at a university. A first-year student's parents, brother, and sister were all killed in a car accident. The RD and the president got together and decided that they were going to be the ones to tell the student what happened. Not only that, but they were going to support her very intentionally from that point on. The RD practiced the ministry of presence to the student. She told the student, "On nights where it's too much for you to be alone, come and sleep on the couch in my apartment." In addition, she extended her commitment to this student beyond her time at the university. In the past decade since the event, the weekend of the death of the student's family, the RA and the student take a pilgrimage. They go to where she first heard the news, then they go to the home, and then they go to the cemetery. During that time, they process through intentional conversation: "Where are you now, as you continue to work through this trauma in your life?" As Ashley told us, "It is a great vision to me of what student development should look like on a Christian campus."

Programming

We asked residence life SALs for examples of substantive programming or activities they oversee that enhance the Christian mission of their college or university. To this question, participants gave us three types of responses. First, they mentioned nurturing common Christian practices one might find in a church setting, such as residence hall Bible studies, worship times, prayer groups, spiritual retreats, service events, or mission trips. Interestingly, prayer groups were the least mentioned spiritual practice.

Second, a few participants described creative residence life programming. For instance, one mentioned a "Sex & Chocolate Panel" composed of individuals at various levels in their relationships who discussed "what it means to be a sexual being as Christians and live it out in different aspects of relationships." Another participant described a Freedom in North Korea event that involved bringing in an outside nonprofit to educate students on current issues in North Korea. It was in this area where we found two types of residence life SALs. Some were quite willing to venture into difficult conversations, while others felt like their campuses played it safe (e.g., those quoted at the beginning of this chapter). Representing the former, Noah described this experience regarding conversations about sex:

> And so, I'm just like, "No, this is something we're going to talk about. This isn't this un-Christian thing. No, we're going to talk about it, and we're going to talk about it explicitly. We're going to allow people to ask their questions about sex." And if we don't have answers to these questions, invite different professors from around campus . . . to [host a forum for] those questions in the residence halls. . . . We don't want to do it anywhere else, because this is going to be a safe space. Then we're going to have these kinds of events in the residence halls, in an open space in the residence halls. Structure it, because we don't want anyone to feel ashamed, but we're going to have these types of conversations in the residence halls.

This kind of programming varied from occasional events to weeklong or even yearlong programming around a difficult topic.

Finally, participants described more intimate mentoring or relationship-building activities. One mentioned, "In a micro-sense, I believe my one-on-one meetings with students enhance the mission. Rarely do I meet with a student and not talk about how their faith integrates with their learning, whether that be in or outside of the classroom."

Only a few activities ranged outside of the aforementioned categories, which perhaps speaks to the need for more creativity in residence life. One area where some residence life SALs mentioned seeing this creativity happen is through the design of different types of living-learning communities (LLCs). Natalie talked about how all six of their LLCs are based on the Christian mission of her institution. One of the LLCs is a healthy living hall that focuses not just on physical health and healthy eating, but also on spiritual wholeness. Another LLC is called the Global Village. Both international students and domestic students can elect to live there. There is also a faculty-in-residence who leads programming. Natalie noted, "So, we're going and making disciples and we're hopefully influencing the students' lives, particularly the students that don't have a faith background that are coming or have a very different understanding of what the Christian faith is from outside a Western perspective."

Another type of creative initiative involved curricular partnerships. These partnerships revolved around a certain theme. For instance, Avery mentioned, "We have a service-learning class that's talking about servant leadership and Christ-led leadership." Another SAL, Helen, pointed out, "We have one RD on our campus who does these pilgrimages into the wilderness, and they're for holistic student development—thinking about the spiritual life, the interior life, student health, relationship[s]." Beyond these creative suggestions, few mentioned other endeavors. Overall, although clear areas of creative programming exist, we think more work could be done. The following section outlines some additional areas for growth.

Theological Evaluation and Suggestions

In this last section, we will offer some theological evaluations and practical suggestions. Though not exhaustive, we hope that the following reflections will help improve the practices of Christian residence life.

First, we think SALs must continually cultivate the skill of looking at residence life through the Christian story. Residence life provides an opportune setting to not simply build learning communities but also to create communities of character. This results in residence life being one of the main settings where students can practice virtues to become more like Christ (e.g., loving your neighbor, sacrificial love, humility, service, forgiveness, grace). Additionally, SALs have the responsibility to address the fall by establishing specific boundaries, enforcing rules, and disciplining students. Residence life also provides SALs the privilege to participate in Christ's redemptive work, such as helping students understand discipline within the Christian story, guiding students to be more like Christ, and assisting in students' holistic transformation (i.e., mind, body, and spirit) for the purpose of glorifying God. Our hope is that articulating residence life through the Christian story helps SALs distinguish the distinctive components of Christian residence life.

Second, we believe SALs working in residence life should continue to be the "front lines of fall control" by recognizing sin and acknowledging brokenness. We want to emphasize this point because this is one of the most difficult aspects of residence life, as articulated by our participants. We believe that one's ability to recognize sin and accept brokenness—and address it—is an essential competency for those desiring to work within residence life. Indeed, SALs must be able to address the fall by enforcing the rules and trusting in the established disciplinary process as an avenue of redemption. Given that we live in the eschaton of the already and not yet, SALs must understand that brokenness is a consequence of the fall and cannot be avoided. This requires SALs to have a specific posture when encountering sin and brokenness: be saddened but not surprised. Moreover, it entails SALs to have specific competencies in accepting and addressing sin and brokenness: (1) the ability to directly confront sin and discuss it; (2) the ability to articulate brokenness within the Christian story and why rules, regulations, and boundaries are necessary when building a faithful Christian community; and (3) the ability to referee community life.

Third, student affairs divisions must allow residence life staff to draw boundaries. In fact, we believe that residence life staff can often be abused in this area, which likely results in burnout and high turnover rates. For example, Mason spoke of the challenge of being an RD at his institution:

> As of right now, our RDs—unless you are using vacation and are gone—you are on call 24/7. Each RD is on-call 24/7 for your residential area. Then if somebody is on vacation, you're on-call for your area and you sign up to also be on-call for somebody else's. That can just be a real struggle, even if I want to go hiking in the middle of nowhere and leave my phone in the car. . . . If I did that and something happened and I was not able to be reached, it would not be that big of a deal, but it's still in the back of my mind—this "I need to be constantly available" thing. Yes, which is super stressful. It is. It is. It really, really wears on you.

Moreover, Emma shared that she felt tension between being an "RD and [being] connected to the church faithfully." She shared that she has difficulty committing to a church because "I'm on-call or I have to check out if there's an event." Regretfully, she told us, "It does feel church community always comes second tier to my job."

We believe that the challenges described above are common struggles faced by residence life SALs. Of course, residence life SALs must be willing to embrace various interruptions and inconveniences; not only is it a part of their responsibilities, but it is often in these moments of interruptions and inconvenience that SALs can model Christ's love toward students. Yet this does not entail that SALs should give up basic commitments to their family, community, and the church to be a "good" RD. We would argue that if RDs are not given a Sabbath rest and are not given space to be involved in the larger church community, the Christian college is failing to model some of the most fundamental things it tries to communicate to students— the need to steward one's body and time, the need to care for others, and the need to worship God and fellowship with other believers in the context of the local church. In order to help draw boundaries for SALs, deans and vice presidents of student affairs should encourage all—including residence life SALs—to observe the Sabbath. Practically speaking, residence life staff should not be expected to answer calls or answer emails during the Sabbath. Moreover, programming on the Sabbath should be discouraged. Regarding after-hours emergency situations and on-call protocols in residence halls, this would mean RDs should not have the unending, 24/7 responsibility over their residence hall; instead, the institution should have a rotating on-call system that creates boundaries and allows space for rest for SALs.

Fourth, Christian SALs should be some of the best at implementing new and creative residence life programs. Although we admire much of residence life and believe that it is a strength of Christian student affairs, we do believe that residence life programs can benefit from more creative programming. We will suggest two possibilities: (1) faculty-in-residence programs and (2) living-learning communities focused on a particular contemporary theme of importance. First, given the need to increase the partnership between the curricular and the cocurricular, as well as the literature of the importance of faculty and student engagement, we believe that a faculty-in-residence program can lead to great benefits. Yet many Christian campuses do not have faculty-in-residence programs. According to Rishi Sriram and Melissa McLevain, faculty-in-residence programs offer "faculty members the unique opportunity to live and learn with students in residential communities."[1] Not only do these faculty members serve to assist residence hall staff; they support the intellectual, social, and spiritual programming of residence halls. Moreover, these faculty members help students understand their life and vocation within the Christian story. Ultimately, faculty-in-residence, when properly implemented, can assist in achieving the ends of Christian student affairs we discussed in Chapter Five.

The second program innovation we suggest is a living-learning community that focuses on a relevant biblical theme with contemporary relevance. For instance, we could imagine a community devoted to cultivating the awareness, knowledge, and skills of racial reconciliation. We believe such an innovation is needed in light of the challenges of creating racially inclusive climates (Chapter Ten), as well as the reality that many of our students come from racially homogenous churches, schools, and neighborhoods.[2] There are two main benefits of this type of living and learning community. First, it allows students, staff, and faculty—while living in community together—to engage biblically and theologically with one another on key issues. Second, it creates conditions for intentional, prolonged, and holistic engagement on these issues. For instance, scholars have revealed that racial engagement and programming must be sustained over time; isolated programmatic efforts often fail at achieving desired outcomes.[3]

Finally, SALs should embrace both the ordinary as well as the extraordinary aspects of residence life. Part of residence life is embracing the ordinary, or what some SALs call the "grind of residence life." This means faithfully carrying out the ordinary tasks (e.g., check-ins, check-outs, work orders, and even handing out fines). It also means consistently building community and showing hospitality through ordinary means (e.g., eating together, praying together, spending time together) and not necessarily through grand events. We also believe that SALs must embrace the extraordinary aspects of residence life—recognizing, for example, that a Christian community is created not by our own efforts but by God. Dietrich Bonhoeffer stated, "Christian community is like the Christian's sanctification. It is a gift of God which we cannot claim. . . . Christian community is not an ideal we have to realize, but rather a reality created by

God in Christ in which we may participate. The more clearly we learn to recognize that the ground and strength and promise of all our community is in Jesus Christ alone, the more calmly we will learn to think about our community and pray and hope for it."[4] Ultimately, the most extraordinary aspect of Christian residence life is that building a Christian community is, in the words of Bonhoeffer, a "gift of God." This proclamation is one of the most distinctive aspects of Christian residence life.

9

HOW CHRIST ENLIVENS STUDENT CONDUCT AND ALCOHOL EDUCATION

Survey Question: What would you list as a best Christian practice of student affairs professionals at your institution?

Participant: Simply put, restoration. We strive to give students in all areas a chance at restoration. . . . I was restored of my past of not representing Christ well through learning how to in a dorm at a Christian college. Others experience restoration as they sit across from our Director of Residence Life during a student conduct meeting. We want to offer restoration to every student.

Survey Question: How does the Christian faith inform your message about alcohol?

Participant: We don't really have a message about alcohol, aside from "don't do it."

If there are two ends of the spectrum regarding how Christ animates student affairs, they are student conduct and alcohol education. On one hand, student affairs leaders (SALs) continually pointed to student conduct as one of the most significant areas in which Christ animates practice. In fact, 89 percent of our survey participants said there was something Christian about their discipline process. For example, after asking about the greatest strength of student affairs on their campus, we received comments such as the following:

- "We have probably the most prolific restorative justice practice in Christian higher ed in the country. Our model of discipline is inseparably linked with restorative practices."

- "The use of restorative justice (or even transformative justice) in the realm of student judicial matters—or at least some variation of it."
- "Our redemptive discipline philosophy. Those who break rules are whole people and can't be reduced to a student conduct code violation. We strive to know their stories and help them grow and make better decisions in the future. This is all with the hope that it will help them understand God's grace and how it impacts their lives."

On a list of best practices, how Christian institutions exercise discipline would surely be near the top.

On the other hand, when we asked participants about how their Christian faith informs their message about alcohol, we found the opposite. We expected these answers to be routine and uncontroversial. We were wrong. It appears that a significant percentage of Christian universities do not even integrate anything distinctively Christian with their alcohol message. One-third of our participants gave responses such as the following:

- "It doesn't."
- "I'm not sure."
- "Not sure. The expectation for students is clear but the rationale is not. Neither the expectation not the rationale for faculty and staff members are clear."
- "I don't talk about my relationship with alcohol, because it is too touchy of a subject on my campus."
- "It does not actively inform the message we present."
- "I don't even know what the policy is. . . . I just know you can't drink."

Amazingly, on one of the key cocurricular and disciplinary issues facing students, SALs recognized a clear lack of Christian input or discussion. Alana summarized one core problem: "We have a really hard time on our campus explaining all the time the 'why' behind things. We have a 'no alcohol' policy for our students. Why do we think that is a healthy, good practice for these four years of your life? Where does that come from?

Where does it not come from? So, things like that." For the most part, a significant percentage of Christian campuses do not place alcohol education within a Christian story when they educate students and perhaps do not even engage in significant alcohol education.

The contrast between these two matters is startling, since these two issues often go together. Unsurprisingly, many of our conversations about student conduct issues centered on alcohol misuse, whether a policy violation and/or substance abuse. One would think that institutional leaders would want to focus on preventative efforts and not merely redemptive discipline, which occurs after the fact. In this chapter, we will highlight the exemplary work the Christian SALs do in student conduct, as well as examine some of the helpful alcohol education practices we found. We also identify some important ways Christ can further animate alcohol education.

Student Conduct

Although we could cite several cases here, we think one particular instance provides a helpful example of a unique Christian approach to discipline. Mark, a vice president of student life, talked about how the process originally started:

> So, when I got to [my institution] it was very transactional. If you went out and drank on the weekend, which is against our policies, you would typically end up with a fifty-dollar fine, you'd be assigned an online course, and you'd have a conversation with the dean of students. When I came in, it was like, "Why are we doing this?" [Answer:] "Well, because it's always been done this way. These are all the rules; this is why we're not supposed to behave the way that we are." I said, "Well, we're a Christian university, yes? Why are we not also talking about where they're at faith-wise?"

This question began a transformation of the disciplinary process. Two parts now stand out. First, the discipline meeting itself has changed. Mark now tries to find out if the issue is one of integrity, peer pressure, substance abuse to cope with depression, or something else. He says, "We've gotten down to the heart of that in that conduct meeting." Next, Mark asks students how he can help them grow:

> Then my job is to help them figure out: What is that next
> step? "Besides going to chapel, how else can I encourage you
> to grow?" Sometimes I'll give them some suggestions because
> they're kind of like, "Whoa, wait. This meeting was [supposed to
> be] you yelling at me. . . . All of a sudden, the tables are turned."
> It just sets it in a very different tempo. In terms of reoffenders,
> we've had very few. Where before it was like, "How can I skirt
> the system? How do I get around it?," . . . what I saw was by not
> approaching everything from the inside out (faith community
> and life all the way around), we were putting a Band-Aid on
> it, but we weren't fixing the internal components of what went
> awry. What was missing was the heart intent.

Second, the process now contains a component that is a restorative justice contract between the institution and the student. It looks at how the student violated community and what they need to be restored to the community. As part of this process, the office connects the student with a mentor in the community, or faculty or staff member, who is going to pour into his or her life. Mark noted that he often asks pastors, "Hey, who've you got who's retired out there who's a great member of your congregation, who might have a heart for college students who are walking through a tenuous time with us?" He offered one example of how this mentoring worked:

> There was a freshman female who had come from Florida. . . .
> She ended up getting in trouble with us, and I ended up find-
> ing another person who was a mentor at a local church. It was
> actually a pastor's wife . . . and she happened to be from Florida,
> too. . . . So, I put the two of them together. It turns out they
> had community members back home that were in relationship
> and other things. . . . She went back for Thanksgiving and then
> Christmas at home and connected with other people back at
> home. Like, "Can you believe I just met so-and-so," and all of a
> sudden, they'd started connecting all the different pieces. But for

her, it was a moment of true transition. She was not a fan of me, and she for sure was not a fan of our resident director, who typically would be an easy mentor in that regard. But because of the conduct, because of several other social issues that were there, this was a perfect person to walk alongside her. So, they started doing devotions and meeting for coffee every other week. She started to pour into her spiritually and emotionally, and all those pieces. Now she's a junior at [institution]; hasn't gotten in trouble again since that point. She has spoken highly of, "Hey, I went through a process of transformation and I'm different than how I came into the university, and I'm thankful for that."

This kind of redemptive discipline process, as well as others like it, contained a couple of key components—whole-person care and restoration to the community.

Whole-Person Care

Within the conversation on discipline, many of our interviewees discussed the focus on caring for the whole personhood of the student, rather than just focusing on their misbehavior. In order to live this method out well, SALs shared that having a conversation with the student about the misbehavior was key, rather than having a "disciplinary" or "conduct hearing." In order to understand the behavior and the underlying needs of the student, one must listen to the student and ask questions in order to cultivate a relationship of care.

According to most of our participants, the conduct process for Christian SALs aimed to be educational, developmental, and redemptive (the most common process descriptors). Mark shared this about the discipline process: "So, all of our outcomes are educational—and again based in that redemption educational process—and it's gotten to the point where we've had students now saying, 'Yeah, that was the worst day maybe ever that I had, but I'm really glad that it happened.' And my favorite thing is we had a student get caught for alcohol on campus, and he was telling his buddy [who later got caught]. He was like, 'Look, you're going to be glad that this happened in the end.' And I was like, 'It's working!'" Something must be working if students that went through the discipline process can testify to its positive influence.

Along a similar vein of developing students personally through the conduct process, our participants also discussed the focus they as administrators had on really getting at the heart of the matter rather than simply the behavior. It was not just about holding students accountable for their actions, or even developing them as humans—it was about helping students become more like Christ through this process.

As Mark's example described above reveals, one key was using mentors. Some of our interviewees discussed using the Education Policy Innovation Center (EPIC) model for developing educational sanctions for conduct violations.[1] Within this framework, mentorship is a key sanction utilized. Mark shared the key to this experience: "And the number one thing for the students that I've engaged in that EPIC mentoring with . . . the number one thing they've come back with of what they want to work on is their relationship with God." Thus, the marriage between both spiritual development and the EPIC model comes together through mentoring.

Restoration to the Community

Beyond care for the individual, the majority of SALs we interviewed and surveyed all said that a distinctively Christian element of their conduct process was the restoration of the individual to the community. Many interviewees mentioned utilizing a restorative justice model for their conduct proceedings. On these campuses, a process exists to restore that individual back to the community and bring healing to those affected by the misconduct.[2] Ashley shared, "We buy into this idea that discipline is not an end in and of itself, that it's not for the sake of punishing; that it's for the sake of restoring someone to community. In the process of talking with the student about a violation that they've made, we're going to talk about what [it meant] for the rest of the community? How did that affect them?" In order to restore someone fully to the community, our SALs iterated the importance of extending grace and offering the individual redemption—a clean slate.

Overall, our participants advocated for a better approach to discipline beyond taking punitive measures. They all promoted some form of whole-person care and the need for SALs to come alongside students during times they have strayed, to bring students back into right relationships with the community. In many ways, our participants said student affairs work is about being the shepherd that leaves the rest of the flock to go find the one lost sheep and bring it back to the fold (Matt. 18:12; Luke 15:4).

Alcohol Education

By far, the most frequently used example of student conduct issues on Christian college campuses is related to alcohol. It should be noted that different Christian colleges take different approaches to alcohol policy on their campus (see Table 9.1). The key commonality is that not one institution we surveyed allowed alcohol on campus.

Table 9.1 What is the alcohol policy on your campus? (*N* = 46)

	n	%
All students are asked to abstain from alcohol	28	60.9
Students over 21 can drink, but alcohol is not allowed on campus	15	32.6
Other	3	6.5

Note: Survey participants indicated they deal directly with conduct issues on their campus.

Our survey also asked SALs how Christian faith informs their message about alcohol to students. The most frequent themes, discussed in more detail later, were (1) it doesn't, or the topic is avoided altogether; (2) the SAL references biblical standards or a passage about alcohol; (3) there is no drinking in excess or getting drunk; and (4) the institution promotes abstinence, particularly for the sake of the community. In our interviews, we wanted to know about the role that Christian theological thinking played in approaches to alcohol education. What makes the Christian approach different, if it all?

To be frank, what we found disappointed us. We wondered if our participants were simply not that familiar with their institution's teaching on this matter, so we looked up the policies. Unfortunately, we found that alcohol policies were no better. Often they just stated the policy (e.g., our institution prohibits drinking of any kind), engaged in general moralizing (e.g., visiting bars is counter to our Christian values and lifestyle), or stated nontheological reasons for the policy (e.g., law, general social concerns), but they failed to offer any theological story or rationale for the policy. Although we understand why the student handbook or community covenant may not be the best place to provide theological reflections about alcohol, we then wonder where such reflection takes place in the lives of students. We found few healthy models. Thus, in this section, we both relate some positive examples but also set forth a more thorough vision that we believe can inform alcohol education on a college campus.

Does Christ Enliven Alcohol Education?

This problem with alcohol education seems to be particularly pronounced at institutions with a strict "no drinking" policy that lasts for the duration of a student's matriculation. For example, Nathan described the situation at his campus, which forbids all alcohol consumption:

> I don't think we're as strong in terms of the faith message as it relates to alcohol. . . . Quite honestly, as a VP for Student Life, I wrestle with how well we're doing with that. I think we could do better. I think it's a place where we could have more honest dialogue with our students. For some of our staff, it's just, "It's in the handbook." It's not much of a conversation. And, again, if we're pushing toward a deeper conversation about integrity, and about choices in life, and about the role alcohol does play or could play going forward, then we have to commit to engage our students in the conversation. At any rate, that's where [my institution], I think, could do better.

Nathan was not alone in his thinking. Overall, on many campuses, the conversation about alcohol—particularly how to think about alcohol in a broader way within the Christian story—is lacking.

Some campuses stayed away from even using a direct theological rationale when talking to students. Patricia noted, "We have articulated in our handbook that our decision about alcohol has nothing to do with God's judgment of alcohol, that it seems clear to us that consuming alcohol in responsible ways is fine, but we've chosen to maintain an educational community free of alcohol for a variety of reasons. You can point to millions of research articles supporting that." One could also see this attitude in what many considered the basic wisdom offered by Mark, who said, "It is associated with unhealthy living, sexual violence, and addiction" and "Under 25 the brain is not fully developed. Alcohol unnecessarily impedes brain development in youth." As can be seen in these cases, SALs appealed to research as possibly demonstrating benefits for a dry campus, but there was no overt theologically oriented alcohol education.

In other cases, SALs appealed to the healthy community the policy produced for individuals. Ryan, a vice president of student life, noted that in his University 101 class at the start of the year, he does the following: "I know that the students are not going to buy something that's canned. So, I've been going around with my iPhone, recording students. I'll talk to them. I'll say, 'Hey, tell me a little bit about your experience here. Where have you found community? Talk to me a little bit about why community is important for you here at [our] university?'" During this time, students shared about the alcohol policy:

> One of the students was like, "You know what? I chose [this] university for a reason, because it didn't have alcohol. I had a chance to go to [name omitted] State. I was going to go to [name omitted] University. But I recognized that there was a uniqueness in [our] community—that I didn't have to worry about the social pressures on a Friday or Saturday night. I chose . . . to fully participate with integrity in that community. It's my right to drink 'cause I'm twenty-one, but I've chosen to give that up to be a part of that community."

Ryan mentioned, "I had another student who was an alcoholic before he came to [our] university and realized that he had to give that up." In the recorded video for students, the former alcoholic said, "I found freedom at [my institution], because I wasn't tempted on a regular basis to go out and party with the rest of my friends. I knew that we could have fun without introducing that as a part of my experience." In an insightful piece of educational pedagogy, Ryan was having students do the hard work of pro-moting the good of the alcohol policy without any mention of the Bible.

The rest of our participants were able to identify some basic connections to the Christian story they or their institution made when undertaking alcohol education. These appeals to Christianity tended to focus on one of four things:

1. "The Bible says . . . obey your leaders and laws" (Rom. 13:1).
2. "A prohibition of drunkenness based on Ephesians 5:18."
3. "Excessive drinking does not reflect care for a person's body as a temple" (1 Cor. 6:19–20).
4. Appeals to consider those with a weaker conscience:
   a. "We place the betterment of the community above our own wants, desires, and legal rights" (1 Cor. 8:9–13, 10:23–31).
   b. "We preach sobriety and that being a part of a Christian community means sometimes we need to sacrifice our preferences."
   c. "Whether a Christian chooses to drink or not should be decided between them and their conscience, and if drinking in the presence of a fellow Christian causes them to stumble, the Christian who feels free to drink should abstain for the sake of the other" (1 Cor. 8:13, 10:28–29; Rom. 14:1–3).

All of these scriptural responses are important parts of a biblical perspective, but when appealed to in isolation, some important elements may be missed. Of course, since some participants are responding to a survey, we expect that they would have more to say on this topic if asked. Yet, even our interview participants tended to focus on one or two of the four elements above.

Still, in these conversations, SALs tried to mitigate against the weakness of focusing upon rules. One of the limitations with a rules-based approach is the tendency to start with and continue to focus on legal or moral rules (i.e., do not drink before twenty-one; do not get drunk). However, rules only make sense within a larger story (Exod. 20:1–2; Mark 10:1–12). Thus, interviewees tended to dwell on the larger developmental context. For example, Carter focused on appeals to protect those with a weaker conscience regarding alcohol's place in their community covenant and the developmental conversation they hoped to produce: "Where I say, 'It's my freedom to do this, but I've made the commitment not to, and the reason I've made the commitment not to is because I want to be a part of this community'—that's a great spiritual discipline. . . . I'm hoping, through this kind of dialogue and this kind of process, we're getting them to ask a different question. It's not 'Who am I hurting?'; it's 'How am I helping? How am I being more a part of this community?'"

Jaxon described his outlook in this way largely using wisdom about an educational environment and answers 2 and 4 from above:

> Our communal expectations can be grouped into two primarily different categories. One is based on biblical conviction. One is that Scripture, specifically, prohibits. So, drunkenness is something that Scripture specifically prohibits. But we have other [expectations] just based on the fact that we believe that having these [rules] is actually conducive to our students having a better educational environment. . . . On ecclesial grounds, because we are a broad Evangelical school, students on our campus have different convictions about alcohol. [But] from the principle of honoring the weaker brother or sister—that's why we have a policy on [drinking].

Certainly, these SALs are seeking to be both biblically grounded and culturally sensitive.

Yet there are several weaknesses if this is the foundation of the approach. First, participants tended to focus on biblical rules instead of biblical wisdom. Not one person mentioned anything from Proverbs—the biblical book that has the most to say about alcohol. Second, as can be seen from these answers, most of the theological contributions tended to focus on the negative aspect of alcohol. Among participants, there was little positive to say about alcohol besides two SALs who noted: "Jesus also demonstrated that there are occasions where imbibing is appropriate" (e.g., wedding feasts, the Last Supper) and "Jesus drank alcohol. His first miracle involved turning water into wine . . . and into really good wine at that."

Overall, the picture of alcohol education on Christian campuses was that it was largely absent, simplistic, and rules-based, or a developmental opportunity for students to focus on what it means to be part of a covenant community. Perhaps the American Christian church is still recovering from the legacy of Prohibition, but we found the dearth of theological reflection and engagement with this issue disturbing.

An Alternative Vision

In our own experience, we find that successful alcohol education involves placing alcohol education in two stories—the personal stories of students and the larger story of Scripture. Undertaking the first part simply involves asking a series of questions in a group setting:

- Pair and share your personal family history regarding alcohol with a partner. What was taught in the home and what stories were shared about it? Then ask partners to share stories in public with permission of the other person.
- When you have seen alcohol used for bad or good in your family or friends?
- What are some reasons students drink in college?
- What do you consider good or bad reasons?
- What moral criteria are you using to evaluate whether a reason or story is good or bad?

What we find helpful about this exercise is that by the time students have gone through these questions, they have heard some tragic stories of how alcohol has influenced and destroyed families, as well as some positive stories of moderate alcohol use. They have discussed how their parents have divorced due to one spouse's alcoholism or how they have seen alcohol used to cover up pain or help a person overcome their inhibitions. They will also likely tell of healthy stories where it was used to enhance celebration and food around a family dinner or special event such as a wedding. Moreover, they are usually already making moral evaluations of alcohol use without the person leading having to moralize. In fact, we find this exercise works well even in a group mixed with Christians and nonbelievers.

A second set of questions, though, would be relevant on Christian campuses: (1) How are the moral criteria you used for evaluation connected to your Christian beliefs? (2) How else does your Christian worldview inform your understanding of alcohol? By the time we got through these questions, students have articulated a fairly robust Christian understanding of alcohol. Yet—and this is a key role of Christian educators—students often have not put this view together in a sophisticated way that addresses each part of ethics.[3] Any sophisticated ethic about a practice needs to place that practice in a larger story and then talk about the ends, rules, virtues, practices, mentors, and models associated with the practice.[4] One of the few SALs who did this gave a combination of three elements mentioned: "Ephesians 5:18 instructs believers not to be drunk with wine but to be filled with the Spirit. Yet Jesus also demonstrated that there are occasions where imbibing is appropriate (wedding feasts, the Last Supper). Whether a Christian chooses to drink or not should be decided between them and their conscience, and if drinking in the presence of a fellow Christian causes them to stumble, the Christian who feels free to drink should abstain for the sake of the other."

Of course, we do not expect any survey or brief interview answer (even this more expansive one) to capture a holistic Christian ethic. Still, since alcohol education will likely not happen in class, it needs to be the job of Christian student affairs. Below we set forth a vision that could inform such a discussion.

A Christian Story-Informed Ethic for College Students

Ends. Students drink, but they often do not ask the simple question "Why?" In light of the Christian story, we can recognize that like any of God's good gifts, it must be stewarded and directed in the right way. Food, alcohol, and sex are all part of God's good gifts. They can be enjoyed in the proper context. Alcohol's ultimate use in certain Christian traditions is to remember Jesus's sacrifice, but it also can be used to enhance celebrations. After all, Jesus will once again drink with us when we celebrate in heaven (Matt. 26:29). Of course, the improper ends of alcohol use, of which there are many, have already been mentioned.

Rules and referees. Considering this larger context, we can understand the rules for drinking. We always need rules in life with any practice with which we engage. The moral rules in the Bible have already been mentioned. Of course, obeying these rules is hardly demonstrating stewardship of one's body.

For those in student affairs, it helps to be clear about the rules and to enforce the rules you have made. Robert provided a good example of this concept: "Our policy is essentially you can drink off campus if you're twenty-one and over, but you have to be under a .05 BAC level. So, when you come back to campus, if we think you're inebriated, we will breathalyzer you. So, in terms of how we communicate that, we have an orientation session at the beginning of the year. . . . The reason that we do allow alcohol is because we understand there's diverse needs of the church regarding alcohol." In addition, there needs to be clarity about whether the rules apply to students when they are off-campus as well as on-campus, as highlighted by Ashley's experience:

> We had a case this fall of a very large off-campus party involving almost all underclassmen . . . all students under the age of twenty-one. That's a policy violation, and so we investigated it. . . . We had a lot of pushback on that one. Like, "Why do you think you have any say in what happens off campus?". . . Parents [were] calling us and saying, "You have no right, this was a private residence, and they weren't harming anything. You have no right to punish them for what happened there." I think that's a real practical struggle we have—kind of knowing, "What do we do with those off-campus situations?"

Of course, although clarity about rules and the proper punishment remains important, it is hardly the core of the Christian ethical tradition.

Missing virtues and practices. One of the surprising things we found is that when it comes to alcohol education, Christian SALs do not appear to talk about virtue or the fruit of the Spirit, or about spiritual practices that would be associated with it. Not surprisingly in our consumer culture, fasting and abstinence (outside of sex before marriage) are the least-discussed spiritual disciplines today. Furthermore, self-control is a fruit of the Spirit (Gal. 5:22–23) and one of the major qualifications of a Christian leader (1 Tim. 3:8; Titus 1:8, 2:2). In contrast, being a drunkard or addicted is one of the characteristics of a rebellious youth in the Old Testament (Deut. 21:20), the characteristic of the unfaithful servant in the New Testament (Matt. 24:49), and the unqualified Christian leader (Titus 2:3). Not being a hypocrite and living a life of integrity, as some SALs did mention, should also be a prime virtue. Instead, as Austin noted, "So it's crazy, especially today. Our students are very much, 'What are you getting in my business for? I'm twenty-one, and I'm off-campus. I should be able to do what I want.' The whole idea of Christian community and making an agreement to live in that life is really being challenged." We need students to understand that being filled with the Spirit, the opposite of being drunk (Eph. 5:18–19), is to have the courage for heroic deeds of self-sacrificial love and care for others, to be uninhibited in one's true self, and more. To binge drink is to try and find courage or a good feeling outside of God. Effectively, it throws away the ultimate meta-dependence on God for an unreliable substitute. God made us for so much more. Instead, as *The Message* interprets Paul's admonition in Ephesians 5, "Drink the Spirit of God, huge draughts of him" (Eph. 5:18–20 MSG).

Conclusion

Student conduct represents one of the greatest strengths of Christian student affairs work, and alcohol education one of its greatest opportunities for improvement. As our participants shared with us, Christian student affairs leads the way in student conduct and discipline through restorative justice, redemption, and restoration back to community. However, a Christian view of alcohol and alcohol education is often missing on our campuses—oftentimes out of fear or lack of knowledge about how to engage the topic well with students. We are not doing our students (or ourselves, for that matter) any favors by not stepping into the murky waters with them. Put on your muck boots and get muddy.

PART FIVE

Current Issues in Christian Student Affairs

Student affairs is a practical field. As such, it is important that we explore how the model we have been constructing plays out practically. To do so, we asked participants to identify the issues they felt were most pressing, and then followed up with questions about how their faith informs their responses to these issues. In our interviews, three topics rose to the surface: multicultural affairs, sexuality, and Title IX. We will explore participant comments and perspectives on these "hot button" topics in the next three chapters.

Although these chapters will be intentionally practical, our discussion of them is not limited to means and methods. We hope, in the coming pages, to demonstrate how God and God's story can animate a comprehensive approach to a single issue. Thus, our analysis of multicultural affairs in Chapter Ten, sexuality in Chapter Eleven, and Title IX in Chapter Twelve will draw on all four facets of our model of the imagination for Christian student affairs.

Figure V.1. The Christian Student Affairs Imagination

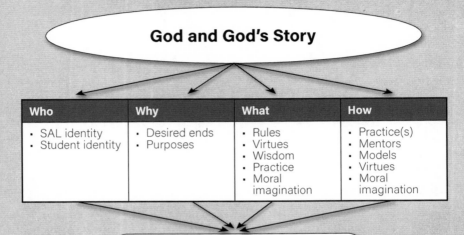

10

HOW CHRIST TRANSFORMS
THE CAMPUS RACIAL CLIMATE

For he himself is our peace, who has made us both one and has broken down in his flesh the dividing wall of hostility.

—Ephesians 2:14

I (Elijah) still remember the day when Angela (pseudonym), a female student of color, called me to let me know that she would be transferring to a different institution. Despite it being her senior year of college and only having a handful of courses to finish, she felt that she could no longer continue. As we unpacked the reasons behind her desire to leave, a theme began to emerge: as a student of color, she continued to feel that the institution was "not made for her." She would go on to describe her feelings of "not fitting in" and her perception that the institution lacked key support measures for students of color. She even shared her belief that student programming was tailored for a specific group of students—white students and not "students like me." I knew changing schools would delay her graduation and increase her student loan debt, but I also knew what she was saying was true—at her institution, the institutional policy, programs, and structures were not created with students like Angela in mind.

The problems Angela faced are not unique to her institution. In fact, at many Christian institutions, students of color perceive the environment as "not made for them." Given this reality, one of the major tasks faced by Christian student affairs leaders (SALs) is how to transform their campus racial climate (CRC) to be more hospitable, inclusive, and equitable for students of color. In other words, how do we help students of color experience a campus that is "made for them?" Of course, responding to this challenge requires SALs understand the nature of the CRC; it is complex and multifaceted, and transforming it requires various stakeholders to carefully and humbly work together towards change. Indeed, altering the CRC of an institution does not happen accidentally or independently; rather, it is done intentionally and collectively. To provide additional understanding, this chapter will be structured somewhat differently than other chapters. First, it provides a brief overview of the literature. Then, it outlines our findings. At the end, it provides some practical next steps in creating a hospitable CRC for students of color based on our findings.

Christian Institutional Context and Race

Before moving on, it is important to situate the perceptions of the CRC by SALs within a larger historical, educational, and religious context— namely (1) Christianity's checkered past, especially Christian institutions, in dealing with issues of race; (2) problematic white Evangelical attitudes toward race; and (3) differing educational outcomes between students of color and white students.[1]

To the first reality, Christian institutions have a long history of both promoting and challenging racial inequality.[2] For example, although some Christian colleges were founded by abolitionists, many other Christian institutions were born out of and maintained by segregationist ideology.[3] After *Brown v. Board of Education* made it illegal for public institutions to deny access to students of color, there is evidence that white Christian families reacted to this federal mandate by either overly resisting the implementation of racial diversity or choosing to attend private institutions. As a result, the exodus of white Christians from public institutions partly fueled the creation and growth of many Christian higher education institutions.[4] This explains, in part, why Christian institutions have lacked racial diversity compared to other institutional sectors.[5]

Second, scholars have documented problematic white Christian attitudes on race. White Christians generally do not perceive or take responsibility for systemic and institutional factors that bring about racism and racial inequality. Simply put, they are more likely to conceive of racism in a narrow fashion (e.g., racism is simply a problem with individuals who are prejudiced) while also advocating for circumscribed solutions to racial inequality—solutions that find their answers in simply having better relationships between individuals from different racial groups. As a result, white Christians are not able to see the structural and systemic realities of racial inequality and racism, which lead them to deny systemic racism, advocate for a color-blind ideology, deny white privilege, and believe that equal opportunity is an objective American reality.[6] According to George Yancey, the distinct white Christian ideology carries over to faith-based higher education institutions, which "promote an individualistic, color-blind ideology."[7] Moreover, Christian higher education institutions are historically known to "perpetuate a predominantly white culture" that comes at the expense of creating an equitable climate for students of color.[8]

Third, scholars have found that students of color attending Christian higher education institutions, when compared to their white peers, have lower levels of achievement in educational outcomes.[9] Specifically, students of color are less likely to be retained at an institution, less likely to graduate, and report lower levels of belonging.[10] Moreover, students of color attending these institutions are more likely to report negative perceptions of the CRC, which can lead to lower levels of student satisfaction and sense of belonging compared to their white peers.[11] These lower educational outcomes and negative perception of the CRC are, in part, due to the problematic racial environment where students of color face various racial inequities, marginalization, and overt and subtle forms of racism.[12] As a result, it can be said that flourishing is racially stratified within Christian higher education institutions; unlike white students, the racial inequities faced by students of color negatively impact their ability to flourish.

Perception of the Campus Racial Climate

When first discussing the CRC of their respective institutions, many SALs were quick to identify the changing racial demographics of their student body. In fact, many cited that the growth of students of color tripled or quadrupled in the last decade. From the SALs' perspective, the growth of the students of color at Christian colleges stood in contrast to the racial homogeneity of a couple decades earlier. Yet these SALs also understood that despite the growth, simply increasing access of students of color did not naturally equate to their success. In fact, given the complicated relationship between race and Christian higher education institutions mentioned above, we were not surprised to hear the following answers when we asked SALs for their perception of their institution's CRC:

- "It's complex."
- "I think for all of our institutions we have a long way to go, but we have done a lot."
- "On our campus, we're in transition."
- "As an institution, we've really wrestled with how to do this well."
- "Terrible."
- "I think, for students, it's poor as well. I would say it's terrible."
- "Yeah, we're pretty bad. We're pretty bad."
- "OK. I would say they are challenged by it."
- "Bad, bad, bad, bad."
- "I think Christian colleges are behind the secular [colleges] here, but we should have never been."

Of course, although some SALs described their own CRC as "improving" and "doing well," the majority of SALs were hesitant to describe their CRC in overtly positive terms. In fact, only one SAL was willing to say, "The climate is good."

How the Fall Inhibits the Creation of an Inclusive Campus Racial Climate

Why were SALs hesitant to describe their own CRC in positive terms? Overall, SALs discussed four specific barriers that hindered their efforts to create hospitable racial environments on their campuses: (1) racism and racial ignorance, (2) the lack of faculty and staff of color, (3) the lack of white student engagement, and (4) the paradox of religion supporting or hindering efforts to create inclusive racial environments.

Acts of Racism and Racial Ignorance

Due to the fallenness of both individual students and institutions, many SALs identified racism and racial ignorance as the primary barrier to promote inclusive environments. SALs shared a variety of appalling acts of racism and racial ignorance on campus—white students calling African Americans the "n-word," white students wearing blackface and saying insensitive remarks about students of color on social media, students wearing culturally inappropriate Halloween costumes, and professors making insensitive racial remarks. According to participants, all of these acts— whether intentional or unintentional—created negative racial climates for students of color. For example, Ryan spoke about an atrocious racist incident that happened in chapel. When a female African American student came to speak during chapel, an individual stood up and shouted, "You [n-word], get off the stage, now!" According to some SALs, these inexcusable acts of racial hatred revealed an underlying reality of their institution—an inequitable CRC for students of color.

In addition to outright acts of racism, some SALs shared acts of racial ignorance that created a negative campus climate for students of color. Noah described that some students on campus would unequivocally deny even the existence of racism while proudly flying the Confederate flag in their truck beds. Moreover, some racial ignorance embodied itself through white students pushing back on efforts to create more racially inclusive environments for students of color. One SAL shared that any time minority students or student affairs staff would discuss issues of racial injustice, many students—a majority of them white—would argue that those who focus on racial injustice are simply "whining" or embracing "a victimhood mentality." These statements and pushback from other students created an inhospitable environment. As Helen shared, "It's really painful for our students of color, in particular, to have white students—ignorant, angry white students—empowered to say hurtful things."

Sadly, racial ignorance was not limited to students; it involved parents and faculty as well. Helen openly described the types of phone calls she would receive after implementing programs to create inclusive environments: "I had a number of phone calls from white parents who are like, 'I have no idea why you're talking about white privilege. Why are you talking about white privilege in chapel? First of all, white people don't have privilege. . . . I'm going to take my child to a school that doesn't talk about white privilege.' I'm like, 'Good luck finding one.'"

Some SALs discussed problematic faculty actions that unintentionally created an inhospitable racial environment. Anthony described an incident at his institution: "We had a faculty member who at the beginning of class said, 'I want all the black students to stay after class.' And the reason was she wanted to address them about wearing their hoodies up while they were in class. Now, only two of the guys had ever done that. So, [all of the black students] were highly offended that the black students had to stay. . . . You would think in this day and age a faculty member would be smarter than that." For Eden, unintentional racial ignorance did not excuse one's culpability: "It's not intentional that they may have said or done something, but we can say it's intentional that you didn't try to learn about it, or from it."

Overall, SALs identified individual acts of racism and racial ignorance perpetrated by various stakeholders. The sin of racism and racial ignorance did not discriminate; no individual stakeholder group, whether that be students, administrators, faculty, or parents, was immune from resurrecting the "wall of hostility."

Lack of Faculty and Staff of Color

When asked about the challenges of racial diversity at their institutions, the majority of SALs of color, as well as a small number of white SALs, pointed to a specific institutional problem—a lack of faculty and staff of color. Specifically, SALs argued that the racial diversity among staff and faculty clearly lagged behind an increasingly diverse student population. When asked about ways that his institution could improve the CRC, Elias stated without hesitation, "Well, obviously, first the easiest step would be to hire more student development professionals, more faculty, more administrators that look like [the] students that they serve." Mark expressed the importance of hiring faculty and staff of color in relation to issues of student success. He thought that racial representation—especially having a mentor, faculty, or staff of color—would help support the success of minority students. Additionally, Nolan explained that by having more minority faculty and staff, the institution would be able to have leaders who understood the unique cultural, ethnic, and racial experiences of students. He explained, "It is really critical to make sure that our students have people who have their experience, or share their experience, working at the institution. So, we need to see female faculty, we need to see faculty of color, because our students look to them as mentors and as guides for how to navigate a majority culture." Cali reiterated Nolan's points by stating that institutions need to be "aware" of who they hire: "Do they continue to represent our student population? Do our students feel that they have someone to look up to and someone who emulates the culture that they're familiar with? Are we hiring faculty and staff who represent our student body?" When asked about what she sees as the most important aspect of creating inclusive racial climates, Heather openly stated, "I think it starts with representation."

A few SALs of color were uncomfortable simply having "token" minority hires and "not giving them the power" to create institutional change. For example, Christopher argued that many Christian institutions "hire safe people of color . . . [w]ho essentially think along white ways. So, you can have a lot of people of color within an institution that don't bring any diversity and . . . [who] don't bring any diversity benefits to the table." In fact, Christopher continued to discuss that hiring minorities simply based on their skin color was not adequate; institutions need to hire staff and faculty of color who are willing to challenge the status quo and the normativity of majority culture.

From the perspective of SALs of color, when faculty and staff hiring lagged behind the racial diversity of the student body, it negatively impacted the success and belonging of students of color. Thus, SALs provided specific clarity on how to improve the CRC: hire more faculty and staff of color.

Lack of White Student Engagement

Another institutional challenge voiced by participants was the lack of white student engagement on issues of racial diversity and inclusion. Despite highlighting various types of programming implemented to engage the entire student body, many SALs reported that white students failed to participate. For example, Noah bluntly stated that white students "are not really engaged at all." Noah went on to explain that the Martin Luther King Jr. chapel was the "least attended chapel of the year," implying that many white students chose not to attend the chapel because they knew the topic of race was going to be discussed. Sadly, Zachary made similar comments that white students complained that the topic of race was being discussed too often in chapel—to which Zachary responded, "It's not talked about often."

For many SALs, the lack of engagement by white students created challenges in creating inclusive racial climates. Although SALs perceived their role to "set up an environment in which people can talk about [issues of racial diversity]," the problem was "the same student show[s] up every time."

Overall, many SALs articulated their frustration in trying to create programming efforts that engage majority students. Due to majority students avoiding important programmatic events that could potentially create common ground and understanding, SALs perceived a lost opportunity—white students were losing the chance to increase their racial consciousness as well as understand the experiences of students of color. And, more importantly, white students were squandering an opportunity to imitate Christ and "love one's neighbor."

Paradox of Religion

Various SALs discussed the paradox of religion in supporting or hindering efforts to create inclusive racial environments. For example, some SALs believed that Christianity hindered diversity efforts. Melissa argued, "To be really honest, I think Christianity has kind of got in the way [of diversity efforts] . . . because Christian higher ed has been such a majority white culture, just operating out of this 'good ole' boy's club.'" Although Melissa acknowledged that she was speaking in generalities, she believed that her accusation was generally true for many Christian institutions. In fact, she continued to profess her discomfort with a Christian culture that attempts to flatten racial and ideological diversity by "making assumptions that we all know we're all on the same page; we all believe the same; we all think the same; we're all very much one happy same family. It's just bull."

Reiterating Melissa's point, Zachary described how white Evangelicals used Christianity as an instrument to "keep some things out," especially issues concerning racial diversity. From Zachary's perspective, Christian institutions used religion as a "weapon and a wall" to limit diversity efforts. He continued, "I feel like the Bible is used as . . . 'We're all one in Christ. We don't need to talk about this. We're going to be about unity, which seems to be something Jesus was about.'" Zachary stated, however, that this position leads ultimately to disunity. Similarly, Heather argued, "There's still some sort of unrelenting aspects that I think affect many people of color that come to this institution, where everything is influenced by white Evangelicalism." Yet, according to Heather, "it was really hard for administrators and many people who work at Christian schools to admit that, because it feels like we're betraying something that we know to be true to ourselves and our experience." No SAL argued that institutions should cast away their religious beliefs. Rather, participants articulated that faith-based institutions should dismantle distorted religious understandings and leverage true Christian faith which embraces diversity.

Rationale for Racial Diversity and Inclusion

After identifying the barriers to creating an inclusive CRC, SALs then turned to various rationales that support racial diversity and inclusion at their institutions. Interestingly, only a small number of SALs articulated their support for racial diversity using economic or civic rationales, which is the primary rationale to engage in racial diversity at secular institutions.[13] For the majority of the SALs we interviewed, however, the primary justification for engaging racial diversity stemmed from theological conviction. From the SALs' perspective, clearly articulating a theological rationale became necessary for three specific reasons. The first reason arose from SALs' desire to *differentiate* themselves from secular institutions. For example, Steven stated that Christian institutions must "articulate a compelling theological reason why diversity is at the heart of our mission as a Christian school." Other SALs discussed the need to articulate a theological understanding of racial diversity that was different from secular institutions and be aware of "reimporting" secular ideas of diversity to Christian campuses that did not align with the institution's mission. Mason discussed the difference between a secular and Christian institution's engagement with racial diversity by quoting a theology professor at his institution: "A lot of schools think that diversity is nice. That it's 'nice' to have a diverse student population. We believe that it is necessary, because if we are called to look like the body of Christ, we have to look like everything the body of Christ looks like."

The second rationale identified problematic *perceptions* of racial diversity efforts as being "unbiblical," "a distraction," and "liberal." Several SALs described the pushback they received when engaging in racial diversity efforts. For example, Jaxon described responses from faculty members at his institution: "I've had faculty members who have said to me that diversity is a distraction to the gospel . . . that it's actually taking us away from just proclaiming the good news of Jesus Christ." Due to these realities, SALs emphasized the importance of articulating a clear theological rationale in order to show that racial and ethnic diversity efforts were grounded in the Christian story.

Finally, SALs felt a theological rationale was necessary because they saw engagement with racial and ethnic diversity—and caring for students of color—as a *biblical mandate*. Simply put, for these SALs, the trajectory of the biblical narrative affirmed that racial and ethnic diversity was—and is—a part of God's unfolding plan from beginning to end. When asked about why he engaged in racial and ethnic diversity efforts at his institution, Jason shared that his Christian faith required him to do so. Specifically, he carefully articulated his understanding of racial diversity within the biblical narrative:

> You go throughout the Bible, from Genesis 15, you're blessed to
> be a blessing, and yet it seems like white Christians and white
> higher educational institutions that are Christian think that
> "blessed to be a blessing" is "blessed to be a blessing" only for
> people who agree with them, or who are within the lines of their
> ethnic and racial makeup. I don't think that Christianity should
> ever depart from biblical orthodoxy. But I think that some of
> our interpretations of biblical orthodoxy and our applications
> of them are significantly off, especially the hyper-individualism

and the meritocracy that exists. But all throughout Scripture you see a consistent biblical vision for racial justice and racial equity and racial harmony . . . from the Trinity, where God is three in one, diversity and unity, to revelation, where everyone will gather together from every tribe, nation, tongue, people group. There's a diversity there, and we're all centered around Christ.

Similarly, other SALs discussed their motivation to engage in issues of diversity by using rich theological language and biblical categories. Participants told us they engaged in racial and ethnic diversity because it was "the heart of God's desire," an implication of making "disciples of all nations," a "biblical mandate," an implication of "representing the full body of Christ," and an important value to God since everyone is "made in the image of God." Moreover, SALs used a variety of theological language, such as "biblical justice" and "God-ordained," to describe the importance of racial and ethnic diversity and inclusion. Jacob shared his core theological assumption regarding racial and ethnic diversity by emphasizing our need to affirm "the value of human diversity and the requirement of it and the beauty of it." Overall, for these SALs, racial and ethnic diversity was not an afterthought but "has always been a part of the main plan and purpose of Christ."[14]

How Christ Transforms Efforts to Cultivate a Hospitable Campus Racial Climate

After describing the barriers faced by students of color as well as their own desire to improve the CRC, SALs described efforts from different institutional units as well as multicultural best practices that made their institutions more hospitable for students of color. The two most mentioned units or offices on campus that improved hospitable campus climates for students of color was the spiritual formation office (mainly through the chapel programing) and the multicultural office.

Many SALs believed that chapel was the best avenue to touch upon issues of racial and ethnic diversity from a biblical and theological perspective. Despite knowing these conversations would be difficult and challenging—as well as knowing some students would complain that racial conversations were unnecessary—SALs saw a "real opportunity" to challenge all students to cultivate a biblical foundation for racial and ethnic diversity through chapel. Moreover, Helen mentioned her institution's efforts to structurally connect the spiritual formation office with the multicultural office so that conversations of race would not be "silo[ed]" to one department or simply to students who already acknowledged the importance of this topic. In addition, through implementing different worship styles and having racially diverse chapel leadership teams, SALs believed that they could acknowledge the beautiful diversity represented in "every tribe, nation, and tongue." As Helen also told us, "We've been working super hard to have chapel be a diverse place of worship, a multicultural worshipping community."

Other SALs also mentioned the efforts of their multicultural office. These offices were sites that supported multiple ethnic student groups and initiated multicultural programming efforts. The multicultural office became the specific "space" and "place" where students felt a sense of belonging and support. Henry argued that because students of color often face additional barriers, the multicultural office was a place where "students could go in there and feel at home." He hoped this place could be a site where students of color do not have to "code switch all the time," implying that students of color constantly bear the burden of adapting to white culture in other spaces. Lucy described her institution's efforts to create hospitable spaces: "As an institution, I think we have been really challenged to be more accountable to creating hospitable spaces because we are a Christian institution." Overall, SALs hoped that the multicultural office was a place where students felt a sense of belonging and support, and experienced Christ's love and hospitality.

In addition to chapel and multicultural offices, participants described other racial diversity efforts employed by their institutions, such as racial diversity training; educational programing for staff, faculty, and students; the creation of bias response teams; and collaborating with faculty to make the academic curriculum more "diverse." Carter shared a creative program that integrated the curricular and cocurricular to increase racial consciousness of students: "Our honors program, along with our office of intercultural programs, does a student civil rights tour. They take [a diverse group of students] on a five-day civil rights tour. I had a daughter [who is white] who traveled to it. It was just a mind-blowing experience for her. [It] changed the trajectory of her life. Really." We highlight this programming not only for its ability to merge the curricular and cocurricular, but also because it was constructed in a way to increase the racial consciousness of all students through prolonged cross-racial engagement. In fact, it helped white students engage in matters of racial and ethnic diversity—a weakness that was identified by our participants. Through these efforts, SALs desired students cultivate specific virtues such as acknowledging that everyone is made in the "image of God," learning "cultural humility," and "lov[ing] their neighbor."

We want to highlight one SAL's response to how Christ transforms the CRC. We found John's response to be extremely thoughtful and informative. He did not believe a single effort can transform Christian higher education environments to be more hospitable for students of color. Rather, John believed that institutions must think in a multifaceted manner:

> We've seen the benefit of working harder at identifying [a] quality pool of candidates of color—the impact not only on students of color but on the whole campus. It's significant. [We are more] intentional now about weaving in engagement with diversity into the curriculum. . . . I think that communicates to students of color, "OK, faculty are really talking about this in the classroom." The chaplain is doing a really good job of mixing up the worship style in chapel. And students really notice that . . . there's a variety of worship styles. We've identified we need to do more training with our chefs in the dining hall to cook more authentic food. It's a growth point for us, so we're not there yet. But I think students appreciate that we recognize that when you say this is Latino food and you eat it and it doesn't taste authentic . . . it would be better to just not even serve it than call it ethnic and it not really be authentically ethnic.

John understood that creating hospitable CRCs is a multifaceted endeavor. He had a complex understanding of the racial problems, as well as a robust imagination regarding the solutions. He did not isolate Christ's enlivening power to a single program or office, nor did he limit Christ's animating power to simply improving individual relationships. Instead, John desired for Christ's transformative power to influence systemic aspects of institutional life, including hiring, curriculum, spiritual formation, and even food!

Overall, SALs articulated different institutional efforts (some more than others) to create inclusive environments for students of color. Yet many shared the same goal. Conner shared his desire to see his and all Christian institutions create climates for students of color that are "not just a place where you're a welcomed guest, but where you're able to move the furniture."

What Is Missing?

We admire SALs' intentions and efforts to cultivate hospitable environments for students of color. These efforts stemmed from the desire to care for students of color and to "not just make a statement." Yet we do believe divisions of student affairs suffer from two particular weaknesses. First, SALs collectively have an anemic view of the fall. As Elias told us, Christian institutions must be better at understanding how sin includes not only "individuals" but also "communal guilt . . . and communal sin." Indeed, the doctrine of the fall requires us to understand its immense scope—it not only warps the hearts and minds of individuals, but also institutions and organizations. Although many SALs—especially white SALs—were quick to identify individual acts of racial sin (primarily acts of racism and racial ignorance), many failed to acknowledge the organizational and systemic acts of racial sin (the more invisible forms of racism) within the institution. In other words, barriers (i.e., the sins) to inclusive campus climates were conceived of only individually (i.e., individuals who are racist or enact various forms of racial ignorance) rather than also structurally (e.g., lack of faculty and staff of color, structural issues that bring about racial inequality). We commend SALs' commitment to denounce individual acts of racism. Yet they also must attend to aspects of institutional racism—and fight against it.

Second, many SALs had a limited imagination of ways to improve their CRC. Creating hospitable environments is a robust and multifaceted effort; the responsibility of creating one cannot fall on the shoulders of a few staff members or isolated to a few offices—it must be the effort of the whole institution. If the responsibility does fall on one or two offices (such as the multicultural office or spiritual formation office), creating a transformative climate—one that is truly hospitable to all students—is likely to be short-lived and superficial. Our concern, however, is that this is a reality for many Christian institutions. When asked about the positive efforts put forth by the institution to create a hospitable CRC, many SALs were quick to identify the work accomplished by the multicultural office or the spiritual formation office. On the one hand, this quick identification highlights the remarkable work done by these two offices. On the other hand, we are concerned that the general lack of identification of other stakeholders and offices potentially points to two particular problems: (1) one or two offices shoulder the responsibility of racial diversity efforts, and (2) racial diversity efforts are siloed rather than integrated into all aspects of university life. This is concerning because when racial diversity efforts are conducted by a few leaders and isolated to programmatic efforts or offices, they are doomed to fail.[15] Although isolated approaches to diversity can have sporadic success, they will not achieve deep and lasting transformation that is truly inclusive of all.

Suggestions to Improve Campus Racial Climates

In light of our findings, we offer some specific suggestions for student affairs to improve their CRC. These suggestions are not exhaustive, nor should they be considered the "magic pill" that suddenly creates a welcoming environment for marginalized students. Rather, they are the result of reflecting on our findings. Although there are multiple suggestions for how individual SALs can cultivate multicultural awareness, knowledge, and skills (we acknowledge this is important), due to our limited space, we will focus mainly on institutional efforts.

Commitment to Use Theological Language

One of the biggest strengths we saw regarding diversity efforts was SALs' use of rich biblical and theological language when describing racial and ethnic diversity. We would like to offer a specific theological term that could be of benefit when discussing issues or race within a Christian worldview: *racial identity stewardship*.[16]

There are two specific reasons why we advocate for using this terminology and believe it could benefit Christian institutions. First, racial identity stewardship places the responsibility on all students, including white students, to reflect on how they must steward their racial identity. Many white students do not critically engage or reflect on what it means to be white. One reason for this lack of reflection is that many white students are color-blind; they do not reflect on what it means to be racially white in a multicultural world. Yet Scripture is clear: God has made all people in his image and has given all a racial and ethnic identity. And just like other identities we hold (e.g., student, professional, parent, spouse, female, etc.), we must steward these identities for God's glory. This stewardship certainly encompasses stewarding our racial identity. Thus, evoking the term *racial identity stewardship* challenges all students—especially white students—to think about *how* one should steward their racial identity for God's kingdom.

Second, racial identity stewardship, within the American context, means that certain races bear the burden of properly stewarding their identity more than others. Although all races bear the responsibility of stewardship; the level of stewardship depends on social, cultural, and historical contexts. Within the racialized American context, it is undeniable that white Americans bear a large portion of responsibility to steward their racial identity for the purposes of racial reconciliation and justice. This stewardship cannot be optional if one truly wants to love his or her neighbor.

Inclusion in Espoused Mission

It is important for Christian institutions to articulate why embracing and seeking racial and ethnic diversity is not simply a peripheral issue or an added benefit, but rather a fundamental component to the Christian mission of the institution. We believe that this clarity should manifest itself in a clear, biblically derived diversity mission statement, outlining a holistic vision that affirms the dignity and beauty of all. This will have multiple benefits. It will help make racial and ethnic diversity an institutional priority within a Christian college context, and bring diversity efforts from the periphery to the focus of each institution.[17] Moreover, theological clarity will help combat the problematic underlying assumption that engaging in racial and ethnic diversity is simply a political or secular issue.

Enact the Mission

Christian institutions should have a specific short- and long-term strategic plan coupled with specific measurable outcomes regarding diversity. In our interviews, SALs did not articulate clear short- and long-term organizational direction or how success in racial and ethnic diversity is measured. For example, what are the specific goals to increase faculty and staff of color within the next five years? How will an institution reduce the gap between white student graduation rates and students of color in the next ten years? What institutional efforts will be implemented to reduce students of colors' negative perception of the CRC? What virtues are we going to cultivate so that each student can love his or her neighbor well? How will the success of these efforts be assessed? The espoused mission must be joined with the enacted mission.[18] Without action, the espoused mission is merely a statement of sentimentality.

Hiring and Retaining Faculty and Staff of Color

Institutions should commit to hiring—and retaining—more faculty and staff of color. Arguably, this is the commitment that might be the most important practice in creating a hospitable racial climate. Creating racially hospitable environments is virtually impossible without intentionally hiring leaders who represent the diversity of the student body. Representation matters. Creating an inclusive CRC is more than simply denouncing individual racism or improving individual relationships between those of different races through programmatic efforts. It is also about thinking organizationally and structurally, particularly as it relates to current distributions of power and representation within higher education leadership.[19] As our interviews revealed, SALs perceived that Christian institutions lagged behind in diversifying their faculty and staff. In fact, many saw this deficiency as a hindrance to the educational experience and success of all students, but especially students of color.

Look Beyond Compositional Diversity

SALs should commit to look beyond compositional diversity (e.g., racial demographics) of the student body and focus on inclusion.[20] Compositional diversity is primarily concerned with numbers, but inclusion focuses on empowerment, belonging, and dignity. Compositional diversity is simply the presence and percentage of students of color at an institution, while inclusion is giving those students the freedom and power "to move the furniture." Indeed, on its own, compositional diversity does not result in inclusion. As our participants revealed, the growth of the minority student population (i.e., diversity) did not necessarily correlate with hospitable campus environments (i.e., inclusion). In fact, in many cases, simply increasing the population of students of color without equitable systems, structures, and programs led to hostile racial environments. This is because, as research shows, compositional diversity is only the beginning.[21] Inclusion is not a natural outcome of compositional diversity; rather, inclusion must be carefully cultivated.[22]

Incorporate Christian Institutional Practices

SALs should commit to incorporating specific Christian practices into university life. One Christian practice that could serve to orient our posture is the practice of confessing the sin of racism and lament its pain—both individually and structurally. This is the practice of what Alleman and Glanzer describe as "institutional confession."[23] Institutional confession is a "corporate commitment to practices through which the acts of violence, oppression, neglect, abuse, and other moral failures resulting directly or indirectly from institutional policies, practices, and norms are owned and acknowledged so that healing, altered behaviors, policies, and practices might commence."[24] We believe that due to the fall, Christian institutions continually fall short of loving all students as God's image bearers. Specifically, history reveals that Christian institutions have a checkered past in promoting equal access and opportunity for students of color. For many Christian institutions, policies, cocurricular efforts, and curriculum were not developed with students of color in mind. In light of this historical reality, as well as the current manifestations of racism and racial ignorance within each institution, we believe the practice of institutional confession should be a normative practice within the life of the university.

How, then, should institutional confession be implemented practically? Alleman and Glanzer provide a two-step template: (1) ritual confession and (2) situational confession.[25] We believe that a yearly ritual confession of racism should be incorporated into regularly structured events such as chapel, new student orientation, new faculty and staff orientation, or commencement. As institutions participate in the ritual confession of racism, they acknowledge that they, as an institution, have fallen short of loving God and neighbor, and that they have ignored—whether directly or indirectly—the pain and cries of our minority brothers and sisters in Christ.

The opportunity to practice situational confession, on the other hand, should occur when specific instances arise where the institution must confront specific forms of racism. To be sure, the decision of when and how the institution failed to acknowledge the humanity and dignity of all students could prove to be difficult. Although overt and direct forms of racism could be easier to prove, there are always covert and indirect forms as well. Regardless, we believe that institutional confession is a necessary liturgical practice—in light of the historical and current manifestation of racism—that should be incorporated into the fabric of institutional life.

Commitment to Celebrate

It is imperative to have moments of genuine celebration of racial progress. Creating hospitable racial environments is difficult. Fighting issues of racial injustice will bring on feelings of guilt and shame. Many will feel convicted of their racism and racial ignorance and confess their sins. Yet an institution should not simply stop by uncovering and confessing the sin of racism. This is just the beginning. In fact, we believe that it is imperative for institutions to celebrate progress toward diversity efforts. By doing so, institutions can acknowledge where they have been complicit in their racism, as well as places where they have been courageous in fighting racial injustice.[26] It is important for institutions to lament where they fall short, as well as celebrate the progress made—while understanding that celebration does not negate the progress that still needs to be made.

In practice, the processes by which institutions determine points of celebration will vary. Yet we believe a special committee commissioned by the president could prove to be helpful—for example, a committee made up of racially diverse students, faculty, and staff. The reason why we advocate for a racially diverse committee is simple: it guards against false notions of racial progress or symbolic gestures of racial progress that could be often advocated by those in the majority.

Conclusion

Racial and ethnic diversity is important because it matters to God. Christian SALs are called to love others, enact justice, and participate in the redemptive process of redeeming all things to Christ (Lev. 19:15; Col. 1:17). Part of this process involves redeeming fallen institutional environments that value the dignity of some but not others due to the hue of their skin. A true mark of a Christian university is to hold firm to the truth of the gospel and to "do good, seek justice, and correct oppression" (Isa. 1:17). Although this redemption process—creating hospitable racial environments—will require intentional leadership, patience in times of difficulty, endurance of suffering to correct injustice, and countless hours of sweat and toil, we are ultimately hopeful in the promise that God is already doing the work, bringing all people from all nations to himself. We hope SALs will play a significant role in creating a space for Christian colleges to foster racial diversity, inclusion, and equity among their greatest strengths.

11

THE STEWARDSHIP AND REDEMPTION OF OUR SEXUAL SELVES

Christian sexual ethics have everything to do with who God is and with what it means to be human.

—Beth Felker Jones[1]

Each year, I (Perry) am surprised by my graduate students' answers to certain questions about sex. These questions emerge as I always end my course on moral and faith development by requiring these future student affairs leaders (SALs) to read a book about the sexual behaviors of college students. Before discussing the book, I ask students if they received sex education from their parents, schools, or the church (including youth groups). What continually surprises me is the lack of sexual education in general, particularly in a church context. In fact, in my informal surveys, the church always finishes last. In my last two classes, only three of thirty students said they had discussed this topic in a church context. I am always perplexed by my findings because honest and theologically informed discussions about sex, dating, and marriage were quite common in my own church and parachurch experiences.

Unfortunately, we found reason to believe that my graduate students are not alone. For instance, when we asked Christian SALs whether they were adequately trained to handle pornography issues with students, 40 percent disagreed and another 30 percent only slightly agreed (see Table 11.1). Furthermore, more than half of the SALs indicated their campus lacked a resource with regard to sex education.

Table 11.1. Our staff is adequately trained to handle pornography issues with students (*N* = 222)

Response	%
Strongly agree	5%
Agree	26%
Slightly agree	30%
Slightly disagree	17%
Disagree	18%
Strongly disagree	5%

When asked about what was missing, SALs touched on a variety of needs. One of those needs was simply more communication and education, as indicated by the following SALs:

- "[We need] more training and more conversations about sexuality in our campus community and with other student affairs professionals."
- "We don't talk about it enough."
- "The conversation is lacking."
- "I think that we are lacking the courage to have a real conversation about sexuality issues and how they are impacting our students."
- "[We need] more time and space to discuss these topics."
- "It's not addressed in large-scale ways, so it feels at times like it's a 'secret group' or issue that can't be discussed publicly. I think we would benefit from bringing it into the mainstream conversation more regularly."

Even if there is training or communication, it may not give attention to how Christ animates sex education, as one SAL complained regarding sexuality: "Our campus educates us on how to handle things from a professional standpoint but not a spiritual one." One SAL highlighted the lack of resources available: "We don't really have any resources provided to us on campus." Clearly, there is room for improvement on this issue and other issues related to sexuality.

Still, the church—or at least Evangelical churches and their colleges—must be doing something right. For six years, I (Perry) asked students to read Boston College professor Donna Freitas's *Sex and Soul: Juggling Sexuality, Spirituality, Romance, and Religion on America's College Campuses.*[2] Her study provided an insightful look into the various sexual cultures on different types of college campuses. Freitas claimed that two basic types of sexual cultures exist: (1) free-for-all hook-up cultures, which she found on secular and Catholic college campuses, and (2) abstinence-only cultures prominent on Evangelical institutions' campuses. While she found various faults with Evangelical campus cultures regarding sex, she remained impressed by the counterculture they created that integrates sexuality and spirituality.

In light of these kinds of self-critique and external praise, it would be helpful to discover what undergirds and nourishes the Christian sex education culture and what could strengthen it. As professionals on the frontlines of student interaction, SALs have a unique perspective and voice to contribute to this larger conversation. This chapter covers SALs' views and discusses some of the strengths and areas for growth they identified in their general campus's sex education.

How Faith Informed SALs' Responses to Questions about Sex

So how does faith inform SALs' responses to issues related to sexuality on campus? We asked SALs this question on our survey and found that their answers could be classified into five groups. We should note that we did not provide a definition of sexuality when asking the question.

1. The Bible Group

Not surprisingly, what we call the Bible group mentioned how they turned to the Bible for answers in the area of sexuality. In fact, some simply stated things such as the following: "I have a biblical perspective in all matters of sexuality"; "I would examine issues in light of what the Scriptures state"; and "Scripture speaks to us about the nature of sexuality, and that helps to shape the conversation." In some cases, they listed specific Scriptures. One

SAL made specific references to 1 Corinthians 6:9, 18 and 1 Thessalonians 4:3–5 regarding sexuality—passages that refer to fleeing or abstaining from sexual immorality and controlling one's body in holiness and honor.

A few others unpacked the content of the biblical perspective. This content usually connected to an element from some of the other categories we will discuss. For instance, they might focus on a biblical moral rule such as this SAL: "We hold to a biblical understanding of sexuality. That sex is only reserved for a man and woman who are married. We have separated women's and men's housing." In other cases, they mentioned theological beliefs: "Everything I believe stems from my belief that what the Bible says is true. Sexuality was created by God for goodness, and our world has tried to twist what that means. When it comes to matters of sexuality, I look to the Bible for answers." Or they might discuss how Scripture provides them with particular virtues regard sexuality: "The Bible is my authority, and it has much to say about sexuality—the positives of femininity and masculinity lived positively as a single or married person. The Word clearly calls us to be pure as *he* is pure and to view our bodies as temples of the Holy Spirit who is within us." Finally, they may appeal to a couple of these categories: "We approach these issues with the clear teaching of Scripture. The biblical desire for purity in relationships, marriage between one man and one woman, to live in a way consistent with the biological sex one was created, etc." The obvious key commonality for this whole group was their insistence upon looking to the Bible for answers about how one is to address the exploration of one's sexual nature.

2. The Rule Group

The second group of SALs tended to focus on a particular biblical rule regarding sexuality. One SAL noted that the Christian faith "sets parameters and standards for what is appropriate and inappropriate sexual expression." Another noted that it provides "moral guidelines for the purpose of sex." Still, another stated, "I don't think I am a judgmental person, but I also believe homosexual marriage is a sin." We should note that this group was actually the smallest of any of the four groups. Most SALs appeared to want to soften the rules on campus by emphasizing other aspects of the Christian outlook.

3. The Theology Group

The theology group sought to place the Christian understanding of sexuality within the overall Christian story or some aspect of the Christian story. One SAL in particular shared about how the whole story changed his perspective:

> My response and opinions on every topic of sexuality (any kind of sexual relationship, LGBTQ+ issues, pornography, etc.) and how we should educate students on those topics would be different if I did not believe in God's ultimate plan. In the same way that Christian students struggle to follow Christ's commands when the world tells them to focus on self-indulgence and personal happiness above all else, I would have a completely different response on how we talk about these issues on campus if I didn't believe Christ was worth sacrificing for and following, and believe his plan is the right one for every student.

While this participant focused on God's plan in general, most SALs referenced that God made us in his own image, created sex for beautiful purposes, and entrusted us with this gift. The following comments from SALs give a sample of these three expressions:

- "God made us all and he made us good, the crown of his creation, whatever our sexual identity."
- "I believe that God created our sexuality, and it is a beautiful part of each human."
- "I believe that our sexual identity is an intimate part of who we are and that it is good. I believe that there is a framework that God created for the expression of our sexual identity that is fulfilling for us and reflects his glory and design."
- "I believe God intended sex to be a source of satisfaction, honor, and delight to those who enjoy it within the parameters of the moral standards. . . . Human sexuality is both a gift and a responsibility."
- "Sexuality is a gift from God that needs to stay in the confines of marriage."

Perhaps what is noteworthy about the sexual connection to the first part of the Christian story is that when participants mentioned that God made us in his image, all but one participant did not list the rest of the verse that describes how God made humans "male and female" (Gen. 1:28).

A subset of the theology group went beyond creation-oriented claims and added the second part of the biblical story (the fall). They usually placed both insights from creation and the fall together in order to help understand both the ideal for humans and the problems:

- "I understand that sexuality is a powerful gift from God that was never meant to create power structures, to fill emotional voids, or to be weaponized. It can be as destructive as it can be beautiful."
- "[We need to understand] the draw of sexuality (since God created us as sexual beings), and also [understand] the sexual brokenness of the world and the temptations that come along with it, knowing that God has the perfect plan for our sexuality."
- "I think I can start with a perspective of viewing sexuality as a gift from God and things that are misuses of sexuality as an attack on what God created sexuality to be. Sexuality is an identity, but it's also a way of experiencing the intimacy that we're created to experience. When we can instruct students in the value of that, we're able to address the myriad ways that sexuality has been distorted and why."

Whereas the SALs in the rules group tended to emphasize and prohibit a few ways sexuality goes awry (e.g., sex outside of marriage between a man and woman), a number of SALs noted that there are many types of departure from God's plan for sexuality. One SAL conveyed this concept quite directly: "We attempt to proactively communicate a biblical view of being created in the image of God, which includes sexuality. *Many* things are a departure from that ideal, not simply X or Y trending social issue. Such social issues should be viewed in the larger context of seeking a whole a flourishing sexuality and not simply listing the things that are good/bad." Certainly, adding an emphasis on both the creation-oriented ideal and the fall filled out this larger view.

Interestingly, few in the above groups discussed the redemption of sexuality, and only one mentioned restoration. The most thorough theological vision provided by our participants included all aspects of the Christian story. This SAL wrote in our survey:

> My hope and prayer are that my biblically rooted faith gives
> me a deep understanding of the significance of the body in
> the Christian life and a deep appreciation for the way in which
> human beings are made for relationship with one another, and
> that these two theological foundations inform my sexual ethics
> on a host of topics. Put more simply, I start with the two con-
> victions that bodies matter and that relationships matter in
> the Christian life. Bodies and relationships were created good
> but are deeply broken by the entrance of sin into the world.
> That means much of what our bodies and hearts long for is not
> what will ultimately satisfy. Our loves are disordered. Part of
> the redeeming work of Jesus is redeeming our bodies and our
> desires to love the right things in the right way, and to love God
> first of all. God promises to sanctify us, and we ought to contin-
> ually pray to be made new. We are called to holiness in all areas
> of life, including our sex lives. But on this side of the new cre-
> ation, we are all awaiting the redemption of our bodies. As such,
> we must have humility in acknowledging our brokenness before
> one another and before God.

As this SAL reveals, a sexual ethic that takes every aspect of the biblical story into light provides a much richer approach to sexuality.

4. The Virtue Group

The virtue group was different from the theology group in that although they included theological content in their answers, they focused on the importance of Christians demonstrating certain virtues in their sexual lives. They tended to be most concerned about ways campuses might be excluding others (e.g., "Making sure all those who feel marginalized on this campus have someone who knows they will listen, love, and support them always"). As a result, they tended to emphasize virtues such as love, grace, respect, care, humility, and not being judgmental (e.g., "I want to love all people well, including LGBT people"). Or, as one participant put it, "nurturing the fruit of the Spirit even when people disagree with one another."

What we find noteworthy about this group, and the approach of SALs to virtue and sexuality in general, is that they tended to avoid some of the hard, biblical virtues that would apply to the practice of sexuality, such as self-control (Gal.s 5:22), purity (1 Tim. 4:12), and holiness (1 Thess. 4:4–7). This group's core desire is for students to be supported in this area, not necessarily challenged.

5. The Theo-Ethics Group

The final group we call the theo-ethics group. This group paired theological and ethical beliefs together in one of two ways. First, there were those who answered using this form: "Although we believe this, I try to do this . . ." These SALs understood certain biblical rules or perspectives as problematic if they are not complemented by other theological or ethical perspectives:

- "My faith informs both what I believe is acceptable/unacceptable, but also the grace and hope that I hope to communicate when talking about sexuality with others."
- "Though we do not condone pornography, sex outside of marriage, or homosexual relationships, we try very sincerely to treat students engaged in these sexual practices as God's beloved children and bearers of God's image."
- "I do believe in living by what the Bible says about sex, marriage. I also believe you are meant to be the gender you were born to be; however, the greatest command is love, so I treat those who don't believe the same as I do with love and respect as I would any other student."

In these answers, the theological positions were seen as harsh standards that needed to be softened by Christ-like virtues instead of loving insights into a truth that sets one free. One SAL even mentioned, "This has been blurrier. I see very clear mandates to love all people and treat them with respect and in the image of God. However, some Christian doctrine is challenging and is more confusing to me, theologically speaking."

Second, there were those who gave an answer that followed this form: "Because God did (or will do) this, I do this . . ." The following responses give some idea of these types of answers as related to a particular part of the Christian story.

Creation-based

- "Everyone is an image bearer of God; therefore, I want to strive to promote a healthy understanding, value, and respect due to every person. Scripture has articulated how to value and respect others sexually. I want to teach and emulate these teachings."
- "I try to steer my conversation around stewardship of our sexuality, honoring the image of God in others, and all of our pursuit of God's holiness."
- "We are commanded to treat everyone with love and respect. God is no respecter of persons [Rom. 2:11 KJV]; neither should we be."

Sin-based

- "I approach conversations with love and humility, knowing we all struggle with sin."

- "We are each broken and in need of God's grace, and as such I can't be the first to throw the first stone."

Redemption-based

- "Because grace is at the center of the gospel message, my faith incorporates a gracious approach to issues related to sexuality on campus."
- "I operate from a biblical understanding of sexuality and especially prioritize the grace of Jesus Christ in handling these issues. I do not believe in shaming or behavior correction or modification. I believe in extending the love and grace of Christ and the work of the Spirit as the only force that can change a person."

Redemption- and Restoration-based

- "I am called to love God's people. I am not called to dole out justice or to condemn—I plan on leaving that to Jesus. So, I want every person to feel his love because that is what I am called to do; if the relationship is there that I can speak truth with love, then I will use discernment to do that!"

Admittedly, we found these responses the most attractive, because they tend to follow the biblical pattern of how the writers of the Epistles approach ethics. They remind us of God's larger theological story in the first part of these books, and then give instructions to act in light of that story (e.g., see the transition at Rom. 12:1–2, Eph. 4:1, etc.). The following response illustrates this mixture:

> My faith shapes my understanding of two things: (1) All parts of God's perfect creation have been affected by the brokenness of sin, including human sexuality. (2) I am called to love my neighbor as myself. In this light, my faith shapes my response to be one of love, compassion, and welcome to all students, regardless of sexuality. However, I also believe that while marriage is for a man and a woman, ultimately, I don't know the mind of God, and he is the judge of people's hearts, not me.

What we find interesting about this last observation, once again, is that it mixes together insights from creation, the fall, redemption, and restoration, and it combines them with some virtues.

The Best Sex Education

There are rules related to sex within the orthodox Christian context (i.e., no sex outside of a marriage between a man and a woman), but if we only focus on the rules, we miss the important and beautiful vision God has for sex. Ashley even admitted, "Our policies read as very kind of rule-based, like 'You don't do this, you don't do this, you don't do this,' rather than, 'Here's God's beautiful vision for sexuality,' and sort of inviting students into that." SALs recognized the need to communicate a broader biblical vision of sexuality. As one SAL complained, her campus lacked "a healthy ethic of human sexuality and body positivity (not focused solely on not having sex outside of marriage and/or modesty)." This kind of situation can prove deeply problematic in light of what one SAL shared with us:

> We are not talking about the changing culture and the strong influence of culture at large on our students' views and behaviors. Some of the ideological "givens" that guided our policies and perspectives as an institution are not "givens" for our students. Many of our students are professing Christians but hold a very different theology of sexuality. In other words, our students are not just choosing to do the "wrong thing." They don't believe that their views or behaviors are wrong. And in many cases, they are coming to our school ready to advocate against the "wrong" way that the school views and approaches sexuality.

As a result of the numerous cultural scripts guiding students' views of sexuality, they need a deeper form of sex education.

If we piece together all of the SALs' responses outlined above, there does emerge a larger biblical ethic that Christians believe reflects God's moral order. If SALs talk with students about sex, they need to learn how to talk about all of the elements mentioned. I (Perry) have argued elsewhere that a complete Christian ethic must consider the following: (1) our identities, (2) the larger Christian story and its various theological elements, (3) purposes, (4) rules, (5) virtues, (6) practices, (7) wisdom, (8) mentors, (9) models, and (10) moral imagination.[3] Thus, a holistic Christian sex education should encourage students to wrestle with the following questions:

1. *Identity.* What are your most important identities as they relate to sexuality? What is a biblical view of both a marital identity and identity as a person who is single? What does the Bible and the Christian tradition say about being made "male and female"?

2. *Story.* What does it mean to understand our sexual practice within *every* major element of the Christian story? (For example, one SAL listed the following elements: "understanding God's created order and gifts, and understanding the prevalent way that sin distorts this intention and also our understandings of this; the

way that God's grace, shown to us in Christ, restores us as new creations … but may not heal or solve every issue related to sexuality; [and] the obligation we have to see the image of God in all his people."

3. *Purpose.* What are the purposes of sex? We found SALs' answers reference many traditional Christian answers in this area (e.g., imitative spiritual oneness of Christ and the Church or faithfulness, procreation, pleasure, etc.).

4. *Rules.* As mentioned, most students likely know the rules, and most institutions focus on them too much. Focusing on these other elements helps provide a justification for the *why* behind the rules.

5. *Virtues.* What biblical virtues should you demonstrate regarding your sexuality outside of marriage? What virtues should you practice within marriage? After all, not all sex within marriage is moral if it is selfish, nonconsensual, lacks self-control, patience, love, and so forth. Furthermore, plenty of sexual expression that seems "harmless" (e.g., kissing) can be manipulative, selfish, impatient, and greedy.

6. *Practices.* What biblical practices do you need to develop regarding sexuality outside of marriage? Within marriage? For example, do you pray regarding your sexual life?

7. *Wisdom.* How are you acquiring wisdom in this area? What books are you reading? Do you have a mentor from whom you can obtain wisdom?

8. *Mentors.* Do you have mentors regarding sexuality to whom you can share when necessary? What do you need to share with them?

9. *Models.* Do you have models? Who are they, and why are they your models?

10. *Moral imagination.* What are creative ways for Christians to deal with the fallen and redemptive aspects of sexuality? For example, the Christian group in which I (Perry) was involved in at a secular university developed a service for walking drunk students home from an annual tradition called the Night of Decadence

(you get the idea), since a student was sexually assaulted at the event in a previous year.

For those who wish for a helpful primer on these elements, we recommend Beth Felker Jones's short book, *Faithful: A Theology of Sex.*[4]

Furthermore, we think SALs must not merely have conversations about these various elements as they come up or at a single chapel (although those are helpful); instead, we contend that the best models of healthy sex education should be integrated campus-wide and occur with more regularity. For example, we think institutions should foster conversations within the context of a weeklong—or better, a yearlong—program designed to address the numerous issues related to sexuality. We think there are good examples of yearlong programming found at Calvin University, Northwestern College, and Messiah College (soon to be University). Of course, there are likely others we did not encounter. The yearlong approach designs learning experiences throughout the academic year. Ashley mentioned that the focus is "trying to highlight what we're for, instead of just, 'Here's all the things we're against' descriptions." To do so, her institution established a series that met once a month called "Engage." Ashley noted, "We did a session on marriage, a session on singleness, pornography, sexual assault, sexual violence, same-sex relationships, contraception, and family planning, you know, all of those themes—in that first year." Outside speakers, staff, and professors all participated as presenters. In this particular case, the program even became part of chapel requirements:

> The first year, it was fully voluntary. . . . We previously had a chapel requirement, and I felt strongly and pushed that we needed a Christian formation requirement that was more than just going to chapel. There are other ways in which you become formed as Christians, right? So, then Engage became another option for students that they could get credit for. That became kind of a partnership, then, between student development and campus ministry. Then Res Life is kind of a wing event [where] RAs invite their wings to come to Engage, and then they usually go back to the wings afterwards and talk about what they saw and what they heard and continue the conversation. It's

been a really nice program that's tapped into a lot of different things, and has, I think, really raised the profile of and, I hope, increased an awareness on some of these issues.

We believe these kinds of structural changes that make programming around sexuality a constant conversation help students build a well-developed moral framework around sex and can provide the chance for students to develop a holistic and healthy Christian sexual ethic.

Conclusion

C. S. Lewis once wrote, "I wonder whether, in ages of promiscuity, many a virginity has not been lost less in obedience to Venus than in obedience to the lure of the caucus. For of course, when promiscuity is the fashion, the chaste are outsiders. They are ignorant of something that other people know. They are uninitiated."[5] The lure of unknown knowledge often leads students to experiment on their own. Christian student affairs should lead students to the best wisdom about sex. As Nolan told us, "I think Christian student affairs is at its best when it steps into the really hard and messy places that most of their colleagues on their campus are afraid to step into. . . . I think that's really where Christian student affairs shines—when they step into that and say, 'No, we're going to enter into this space and have a conversation about it.' Or, 'No, we're going to explore this, because it's worth exploring.'" Christians have the best insights into sexuality because we know the God who instilled it in us. We know the God who will defeat the evil one who twists it. And we know the God who offers redemption and sexual wholeness in part now and fully in eternity. We should have the courage to share and discuss it with our students.

12

SEXUAL JUSTICE IN A BROKEN WORLD
How Christ Enlivens Title IX Practice

When I (Britney) tell people, "Title IX is my primary research area," they give me a sympathetic look and say, "Oh . . . Title IX." Sometimes this response seems to come from a sense that Title IX is something forced upon institutions (which it is), but it is not an area Christian colleges and student affairs leaders (SALs) have undertaken confidently. Thus, in this chapter, we look at the pressing issues Christian student affairs professionals who are involved in Title IX (e.g., coordinator, investigator) are facing now and how they might be better equipped to respond to Title IX issues.

Title IX of the Education Amendments of 1972 (Title IX) states: "No person in the United States shall, on the basis of sex, be excluded from participation in, be denied the benefits of, or be subjected to discrimination under any education program or activity receiving Federal financial assistance."[1] Undoubtedly, these thirty-seven words have completely changed education in the United States. Yet, other than arguing Christianity's compatibility with protecting women and LGBTQ+ students' dignity and rights, Christians have rarely explored how Christ and Christian faith can animate practices related to Title IX.

Often, Title IX advocates and activists are villainized as liberal feminists.[2] Moreover, Christians have been reluctant to enter the Title IX conversation because they perceive consent as a very low boundary marker for ethical sex.[3] Despite this tension, our study revealed that SALs do not see the two, Title IX and Christianity, as incompatible. Rather, the data we collected uncovered that SALs articulate an implicit compatibility between Title IX and Christian faith, despite an explicit hesitancy to bring the two together among the majority of participants.

Christ and Title IX

Overall, we found general support for those looking to see how the Christian faith can influence Title IX practice. However, some exceptions existed. For example, Mark said, "I've seen campuses who are acting in good faith and trying to integrate their faith [with Title IX], and it's worse." In this case, Mark believed it was better to not integrate faith with Title IX than to do it poorly.

Robert discussed the challenge and need to listen to secular institutions and secularize the narrative regarding Title IX in Christian institutions:

> We need to learn from our colleagues in secular institutions
> that are at a better level and not dismiss them because they're
> secular. We need to tell a better story about Christian student
> affairs. I think if we can create a better narrative for what we do,
> and I think if we can create a better narrative, especially towards
> our secular colleagues, using—this may come off wrong—but
> using less religious language at times, in talking about our work,
> knowing that our faith is impacting our work in dramatic ways,
> then I think that there can be a bridge in there.

On the other hand, there were those who thought Christian institutions should try to take the lead. Mark claimed, "We need to not just do enough to get by. I think we also need to be exceptional professionals in how we do this. . . . The whole sacred, secular calling . . . I think we've done a good job of debunking that, but it still plays out. [Why can't a Christian] be one of the country's greatest Title IX experts and be at a Council for Christian Colleges and Universities (CCCU) school? That's just as much a part of the calling and honoring of Christ as just meeting the minimum standards."

Unfortunately, we found that Christians were not always taking the lead with excellence. Our participant responses to questions about faith and Title IX generally fell into two categories we labeled (1) limited moral imagination and (2) theological understanding. Moral imagination refers to how SALs are thinking (or not thinking) about faith and the implementation of Title IX, whereas theological understanding represents the integration of faith with Title IX.

Limited Moral Imagination

Within the first of these two categories, we heard responses reflecting a limited moral imagination relating to all three areas of Title IX practice: training and prevention, policy, and investigations.

Training and Prevention

The training and prevention arm of Title IX is focused on educating students, faculty, and staff on issues related directly or indirectly to gender equity, harassment, sexual assault, and so forth. Our participants, in describing how they think their faith influences these conversations, could not identify anything specific. Madelyn said, "I don't think I would say that it is. . . . I don't know how to say this. . . . In the trainings that they're given, I don't know that there's ever a point where we're saying, 'We're Christian, so we do it this way.' Instead, I think we go about it in a way of just in general, 'This is the way this should be done because we are human.'" Mark iterated a similar statement: "Again, it's core of who I am, so it's never not informing. But the more training, the more things that go on with Title IX—I just feel so handcuffed of what we can and can't do or can and can't say." Mark exemplified the growing frustration among SALs regarding federal oversight into private, faith-based higher education.

Policy

Institutional policy can easily become a check-the-box item when it comes to integrating faith into any function of the university. For some institutions, it is easy to make a statement of policy; it is more difficult to fully embody that policy. For many of our participants, Title IX policy was viewed as a good place for the institution to say, "Don't do that [behavior] because it's not right." Is the behavior not "right" morally? Biblically? Ethically? Christian SALs often did not clarify that point. For example, Ryan said, "Yeah, I mean, abuse and violence and harassment of . . . all of those things are wrong, and I immediately feel like those things should be addressed and taken care of. So, I don't know that my Christian faith informs that in any way. I think I'd feel that way, but yeah." For Ryan, policy was written from a basic moral premise, but he was unable to articulate how to connect the premise to the Christian tradition.

For others, policy becomes merely the regulation one follows to avoid litigation. Moreover, trying to insert a Christian virtue, such as grace or mercy, may actually create further injustice.

> We can't be heroes when we're dealing with people. We need to follow our policy that's been vetted through our lawyers and everything else and stick to it. Because when we don't, that's when we get into the most trouble, I think. And it makes us look bad to the population at large. I feel like most of our worst stories are kind of out of that vein. We were acting in good faith, and we're trying to be Christians, and whatever. And this guy, he recognized he made a mistake. He's still around. Well, what about the person who was on the receiving end?

According to this participant, trying to be a hero (as Christian institutions) makes our response worse. Sadly, we believe this too frequently becomes the mantra of Christians: "Give up trying to get it right, because along the way you get it wrong. It's better to just go with the flow than to do something radical for fear it might make things worse."

Investigations

The final branch of Title IX implementation is the investigations arm. When it comes to investigations, participants were able to articulate a general, broad moral imagination for reflecting their faith amidst a Title IX investigation, whereas many participants were able to articulate a more specific theological understanding (described in the next section). Austin imagined: "I think Christianity influences how you're working with Title IX. A lot of what Title IX is just talking about treating people with decency and respect. And I think that the foundation of Christianity is all about that." Similarly, Mark stated that it was important for him to "recogniz[e] no one is defined by their worst decision" and articulate that truth to respondents in Title IX investigations.[4] Again, this participant provided a view of how a Christian perspective about identity informs their Title IX work when it comes to investigations.

Overall, some SALs struggled to articulate a moral vision for how faith could be integrated with Title IX practice. Some simply believed that Title IX is a completely compliance-based practice that is mandated by the federal government. Although this is true, it also exemplifies the lack of imagination for faith integration. For example, when asked if and how faith is integrated with Title IX practice, Zachary said, "I don't think so. I think our Title IX response follows just like the federal law of Title IX. I don't think there's anything that we specifically do that would say, 'Oh, here's our Christian spin or our Christian flavor in it.'" Zachary's response revealed that some campuses, despite boasting a robust integration of faith and learning, view Title IX as an exception. For some reason, Title IX is viewed as an issue such as the disbursement of federal financial aid—completely compliance-based with no "Christian flavor" to it, as Zachary coined. Mark fully embodied the reasoning behind the necessity of said conversation: "How do we do Title IX as Christians? I don't know."

Clearly, what is missing is the acknowldgement that some provision exists for religious exemptions to Title IX. That certainly is not a comprehensive solution, but also Christian institutions too easily fall prey to the assumption that the federal government is "handcuffing" faith-based institutions in how they express their faith amidst Title IX situations. Perhaps a moral imagination is still lacking. Nowhere in the guidance from the Department of Education does it say that Christian institutions cannot talk about sin, the fall, grace, redemption, love, forgiveness, accountability, consequences, or compassion.

As Christians in student affairs work, we need to develop the moral imagination for how we can infuse our Christian faith into *every* area of campus and of practice—even Title IX. We still need heroes. We need risk takers. We believe that the risk is worth the reward in demonstrating that we can implement policy that both addresses sex-based inequities *and* points people to biblical principles.

Theological Understanding

A few participants were able to articulate a theological understanding and, thus, implementation of an integration of faith and Title IX practice. In doing so, they reflected the theological concepts of (1) *Imago Dei*, (2) sin, and (3) redemption and restoration. Each of these theological terms/concepts relates directly to one of the three branches of Title IX: training and prevention, policy, and investigations, respectively. It is through these biblical concepts that integration of faith and Title IX practice can take place.

Imago Dei

As we have explored in earlier chapters, *Imago Dei* refers to the biblical concept of being made in God's image or his likeness.[5] Fundamentally, communicating that all people are loved and valued by God and that God made each and every person in his image drove the conversations in training and prevention of sex-based discrimination within student affairs. To us, participants who were using biblical language and reasoning to explain why we treat others with respect, care, love, and honor demonstrated a deeper theological understanding of connecting faith to Title IX work. Participants such as Nolan provided multiple examples of how this language was put into practice during training and prevention scenarios:

> I think a distinctly Christian approach to Title IX, rather than just saying, "That's from the government, so therefore it's not Christian," could say, "No, a Christian approach honors and values the body, because Scripture informs our approach to the body so heavily that we honor one another and honor one another's bodies, which then informs the way in which we interact with one another. That goes beyond just, 'Here's what you can't do.'" Right? Here's what you need to stop doing, or not do when it comes to Title IX–related incidents, but instead, here's what a college campus should look like when it is honoring one

another's bodies—when it is valuing a distinctly Christian view of sexuality and the body.

Nathan described his institution's Title IX student training session bringing in both the campus pastor as well as a local lawyer to integrate the discussion between faith and legal obligations:

> I'm going to have our campus pastor do an introduction about that very thing. "What does Scripture say about how we treat each other's bodies?" And just kind of set the whole thing up. [The lawyer] come[s] at it. . . . She's a believer as well, and she'll come at it primarily from a legal and a racial standpoint, but she certainly will be able to lead back to some of what [the campus pastor] says as well. So, I think it's going to be a nice combination of voices that are going to be on the stage.

In these conversations SALs are having with their students, a clear connection is made between Title IX parameters and valuing the body, as we are all made in the likeness of God.

One of the hiccups for Christians engaging in Title IX training is the topic of consent. Certain Christians believe that if we are talking about consent, we are necessarily endorsing premarital sex. So, their "solution" is to simply not talk about consent. Of course, students at Christian colleges are having sex. We have to talk about consent, because we do not want a timid young female or male being pressured or coerced into having sex with their boyfriend or girlfriend when they do not want to, and then not talking to anyone about it, getting depressed, feeling violated, and feeling like they cannot talk to anyone about it because "good Christian boys and girls don't have sex—ever."

So, what are the different reasons to talk about consent? How do you talk about consent from a Christian worldview? On the one hand, we think there is an aspect of "fall control" here. In other words, God has given his children (his creation) a physical body and, as an extension, the ability to speak (words), which have dignity and power. Thus, violating someone's body or words is explicitly denying someone's humanity. And marking the boundaries explicitly is not some type of endorsement that one should have sex but that human dignity should be protected—at all times.

On the other hand, there is a positive spin as well—particularly as it relates to *Imago Dei*. We should talk about consent because (1) we want student relationships to flourish, (2) we want relationships to reflect God's love, and (3) that when a person speaks, those words have power because they are made in the image of God.

Ashley discussed how she handles the topic of consent from a biblical perspective this way:

> That's my segue into, "Well, is consent everything?" Then I talk more broadly about, "As Christians, it's not just about consent. That your sexuality is meant to be . . . God has designed it for husbands and wives to be gifts to one another. And not to objectify, not to treat the other person as a means to an end." So, that's where we bring in a more Christian understanding of what sex is for. You know? And it's not just this kind of biological thing that you have to have consent for and then everything is OK.

Ashley demonstrated that you can have a real conversation about consent and what it means to honor one another's bodies, and yet still uphold, value, and honor your biblical commitments.

In many ways, we believe this is what a majority of our Christian campuses desire—to fully engage in any topic from a faith perspective. Take away the societal pressures and the dancing-around-the-issue awkwardness. Let us just be real with our students. Let us not be afraid to engage in difficult (and often awkward) issues. We will all be better for it.

Sin

The theological concepts of sin, brokenness, and the fall were occasionally presented in participants' discussions of Title IX policy. Jaxon made a profound statement alluding to our brokenness and, thus, the need for Title IX policy: "Of all the places where sexual harassment and sexual assault should not be happening, it shouldn't be a Christian campus. Because again, going back to *Imago Dei*, we are all images of Christ. Because of

Christ's modeling of caring for those who are marginalized, of honoring one another, we should be the last place where sexual harassment and sexual assault incidents take place." Jaxon continued, describing how discussing the issue of sin as it relates to Title IX has been important to the integrity of his institution, as well as students' well-being: "The way we get everyone's attention is [by saying], 'We all theologically and biblically know that we live in a broken and sinful world. So, we're not surprised when these things happen.' So, I think we have done a really good job right now of not sweeping anything under the rug." Jaxon and other SALs recognized that we have to engage the difficult conversations with our students in order to best care for them on our campuses.

When SALs did talk about sin, it was often in conjunction with the language of redemption and restoration. Indeed, as we noted in Chapter Nine, this is a strength of the field. But this has led to issues in SALs' approach to Title IX. An overemphasis on developing students who have conduct issues has, at times, led our field to forget about those who have been affected by the misconduct. Mark shared a helpful reminder in this regard:

> We're always carrying this tension of the safety of the individual . . . or the good of the individual and the good of the whole of the campus. And I think sometimes our tendency towards love and grace can be grace towards the offender, but what about for the survivor? He or she needs to feel safe and loved on this campus, too. And if we've reached the point of decision, according to our policies, that our policy was violated, and at the core you're saying that you did this thing that violated another person, I think the risk to the community is too great to allow them to continue to be there.

Mark raised a great question that other SALs must deeply consider: How can our policies provide care for the whole campus *and* the one who is hurting *and* the one who needs to be held accountable, simultaneously? Jesus left the ninety-nine to find the one and bring it back to the flock (Matt. 18:10–14), so we cannot be willing to miss caring for each of our students—particularly those who are hurting or who have lost their way.

Redemption and Restoration

Several SALs embodied theological understanding in their Title IX investigative work. They described the investigative process as being both redemptive and restorative. Steven reflected on the promise of redemption in the face of assault and abuse: "I think the concept of redemption is huge. And restoration. How [else] do you sit with a student who has assaulted someone and say, 'This isn't your identity. This isn't the end of your story. . . . There's an opportunity for redemption here. Yet, that may mean that you're removed from our school; that may mean you're . . . [pause] This is going to follow you, but that doesn't mean it's defining you.'" Steven points us toward the very heart of redemption in student affairs work: "This is going to *follow* you, but that doesn't mean it's *defining* you" (emphasis added).

As student affairs practitioners, we have the opportunity to help students learn and grow from their mistakes. That does not mean we do not hold them accountable. Certainly, in Title IX situations we must hold students accountable. But that does not mean we're teaching our students they *are* their past sins. Rather, it is an opportunity for us to both preach and live out the gospel with our students.

Jacob described his perspective of the gospel narrative preached throughout the Title IX process:

> I think the Christian faith, broadly speaking . . . informs the
> way we interact with students, but we communicate to them
> very differently during a Title IX process, right? I think it's just
> one of those deals when we see the narrative arc of the gospel of
> humanity's fallenness, broken, but then also the life and resto-
> ration of the kingdom of God. When it comes to broken human
> sexuality, there's restoration that can take place. When it comes
> to victims, there's healing that can take place. And even, too,
> in the middle of that, there's comfort that could be achieved
> through relationship with the Holy Spirit. And even through
> Christian community. I think, too, in time there's always space
> for forgiveness and reconciliation as well.

In another example, Heather, a director of residence life (who also serves as a Title IX investigator), expressed her prayers that the Holy Spirit would work in the lives of her students: "Praying and being hopeful on both sides that these students will be able to interact with the Holy Spirit in a way that will bring true change in their lives. Whether that's healing, whether that's conviction . . ." Both Jacob and Heather exemplified the majority of participants' views regarding the necessity of redemption within the Title IX process.

The redemption process will obviously look different for each person involved. Both the respondents and the complainants are our students, and both are children of God, but they have different needs. Madelyn described her institution's approach to addressing these different needs in this way:

> I think that one thing that has been really interesting is that our care office has different professionals that are charged to work with the survivor [complainant], but there's also staff that works specifically with the perpetrator [respondent], so I think that kind of shows that caring Christian community in that because, you know, we're not just there for the people who have been hurt, but we're also there for the people who have been accused. Because we do believe in that salvation, and we do believe in that love and that grace, and so . . . how can we support both or all those people through that?

These kinds of simple practices can aid in the redemption and restoration process. On a final note though, rushing too quickly toward redemption and restoration may fail to deal adequately with the emotions of those involved. Heather mentioned a very specific biblical practice that we believe is important to engage in prior to entering into these spaces of redemption and restoration—the practice of lament:

> And so, my immediate response is lamenting. I mean, this is egregious that this is happening, and that this is happening on our campuses. That this is happening nationally. So, I think . . . lamenting has been a really key part for me theologically. . . . One of my favorite professors has been studying suffering, and

so I read a lot of her writing. Really reclaiming the sort of "It's OK to lament; it's OK to grieve at the horrors of what humans have done and still do to each other." When I'm in Title IX, I think I kind of start there, that "Wow, this is incredibly tragic for both and terribly sad." So, I think for me the reason why I feel like that's important is I think it also removes any sense of power that I have as a Title IX investigator. My job is simply to collect the facts, the information, to treat both parties with absolute respect, to do the best that I can to determine an outcome, and I think the sad truth is that when you're in Title IX and you do the work and as many investigations or cases I've been on, I honestly don't think anyone wins. It's not about winning. You know? It's painful. It's deeply, deeply painful. So, my heart in the lamenting is to grieve the pain that I know that these students are navigating and to treat them with absolute compassion and, even in the decision to treat both students with absolute compassion, knowing that this will forever change their lives, on both sides.

Although Heather was the only SAL to explicitly mention the practice of lament, we believe other participants captured the spirit of what it means to lament during the Title IX process, acknowledging and grieving the pain that has been experienced.

Barriers/Challenges

In higher education, there are always barriers and challenges to moving forward in any area of campus. As SALs reflected on their Title IX processes at their Christian campuses, specific barriers to successful Title IX implementation were identified. The three most common challenges faced were:

1. Limited budgets and extensive workload
2. Unsustainability and restraint
3. Lack of faculty support

Budgets and Workload

Unsurprisingly, most of our participants noted the financial constraints that contributed to underdeveloped Title IX programming and practices, particularly with the increase in the federal expectations of institutions. Prevention programming, as Jacob noted, is especially neglected: "Yeah, Title IX training and prevention—I think that's an area in which we probably could do a little better. And I think, too, there is the phenomenon that happens. Budgets are constrained. Departments become smaller, but there's still the same amount of work to be done. So, all of a sudden, people are wearing more hats, and so they're not devoting the same amount of time." Budgets are tight, and an issue that is not perceived to be a problem on one's campus does not get monetary attention. However, our survey did show that just over half of our participants' campuses are implementing in-person and online Title IX training, along with residence life programming to educate and train their students on these issues (see Table 12.1).

Table 12.1. Title IX training and/or prevention efforts (*N* = 222)

Training/prevention method	n	%
Online Title IX training	142	64.0
Residential life programming	129	58.1
In-person Title IX training	114	51.4
Title IX educational and marketing materials around campus	99	44.6
Prevention programming	86	38.7
Sharing survivor stories	45	20.3
External consultants brought to campus to provide training to students	28	12.6
Advertising PowerPoint Slides in chapel/dining halls/other common areas	25	11.3
Other	16	7.2

Note: Participants could select more than one answer.

Moreover, it is not uncommon for SALs on a Christian campus to be wearing several hats to make ends meet. Thus, an increase in expectations on schools regarding a federal mandate, such as Title IX, requires institutions to make adjustments that are difficult. Mark shared his experience balancing the expectations amid conflict:

> The lawmakers and these rules are made for state institutions
> and Ivy League schools that have resources that are beyond our

capacity. Just [consider] the fact [that] I serve as the Title IX coordinator on our campus. I am also the chief conduct officer. You're not supposed to do those two things.[6] We don't have a choice. There's no way. And there's certain rules that they have, like, "Oh, we can't have a potential conflict." There's no role on our campus that doesn't interact with students that you couldn't have a potential conflict.

A lack of resources can lead to role conflict when acting in multiple capacities. So, what's the solution? There is no easy fix. It takes innovative thinking and cross-campus collaboration.

Unsustainability and Restraint

Many participants mentioned the unsustainability factor of Title IX in terms of what the government is expecting from institutions. However, some do not see this unsustainability as a negative thing, but as a push in the right direction: "We sometimes get freaked out. 'Oh, we have more Title IX cases.' It was happening. At least now students are asking us to help. That's a sign of health to me, not of dismay. The issue is we've got to figure out is how to sustainably meet that. And that's where we're struggling the most, because everybody's bandwidth is maximized." Moreover, a couple of participants mentioned that they "feel so handcuffed of what we can and can't do or can and can't say." In this respect, campuses are feeling that the law inhibits SALs from fully embracing their Christian identity in the moment (i.e., dealing with a Title IX issue). However, we argue against this point, as evidence shows in the previous section that there are ways that SALs on Christian campuses are effectively integrating their faith with their Title IX practice.

Faculty Support

Few would deny the tension that can exist between faculty and student affairs. Certainly, this tension escalates when dealing with a subject that can be theologically controversial. In our findings, SALs reported pressure from faculty on both sides—those more liberal and those more conservative. Kaylee shared, "Our seminary faculty have some issues with the definition of what the [Title IX] policy says about marriage." Undoubtedly, there are going to be vast theological perspectives on every faith-based campus.

Some SALs mentioned faculty who were unconvinced that Title IX is truly an issue on our campuses. Zachary said, "[Regarding] some of the statistics that were used . . . students—and I think [they were] led by faculty—wrote a lot of articles about how all those statistics aren't accurate. And so even when there's education being offered, there's a lot of pushback that this is not a valid conversation or the problem is not present." Faculty support is needed to bring attention and positive responses to Title IX on our campuses. Rather than living in proverbial tension with faculty, SALs need to cultivate a collaborative partnership with them—particularly those who espouse the need for education around sex equity but also those who are resistant or oppositional to the tenants of Title IX. Our message to students must be consistent—treating people without respect, particularly due to their sex, is unacceptable, unbiblical, and unjust.

Why Care?

So, why should we care about this issue as Christians? Well, as Robert put it, "Title IX does not discriminate between Christian and secular." Title IX issues affect *every* campus, faith-based or not. Beyond that, as Valerie reflected, it is an opportunity for ministry:

> I think it's a huge opportunity for us to handle some of these things in a way that the world wouldn't . . . what you might not see at a state school when you're just walking through the process and people are being kind of sterile, and procedural. . . . I just don't want it to feel sterile and procedural. I don't want you to not be able to see my face. I don't want you to think that this doesn't hurt me, too. So, I think there's a time to be human. . . . Our investigators tend to be a little more, you know, just taking down the facts, but when somebody comes to report to me, I'm going to pray for them. I'm going to talk through other feelings beyond just facts and show some care for their souls. You

know? "What do you think this is saying about who you are as a human?"

In order to be effective in this opportunity, however, our campuses must be well-equipped to deal with Title IX issues. In our survey, participants who disagreed that the staff at their institution were well-equipped to deal with Title IX issues landed at just shy of 10 percent (see Table 12.2).

Table 12.2. Our staff is adequately trained on Title IX issues (i.e., sexual violence, sex- and gender-based harassment, stalking, domestic violence, dating violence) (*N* = 224)

Response	*n*	%
Strong agree	49	21.9
Agree	107	47.8
Slightly agree	49	21.9
Slightly disagree	9	4.0
Disagree	4	1.8
Strongly disagree	6	2.7

Although this seems like a respectably small percentage, when adding the group of participants that only slightly agreed with this statement, the percentage increases to 30 percent. Our campuses still lack some confidence in feeling educated and equipped to handle issues of sexual assault, sex- and gender-based harassment, and so forth.

Second, a large majority of our participants alluded to the concept of Christian community as a reason for doing Title IX well. Mason said, "When someone has been broken, or has experienced a traumatic experience, you know, we as Christians are absolutely called to be love for them. I think that's really important." Similarly, Nathan reflected, "So, without a doubt, something we feel is really important is making sure that folks are educated on their responsibility for caring for each other on campus— and understanding things, not just from a legal standpoint, not so much, but respect for community." We were not surprised to see this emphasis on community by our participants. Ted and I (Britney) both attended a Christian campus for our undergraduate experience and fully benefited from this focus on fostering and protecting our Christian community on our respective campuses. In fact, this sense of community is the fundamental reason why we loved our undergraduate experience and became interested in student affairs work and higher education. But when that community is not supportive of someone who has experienced a trauma—particularly someone who has experienced a sexual trauma—we fall short of our Christian calling to love our neighbors as ourselves (Matt. 22:39).

Finally, I (Britney) think we have a lot of work to do to undo the damage that has been done to sexual assault victims in the name of religious dogma. I have witnessed the shame sexual assault victims have experienced from the church because of inappropriate questions and judgmental comments regarding the circumstances and context of the assault. That is not what the church is called to be. When we are caring for someone who has experienced dating violence, that is not the time to talk about refraining from premarital sex. If someone reports having been raped, let's not discuss the issue of modesty just then. I believe this is an opportunity for Spiritual Life directors to take up the gauntlet that Christians often avoid. Christian campuses need to have conversations about biblical sexual ethics. However, the Title IX coordinator shouldn't be leading the charge, and these conversations definitely should *not* be taking place during a Title IX report or investigation. There is an appropriate time and a place to have open and genuine conversations about sexual ethics in light of our Christian faith.

CONCLUSION
FAITH ASSUMED, FAITH ADDED, FAITH ANIMATING

A t the outset of this project, we sought to answer two questions: (1) "How does the Christian faith animate student affairs practice?" and (2) "How *should* the Christian faith animate student affairs practice?" We recognize these questions are too complex to be answered definitively—we have no delusions of our comprehensive treatment of the first question, nor do we pretend to have definitive prescriptions for the second. Having acknowledged this reality, we will—in these final pages—use our guiding questions to highlight a few significant themes we found throughout the entirety of our research. The themes we observed permeate our profession and warrant further collective reflection and dialogue. In this way, we see this conclusion as a conversation starter for the next chapter of our profession.

How Does the Christian Faith Enliven Student Affairs Practice?
As we hope you have seen throughout this book, the Christian faith clearly enlivens current manifestations of Christian student affairs. Following each of our research trips, we were filled with a mix of joy and awe at the work of our colleagues. There seemed to be no end to the stories of God's faithfulness in the lives of both professionals and students. We saw a strong camaraderie among professionals and a deep desire for student well-being.

It was clear to us that Christian student affairs leaders (SALs) contribute greatly to the Christ-centered missions of our institutions. These contributions were confirmed by the themes we found in the data.

Strengths

It is important to call out the strengths we saw in Christian student affairs because strengths can be hard to identify without the perspective of the whole field. We point out strengths for three reasons: (1) to train up future and young professionals, (2) to help current professionals realize the excellent work they are doing, and (3) to communicate this excellent work to senior administrators and those outside the profession of Christian student affairs.

Sacrificial love for students. Throughout this book, we have demonstrated the unique ways that Christian SALs love their students. This love is more than a mere professional duty; indeed, Christian SALs love their students sacrificially. This sacrifice was not only in their ongoing care, support, and love for students during their time on campus, but beyond it as well. Many participants shared about ongoing friendships and mentoring relationships with former students as if it was the norm for the profession. These relationships signal a connection that surpasses the typical roles of staff and student, and a level of commitment that is not the norm of the student affairs profession. This commitment, however, was not limited to the stories of ongoing friendship between staff and students. The Christian SALs we heard from were committed to caring for their students without condition or qualification. In many instances, this care extended beyond significant political, theological, and ideological differences. Love like this can only be based in the love to which Jesus refers when he says, "By this all people will know that you are my disciples, if you have love for one another" (John 13:35).

Imago Dei. One of the most repeated themes in our interviews was that students were created by God and in his image. As we saw extensively in Chapter Four and at other times throughout the book, this seemingly simple idea has massive implications on the ways we approach our field. And, although it was mentioned in this way less often, this truth has equally significant implications for how we view colleagues we work with and supervise. When we see fellow humans as image bearers of God, we know the dignity they bear and define their flourishing in terms outlined by God himself.

Substantive discipleship. The goal of Christian student affairs extends far beyond "do no harm," as one participant told us. Instead, the goal of Christian student affairs is substantive discipleship, yet in a manner different from what is provided by the local church. The practice that most exemplifies this strength is seen in the area of redemptive conduct. As we explored in Chapter Nine, the Christian faith provides a narrative in which to embed the conduct process. Rather than an overly punitive and dismissive approach, in the Christian student affairs imagination, the conduct process invites students to work through a process of restoration that is grounded in grace and aimed at redemption.

The wisdom of dependence. Burnout was a significant topic of discussion in our focus group with a number of student affairs deans and vice presidents. They collectively worried about the future of the profession, given what they sensed was a high rate of burnout and turnover in young professionals. As the conversation turned to causes and solutions, one vice president highlighted the importance of a sense of dependence on God for personal and professional strength. Professionals needed to depend on God, she argued, not only to sustain themselves but also to have the strength to develop their students. Although this is an opportunity for growth in the field, we list it as a strength because so many of the senior leaders we talked to shared a similar dependence on God for their life and work. When we asked them about their experience in field, a sense of dependence on God was the wisdom they shared most frequently.

Opportunities for Growth

As with any field, there is always room for growth. We would like to highlight four general opportunities for growth we saw across our data:

Missing virtues and practices. Certain Christian virtues and practices were not always central in the content of a Christian approach to student affairs. The virtues we are referring to are what Glanzer and Alleman (2019) call "redemptive" virtues—those virtues which emulate Christ in that they take on suffering in an effort to reverse the fall (e.g., self-sacrificial love, forgiveness, humility, servant leadership). The practices are also those needed to reverse the fall (e.g., repentance, sacrificial giving). To be clear, we saw these virtues emulated in the character of our participants and mentioned in their student affairs pedagogy, but we did not hear participants talk about them extensively when they described their desired student outcomes. We believe the field has an opportunity and a mandate to include these virtues—many of which run counter to prevailing cultural self-actualization narratives—into an expanded Christian vision for what student affairs should cultivate.

Professional development. Although we heard that some campuses were developing their staff teams with excellence, a number of others described a need for additional supports and further exploration of how faith might enliven their work. The SALs we heard from in this category described a lack of development due to a dearth of time, resources, or interest. A significant way to ensure continued growth in the field is to be intentional about how we develop and care for our staff teams. It may not fit in your overfilled calendar, but few commitments are more urgent than ensuring your people have what they need to do their jobs effectively. This may require a short-term sacrifice, but it will set your team up for long-term success.

Theological language. Our interviews were peppered with theological language, but it was concentrated in particular terms and types of responses. First, the types of theological language we heard generally related to student image bearing, love for the student, social justice, and Christian community, with little to no discussions of sin or the coming kingdom. The focus we saw generally emphasized strengthening human relationships and the structures of society, with little discussion about how students are to relate to God. Second, when we asked broader philosophical questions, participant responses frequently included Christian visions of flourishing and faithfulness. But, when we asked more pragmatic questions, some of our participants neglected theological language entirely, favoring well-worn scripts from secular student affairs literature. We fear this disconnect in language might signal a disconnect between our espoused vision for Christian student affairs and our enacted practices of student affairs.[1]

We believe SALs would benefit from thinking theologically about our profession. This is not to be confused with merely adding theological language or spiritual formation practices. We are talking about an intellectual labor that animates the whole of one's work. Neglecting such labor is dangerous because unexamined additions can create less-than-effective Christian knockoffs of established student affairs best practices. We need to think about how theological truth animates our work in ways that are unique to our profession.

Critical engagement with theory. In our analysis, we found little to no critical engagement with student development theory. Many SALs knew theory by name, and most had a theoretical intuition. It was clear that theoretical concepts were embedded in their approach to student affairs, even if only subconsciously. But what we did not find was the type of engagement with theory that questioned the fundamental assumptions that lay behind the theory. Instead, it seemed that most theory, and most empirical research, was taken at face value, treated as if it were fact. For example, many referenced George Kuh's high impact practices when we asked for best practices, but we wonder how many would agree with Kuh's limited definition of student success: "higher-than-predicted graduation rates and better-than-predicted student engagements scores."[2] We simultaneously want to encourage our field to engage with more recent and relevant research, and to do so with an eye that appropriately questions the assumptions hidden in the research.

How Should the Christian Faith Animate Student Affairs Practice?

How can Christian student affairs build upon its strengths and make the most of these opportunities? In order to go beyond current modes of operation to answer the "how *should*" question, we think it is helpful to consider how you approach integrating your Christian identity with your professional student affairs identity. In the data, we saw some SALs respond with Christ as an assumption, others who added Christ on top of secular theory and practice, and still others who saw Christ as the animating force behind every aspect their work. We believe the first poses some potential problems, the second has led to many of the strengths in our field (but also limitations), and the third is most favorable. Participants rarely fit neatly into one of these categories. Rather than a singular approach, participants tended to switch among these three approaches in their responses on various topics. What motivates this tendency to mix approaches? A question of identity.

Christ Assumed

The first and most problematic approach to Christian student affairs is the assumption that "everything I do is Christian, because it's the lens that I wear." The assumption is that the work of integration is something that comes naturally or intuitively merely by being a Christian. Thus, the Christ-assumed approach to student affairs sees the Christian identity as something distinct from the professional identity that only influences student affairs practice through intuition and ingrained behavior. This approach can yield adequate results, but the professional will never be forced to question how faith might be *better* integrated into practice because there is no conscious commitment to work toward doing so. We do not assume that someone is an excellent musician or athlete merely because they claim the identity of trumpet player or baseball player (to give two examples). We only make that judgement after seeing the product of all their thoughtful, deliberate practice in action. Christian SALs should not confuse identifying as Christian with demonstrating excellence in Christ-animating student affairs practices.

Christ Added

The idea of a Christ-added approach is borrowed from Glanzer and Alleman.[3] We found that the identity integration in some Christian SALs mirrored what they found in Christian professors. The SALs we interviewed who employed the Christ-added approach saw the Christian identity as an additional, special facet of a professional identity—a facet that was added to an existing construct of what it meant to be a student affairs professional. The responses in our data that exemplify this Christ-added approach took a typical form. We would ask the SAL an initial question, to which they would respond with secular professional language. Then, we would ask, "How does Christianity inform or contribute to that understanding?" and they would "add" Christianity to their previous response.

For example, we asked SALs, "What leads to student flourishing?" One SAL responded: "Yeah, I would say predictable environments. . . . Within student affairs, we have a lot of control over that, especially on the residence life end of things." Then, when we followed up with, "How does Christianity contribute to that understanding?," we received this response: "I don't think the notion of human flourishing is complete without an element of transcendence. And I think we, as humans, long for transcendence, and I think the gospel gives us a full account of what that means. And again, living incarnationally—you know, modeling the life of Christ— provides that. And so, I think students long for that. And I think that's where Christianity plays into, because it offers us that."

We agree with the sentiment this SAL shared—both his understanding of environments and his belief that transcendence is very important. What we find troublesome is the disconnect between the two. Early in our analysis, we saw a few of these disconnections between the professional response and the theological response. We figured it was merely a matter of semantics at first, but as we continued in our analysis, we found a significant number of responses that followed this pattern.

Interestingly, the Christ-added approach can yield some excellent results. Professionals often added in a commitment about students as image bearers or a commitment to Christ, but for some, these commitments did not seem to enliven how they saw their professional identity. We suspect this sort of thinking is what led to the weaknesses we highlighted as opportunities above. Without cultivating an imagination for how Christ enlivens the field of Christian student affairs, professionals will be reticent to foster virtues that fly in the face of cultural norms. They will not prioritize developing the developers. They will not have an expansive theological vocabulary and know how faith might inform their work. Finally, they will see no need to engage the accepted theory of the day because they will have no greater narrative with which to challenge theoretical assumptions. Thus, the field of Christian student affairs needs a third approach. It is the approach we have been subtly arguing for throughout the pages of this book—Christ-animating or Christ-enlivening student affairs.

Christ Animating

The third approach to Christian student affairs—Christ animating—is also borrowed from Glanzer and Alleman's analysis of Christian professors.[4] When something is animated or enlivened, it is brought to life (think of the vision of the valley of dry bones in Ezekiel 37, Christ's resurrection, or our own necessary experience of being "born again"). Thus, Christ-animated student affairs involves practice that is brought to life—flesh, bones, and all the rest—on the basis of Christ and the story of his "restoring, reconciling grace for all of creation."[5] When Christ enlivens something, he does so completely and comprehensively. Although particular methods of practice may not always be unique, Christ distinctively transforms the very nature of the work that we do.

Central to a Christ-animating approach to student affairs is the way that it orders our identities. Whereas Christ-assumed student affairs can lead to a neglect of the Christian identity and the Christ-added approach tends to subject the Christian identity to the professional identity, Christ-animated student affairs acknowledges the privileged place of the Christian identity. As I (Perry) have said elsewhere, "An essential claim of the Christian tradition is that one's Christian identity is one's most important and fundamental identity over and above other identities (e.g., national, ethnic, familial, vocational, etc.). In fact, one can only properly understand oneself and these other identities in light of one's Christian identity and the Christian story that gives meaning to that identity. This story posits that humans are made in the image of God and therefore only find their proper end or telos in proper relationship to God."[6]

By this account, our field's current tendency to pit our professional identity and our Christian identity against one another falsely assumes that they are on the same level when, in fact, the Christian identity is in a place of its own, above all others. In no way do we mean that this then leads to the diminishment or disestablishment of our other identities—this has been done far too often and with horrible effects in the history of the church and society. What we mean to say is that our professional identity is fully rooted in and transformed by the Christian narrative.

After reviewing all the responses, we found that some of the field's most seasoned professionals ordered their identities in this way. In a focus group of student affairs deans and vice presidents, Rose shared that Christian student affairs practice is not marked by "just a general overall sense of spirituality, but it's about a rootedness and relationship with Christ that we share—[a relationship] that is growing and evolving and developmental." For Rose, the relationship SALs have with Jesus is what ought to define them. Dennis shared a similar sentiment at another table in the same focus group: "Our identity, we believe, comes from Christ, Christ alone. That infusion about how much God loves us, who we are, and how he's made us, to me, buoys everything that I do." What is significant about the statements by these two senior leaders is that the Christian identity they describe is not passively presumed (Christ assumed) or one identity among many (Christ added); instead, it is a wholesale identity that demands to be lived out in all aspects of life. All other identities are only truly enlivened or buoyed when they are lived within the context of this—the greatest identity. The Christian identity is the only identity capable of bearing such a responsibility because it is defined by, and given through, a relationship with the living God. As we saw from the responses that utilized this approach, this relationship—and the subsequent identity—provides a new orientation for the whole of Christian student affairs practice.

A Model in Progress

"Why are we really here? Why are we here? We love the [students], but *why* do we love the [students]?" Emily's incisive questions imply what we have been trying to demonstrate throughout these pages. We are here, just as Emily went on to suggest, because of the love of Jesus. "Jesus is the focus." Our goal for this book was to build a comprehensive framework for Christian student affairs that reflects this reality. We have taken the first steps together, but it is still a model in progress. Without continued dialogue, the benefit of these collective reflections on the field will fade away. We have to have the humility and the confidence to refine our model as we expand our imagination for how the Christian narrative might influence

CHRIST-ENLIVENED STUDENT AFFAIRS

who we see ourselves and our students to be, *why* we pursue the work we do, *what* we hope to cultivate within our students, and *how* we go about actually cultivating it. Said another way, we must refine our model as we expand our imagination for how Christ might more fully animate and enliven our student affairs practice.

APPENDIX A

PRINCIPLES OF GOOD PRACTICE FOR CHRISTIAN STUDENT AFFAIRS LEADERS

By the Triune God's grace and strength, the good Christian student affairs leader . . .

Lives in Light of God's Creation

1. Embraces *all* students as image bearers of God who, as a result, have intrinsic and particular worth and who will experience true human flourishing as they imitate God's character (Gen. 1:27; Eph. 4:24).
2. Celebrates and imitates God's hospitality to us by creating and cultivating a flourishing university environment that welcomes all students, finds a healthy and thriving place for all to belong, and seeks to explore with them all of God's wonderful gifts (Gen. 1).
3. Helps students recognize the pursuit of wisdom (Prov. 1 and 8)—which includes Christian creative and critical thinking— as a sacred calling that is now their primary vocation in the university.
4. Creates and cultivates cocurricular learning opportunities for students to discover how to steward God's gifts to humanity, such as our creative and intellectual abilities, our physical bodies, our

inner life of the heart and soul, food and drink, time, material possessions, friendship, community, work, ethnicity, gender, the university itself, and the wider environment (Gen. 1:28–29; Prov. 1, 17:17; Eccles. 3).

   a. Creates contexts for faculty, staff, and students to discuss human sexuality *together,* and how marriage between a man and woman is God's protected context for enjoying God's sacred gift of sex (Gen. 1:27; Mark 10:1–10).

   b. Mentors students' creation of a culture that recognizes the gift of diverse ethnicities and celebrates the multiple student and human cultures that emerge from this diversity (Acts 17:26; Rev. 7:9).

   c. Leads students to embrace the joyful pursuit of God's calling to a work vocation.

   d. Provides opportunities for habitual times of rest, relaxation, and celebration for students and staff (Gen. 1; Exod. 20:8; Lev. 25).

Recognizes Universities Are for Sinners

5. Creates policies, rules, and procedures that recognizes the sinfulness of all administrators, faculty, staff, and students; the misuse of God's gifts; and the need for human authority, order, accountability, and care (Rom. 3:23, 13:1–7).

6. Seeks to enforce just policies, rules, and procedures by exercising the enforcement power God has granted us with patience, restorative justice, wisdom, and mercy. Shapes policies and procedures in light of redemptive and restorative aims.

7. Cares for students wounded by the ravages of the fall through various forms of holistic soul care (e.g., pastoral and psychological counseling; Luke 10:29–37).

Grounds Students in Christ

8. Communicates to every student the good news of God's love for everyone exemplified by Christ's redemptive teaching and

ultimate sacrifice for our sins. Encourages all students to respond to this good news with repentance and worship (John 3:16–21; Rom. 12:1–2).

9. Invites and accompanies students into the life of the body of Christ where they now have new identities as adopted children of God, and are brothers and sisters in Christ (1 Thess. 2:8; 1 John 3:1).

10. Disciples students to follow Christ in gratitude for God's grace, mercy, and love. This discipleship relates to Christian identity, virtue (i.e., fruit of the Spirit), and practices.

   a. Teaches students to understand how Christianity shapes our identity and motivations (Eph. 1–3; Col. 1–3).

   b. Spiritually forms students to imitate Christ's character and bear the Spirit's fruit (Gal. 5:22–23; 1 Cor. 13) through growth in Christian character qualities.

      i. Sacrificial love
      ii. Faith
      iii. Hope
      iv. Forgiveness
      v. Humility
      vi. Servanthood/servant leadership
      vii. Peace
      viii. Joy
      ix. Self-control
      x. Patience
      xi. Kindness
      xii. Goodness
      xiii. Holiness

   c. Leads and challenges students to join in the common practices of the body of Christ through disciplines such as worship and celebration in song; learning, remembering, and meditating upon God's Word; prayer; confession; testimony and evangelism; presence; fellowship; small group Bible studies; missions; and other practices.

11. Illuminates for students how Christ enlivens all of learning in ways that transform every academic discipline and area of student affairs.

Leads Students to Be Christ's Agents of Renewal

12. Creates opportunities for students to learn how to become wise, empathetic, and compassionate interpreters of non-Christian

cultures to better love them and to serve as agents of renewal within them.

13. Helps students create opportunities to serve those in need, especially the least of these. Constructs opportunities for students to learn from that service, so as to engage in wiser forms of service and the creation and/or redemption of just social structures (James 2:12–26).

14. Equips students to join with Christ in the redemption of communal life by considering how God's story and kingdom, Christian practices, and Christian virtues apply to domains beyond the university.

15. Practices faithfulness and hope by demonstrating thinking and living with an eternal perspective that looks patiently to God's ultimate fulfillment of the kingdom of God through Christ.

16. Cares for the holistic needs of their student affairs staff and develops them to model and mentor students in all of these principles.

Questions to Guide Campus Implementation of Each Principle

1. How is this principle currently embodied or demonstrated on our campus? What specific programs, policies, or practices help nurture its practice?

2. How could we improve our demonstration of this principle? What specific programs, policies, or practices would help? What current programs, policies, or practices might be hindering our pursuit of this principle?

3. What evidence will we gather to judge the current state of affairs? What evidence will we gather to judge improvement in this area?

4. How will we share what we have learned with the field?

APPENDIX B
Research Methods

As stated in the Introduction, the purpose of this study was to answer the question "How does the Christian faith animate student affairs practice?" To effectively formulate an answer, we relied on both qualitative and quantitative methods that reflect our critical realist philosophical commitments.[1] In accordance with a grounded-theory approach, we collected a multitude of data in multiple phases. This provided us with the opportunity to allow participant responses to shape and define the next phase of inquiry at each stage of the process.

Phase I: Identifying Christian Colleges and Universities

Since the end of the twenty-first century, Robert Benne's typology has emerged as the most sophisticated way to make sense of the developing differentiation between Christian colleges that prioritize the Christian mission and paradigm and church-related colleges that use a secular paradigm to organize their vision and ethos.[2] Benne splits each of these two groups into two more groups. The pair of schools that still draw on the Christian vision are divided into what he terms: (1) orthodox institutions and (2) critical mass institutions. These first two types of schools clearly acknowledge their Christian identity and use it as a way to guide the school's functioning. The other two types of institutions, (3) intentionally pluralist and

(4) accidentally pluralist, do not. We undertook our own empirical assessment of Protestant institutions using Benne's typology. Overall, we found 192 orthodox and critical mass institutions, which served as the population of our study.

Phase II: Pilot Survey

Based on the findings of our literature review, we created an initial online survey for chief student affairs officers (CSAOs)—typically a vice president of student affairs/life/development. We sent the survey to 192 CSAOs and received complete responses from 69. The core of this initial survey focused on three questions:

1. On a scale of 1 (not at all) to 6 (extremely well), how well has your formal academic education helped you integrate your institution's Christian mission with student affairs practice?
2. What would be the reason for your answer?
3. If your institution's board were to ask you to identify two or more key practices, programs, stories, etc. that exemplify how your institution's Christian faith commitment animates student affairs practice, what would they be?

We also asked for the educational background of the CSAOs (highest degree and where obtained).

Phase III: In-Depth Interviews

Our analysis of the data collected from 69 CSAOs provided the basis for the formulation of the interview guide that we used for our qualitative interviews. Our interview protocol included questions about who Christian student affairs professionals are, who they hope their students become, why they desire that outcome, and how they help students achieve those outcomes. We also asked a series of topical questions that included questions regarding residence life, student conduct, student vocations, multicultural affairs, and sexuality. Overall, we conducted in-depth personal interviews with more than 70 student affairs professionals at Christian institutions across the nation.

Phase IV: Census Survey

The final phase of data collection involved an in-depth mixed-methods survey sent to all student affairs professionals at institutions within our population. The survey instrument was constructed to gather additional qualitative and quantitative data on similar topics to the interview guide. In addition to these topics, we asked specific questions regarding campus racial climates, campus approaches to sexuality issues, Title IX, residence life, career and vocation, alcohol policies, and faith practices and backgrounds. Potential responses for questions with forced choices were informed by our preliminary analysis of our in-depth interviews. The instrument, containing 61 questions, was sent to student affairs professionals at the 192 institutions within our population. The survey was taken by more than 300 participants from 55 unique institutions.

Data Analysis

For our qualitative analysis, we utilized a theoretical sampling process in accordance with our grounded theory approach.[3] Between each phase of data collection, we analyzed the data using open and axial coding methods, debriefed our analysis as a team, and determined which questions would help us discover how faith informs the practice of Christian student affairs professionals in the subsequent phase.[4] All of these phases combined have led to input from well over 400 Christian student affairs leaders, which amounts to more than 1,000 pages of transcribed qualitative data. Our goal in analyzing the data was to group the data into more abstract categories and create any subsequent frameworks or emerging theoretical constructs. In other words, in our qualitative samples, we were not specifically testing a particular theory or hypothesis. Instead, we wanted to discover the answer to the general question: "How does Christianity inform student affairs practice?"

In addition to our qualitative analysis, some basic nonexperimental inferential statistics were used to compare beliefs and convictions among the subgroups within our data set (e.g., gender, ethnicity, role, institutional type). As noted previously, these analyses were used to expand, verify, and further explore the themes we noticed elsewhere in the data.

SELECTED BIBLIOGRAPHY

Balzer, Cary, and Rod Reed, eds. *Building a Culture of Faith: University-Wide Partnerships for Spiritual Formation.* Abilene, TX: Abilene Christian University Press, 2012.

Beers, Stephen Thomas. "Faith Development of Christian College Campuses: A Student Affairs Mandate." *Growth* 3 (2003): 23–35.

Beers, Stephen Thomas, and Skip Trudeau. *Making a Difference: Empowering the Resident Assistant.* Abilene, TX: Abilene Christian University Press, 2015.

Dahlvig, Jolyn E., and Stephen Beers. "The Status of Student Affairs Divisions within the CCCU." *Christian Higher Education* 17, no. 4 (2018): 215–39.

Estanek, Sandra M., ed. *Understanding Student Affairs at Catholic Colleges and Universities: A Comprehensive Resource.* Franklin, WI: Sheed & Ward, 2002.

Estanek, Sandra M., Michael Galligan-Stierle, Maryellen Gilroy, Lisa L. Kirkpatrick, and Association of Catholic Colleges and Universities. *Student Life in Catholic Higher Education: Advancing Good Practice.* Washington, DC: Association of Catholic Colleges and Universities, 2017.

Estanek, Sandra M., and Michael James, eds. *Principles of Good Practice for Student Affairs at Catholic Colleges and Universities: Second Edition with Diagnostic Queries.* Chicago, IL: Association of Catholic Colleges and Universities, Association for Student Affairs at Catholic Colleges and Universities, and Jesuit Association of Student Personnel Administrators, 2010.

Glanzer, Perry L., Nathan F. Alleman, and Todd C. Ream. *Restoring the Soul of the University: Unifying Christian Higher Education in a Fragmented Age.* Downers Grove, IL: InterVarsity Press, 2017.

Guthrie, David S., ed. *Student Affairs Reconsidered: A Christian View of the Profession and Its Contexts.* Calvin Center Series. Lanham, MD: University Press of America, 1997.

Herrmann, Timothy W., and Kirsten D. Riedel ed. *A Calling to Care: Nurturing College Students toward Wholeness.* Abilene, TX: Abilene Christian University Press, 2018.

Herrmann, Timothy W., Kirsten D. Tenhaken, Hannah M. Adderley, and
    Morgan K. Morris, eds. *A Faith for the Generations: How Collegiate Experience
    Impacts Faith.* Abilene, TX: Abilene Christian University Press, 2015.
Jenson, Brian, and Sarah Visser, eds. *Reimagining the Student Experience:
    Formative Practices for Changing Times.* Abilene, TX: Abilene Christian
    University Press, 2019.

NOTES

Introduction

[1] We use the term "student affairs" rather than other terms we heard from participants (e.g., student development, student life, or student services), to be consistent with scholarly literature.

[2] Perry L. Glanzer and Todd Ream, *Christianity and Moral Identity in Higher Education* (New York: Palgrave Macmillan, 2009).

[3] American Council on Education, "The Student Personnel Point of View," *American Council on Education Studies* 1, no. 1 (1937): 2.

[4] Nancy Evans, Deanna Forney, Florence Guido, Lori Patton, and Kristen Renn, *Student Development in College: Theory, Research, and Practice*, 2nd ed. (San Francisco: John Wiley and Sons, 2010).

[5] Sandra M. Estanek, "A Study of Student Affairs Practice at Catholic Colleges and Universities," *Current Issues in Catholic Higher Education* 16, no. 2 (1996): 63–73; Sandra M. Estanek, Richard Herdlein, and Justyne Harris, "Preparation of New Professionals and Mission-Driven Hiring Practices: A Survey of Senior Student Affairs Officers at Catholic Colleges and Universities," *College Student Affairs Journal* 29, no. 2 (2011): 151–63.

[6] Estanek, "A Study of Student Affairs Practice at Catholic Colleges and Universities."

[7] Michael J. James and Sandra M. Estanek, "Building the Capacity for Mission through Use of the Principles of Good Practice for Student Affairs at Catholic Colleges and Universities: A Survey of Presidents and Senior Student Affairs Officers," *Catholic Education: A Journal of Inquiry and Practice* 15, no. 2 (2012): 143.

[8] Sandra M. Estanek, "Results of a Survey of Senior Student Affairs Officers at Catholic Colleges and Universities," *Current Issues in Catholic Higher Education* 24, no. 3 (2005): 83–99.

[9] James and Estanek, "Building the Capacity for Mission through Use of the Principles of Good Practice for Student Affairs at Catholic Colleges and Universities," 144.

[10] Melanie M. Morey and John J. Piderit, *Catholic Higher Education: A Culture in Crisis* (New York: Oxford, 2006).

[11] Sandra M. Estanek and Michael J. James, *Principles of Good Practice for Student Affairs at Catholic Colleges and Universities* (Chicago: Association of Catholic Colleges and Universities, Association for Student Affairs at Catholic Colleges and Universities, Jesuit Association of Student Personnel Administrators, 2007; rev. ed., 2010).

[12] James and Estanek, "Building the Capacity for Mission through Use of the Principles of Good Practice for Student Affairs at Catholic Colleges and Universities."

[13] Sandra Estanek, Michael Galligan-Stierle, Maryellen Gilroy, and Lisa Kirkpatrick, eds., *Student Life in Catholic Higher Education: Advancing Good Practice* (Washington, DC: Association of Catholic Colleges and Universities, 2017).

[14] Stephen Beers and Skip Trudeau, eds., *Making a Difference: Empowering the Resident Assistant* (Abilene, TX: Abilene Christian University Press, 2015); David Guthrie, ed., *Student Affairs Reconsidered: A Christian View of the Profession and Its Contexts* (Lanham: University Press of America, 1997); Timothy Herrmann and Kirsten Riedel, eds., *A Calling to Care: Nurturing College Students toward Wholeness* (Abilene, TX: Abilene Christian University Press, 2018).

[15] Etienne Wenger, *Communities of Practice: Learning, Meaning, and Identity* (Cambridge: Cambridge University Press, 1999), 176.

[16] Perry L. Glanzer, "Why We Should Discard the Integration of Faith and Learning: Rearticulating the Mission of the Christian Scholar," *Journal of Education and Christian Belief* 12, no. 1 (Spring 2008): 41–51.

[17] Glanzer, "Why We Should Discard the Integration of Faith and Learning."

[18] Perry L. Glanzer, Nathan F. Alleman, and Todd C. Ream, *Restoring the Soul of the University: Unifying Christian Higher Education in a Fragmented Age* (Downers Grove, IL: InterVarsity, 2017).

Chapter One: Who Are We?

[1] Jesse Rine, Perry L. Glanzer, and Phil Davignon, "Assessing the Denominational Identity of American Evangelical Colleges and Universities, Part II: Faculty Perspectives and Practices," *Christian Higher Education* 12, no. 4 (2013): 243–65.

[2]C. S. Lewis, *Mere Christianity* (New York: Macmillan, 1952).

[3]Perry L. Glanzer and Todd C. Ream, *Christianity and Moral Identity in Higher Education* (New York: Palgrave Macmillan, 2009).

[4]Rishi Sriram, *Student Affairs by the Numbers: Quantitative Research and Statistics for Professionals* (Sterling, VA: Stylus, 2018); Daniel Kahneman, *Thinking Fast and Slow* (New York: Farrar, Straus, and Giroux, 2011).

Chapter Two: Developing the Developers

[1]Larry Lyon and Michael Beaty, "Integration, Secularization, and the Two-Spheres View at Religious Colleges: Comparing Baylor University with the University of Notre Dame and Georgetown College," *Christian Scholar's Review* 29, no. 1 (1999): 73–112.

[2]"Liturgies" as defined in James K. A. Smith, *Desiring the Kingdom: Worship, Worldview, and Cultural Formation*, Volume 1: *Cultural Liturgies* (Grand Rapids: Baker Academic, 2009).

[3]K. Anders Ericsson and Robert Pool, *Peak: Secrets from the New Science of Expertise* (New York: Houghton Mifflin Harcourt, 2016).

Introduction to Part Two: Surveying the Landscape

[1]David S. Guthrie, *Student Affairs Reconsidered: A Christian View of the Profession and Its Contexts* (Lanham, MD: University Press of America, 1997).

[2]See, for example, some Christian faculty in Perry L. Glanzer and Nathan F. Alleman, *The Outrageous Idea of the Christian Teacher* (New York: Oxford University Press, 2019).

Chapter Three: Does God Make a Difference for Student Affairs?

[1]Shirley Hoogstra and John Witte, "Listen, Love, Learn: Leading People Who Are Different Than You," in *Making a Difference: Empowering the Resident Assistant*, eds. Stephen Beers and Skip Trudeau (Abilene, TX: Abilene Christian University Press, 2015), 104.

[2]Rachel Killam and Heather Gingrich, "Sexuality among Evangelical College Women," *Growth* 10 (2011): 40–53.

[3]Sandra Estanek, "Walking the Two-Way Bridge: Transgender at Catholic Colleges and Universities," in *Student Life in Catholic Higher Education: Advancing Good Practice*, eds. Sandra Estanek, Michael Galligan-Stierle, Maryellen Gilroy, and Lisa Kirkpatrick (Washington, DC: Association of Catholic Colleges and Universities, 2017), 95.

[4]Kirsten Riedel, Emilie Hoffman, and Jessica Martin, "Teaching Students to Care for Themselves," in *A Calling to Care: Nurturing College Students toward*

Wholeness, ed. Timothy Herrmann and Kirsten Riedel (Abilene, TX: Abilene Christian University Press, 2018), 80.

[5] Kristin Keiffer, Amy Van Der Werf, and Doug Wood, "More Than Just Getting Along: The Role of the Resident Assistant in Developing a Community," in *Making a Difference*, 60.

[6] D. Terry Thomas and David S. Guthrie, "A Framework of Understanding," in *Student Affairs Reconsidered*, 1–14.

[7] Stephen Beers, "Faith Development on Christian College Campuses: A Student Affairs Mandate," *Growth* 3 (2003): 23–35.

[8] Beers and Trudeau, *Making a Difference*, 28.

[9] Hoogstra and Witte, "Listen, Love, Learn," 104.

[10] John Amos Comenius, *The School of Infancy*, trans. Ernest McNeil Eller (Chapel Hill: University of North Carolina Press, 1984), 59.

[11] Thomas and Guthrie, "A Framework of Understanding," 6.

[12] See, for example, Andrew Shotnicki and Colette McCarrick Geary, "College Student Discipline and Catholic Identity," in *Student Life in Catholic Higher Education*, 151–55.

[13] Andre Broquard, "The Role of the Resident Assistant in Confrontation and Discipline," in *Making a Difference*, 147.

[14] Steve Ivester, "Beyond Building a Résumé," in *Liberal Arts for the Christian Life,* eds. Jeffry C. Davis and Philip G. Ryken (Wheaton, IL: Crossway, 2012), 169.

[15] Beers, "Faith Development on Christian College Campuses," 30.

[16] Mark L. Poorman, "The Role of Residence Hall Staff Members in the Mission of the Catholic University," in *Student Life in Catholic Higher Education*, 38.

[17] Michael James, "A Christian Anthropology for Student Development," in *Student Life in Catholic Higher Education*, 67; and Barry Loy, "Faith Development and Student Affairs," *Growth* 3 (2003): 9.

[18] Steve Ivester, "The Role of a Resident Assistant as a Program Facilitator," in *Making a Difference*, 136.

[19] Kristine Goodwin, "Faith Matters: Supporting Students' Religious Diversity," in *Student Life in Catholic Higher Education*, 83.

[20] Ivester, "The Role of a Resident Assistant as a Program Facilitator," 134.

[21] James Maher, "Pope Francis: A Model of Leadership and Management at Catholic Institutions and Guide for Senior Student Affairs Officers," in *Student Life in Catholic Higher Education*, 29.

[22] Thomas and Guthrie, "A Framework of Understanding," 6.

[23] Catherine WoodBrooks, "Character Formation and Moral Development: Creating an Intentional Framework," in *Student Life at Catholic Higher Education*, 72.

[24] Poorman, "The Role of Residence Hall Staff Members in the Mission of the Catholic University," 38.

[25] Poorman, "The Role of Residence Hall Staff Members in the Mission of the Catholic University," 38.

[26] Susan Reese, "Conversation Creates Culture: Student Development and Spiritual Formation in the Christian University," in *Building a Culture of Faith: University-Wide Partnerships for Spiritual Formation*, eds. Cary Balzer and Rod Reed (Abilene, TX: Abilene University Press, 2012), 162.

[27] Reese, "Conversation Creates Culture," 162.

[28] Cara Cliburn Allen and Nathan F. Alleman, "Faith, Work, and Praxis: A Process Model of Integration for Christian Student Affairs Administrators," *Christian Higher Education* 16, no. 5 (2017): 285–302.

[29] John Felio and Jabrina Robinson, "Making Mission Matter: Recruitment and Supervision of Mission," in *Student Life in Catholic Higher Education*, 109–12; Josh Hengemuhle, "Developing a Catholic Culture: Catholic Cultural Competency as a Critical Skill," in *Student Life in Catholic Higher Education*, 103–8.

[30] Nevitt Sanford, *Self and Society: Social Change and Individual Development* (New York: Atherton, 1966). Articles dealing with this issue include Dolores Christie, "Student Affairs and Conscience Formation" in *Understanding Student Affairs and Catholic Colleges and Universities: A Comprehensive Resource*, ed. Sandra Estanek (Lanham, MD: Rowman and Littlefield Publishers, 2002), 75–95; Steve Morley and Sarah Hightower, "The Role of a Resident Assistant as a Peer Counselor: Knowing Your Limits and How Best to Help," in *Making a Difference*, 115–129.

[31] Morley and Hightower, "The Role of a Resident Assistant as a Peer Counselor," 126.

[32] Thomas Morgan, "Educating for Justice and Compassion: Catholic Social Teaching and the Work of Student Affairs," in *Student Life in Catholic Higher Education*, 140.

[33] Rev. Jay Fostner, "The Death of a Student: Lessons from a Catholic Campus," in *Student Life in Catholic Higher Education*, 173–76; Hoogstra and Witte, "Listen, Love, Learn."

[34] W. Bernt King, "Contributing Factors to Persistence among African-American and Hispanic Students in Higher Education: A Phenomenological Qualitative Study at a Diverse Mall Institution on the East Coast," *Growth* 8 (2009): 15–30.

[35] Morley and Hightower, "The Role of a Resident Assistant as a Peer Counselor," 127–28.

[36] Morley and Hightower, "The Role of a Resident Assistant as a Peer Counselor," 128.

[37] Hoogstra and Witte, "Listen, Love, Learn," in *Making a Difference*, 108.

[38] Fostner, "The Death of a Student," 174.

[39] Shotnicki and Geary, "College Student Discipline and Catholic Identity," 152.

[40] Shotnicki and Geary, "College Student Discipline and Catholic Identity," 152–53.

[41] Jay DeBruscio, "The Changing Role of the Athletic Director," in *Student Life in Catholic Higher Education*, 131.

[42] Keiffer, Van Der Werf, and Wood, "More Than Just Getting Along," 63.

[43] Haley Williamson, "The Impact of Monastic Practices and Spiritual Disciplines on Student Leader Development," *Growth* 17 (2018): 51.

[44] Scott Keith and Gilbert Fugitt, "Toward a Lutheran View of Student Affairs: Developing a Learned Piety in Community under the Cross of Christ," in *The Idea and Practice of a Christian University: A Lutheran Approach*, ed. Scott Ashmon (St. Louis: Concordia Publishing House, 2015), 295.

[45] Robert Meyer and Laura Wankel, "Managing a Crisis at a Catholic University—Lessons Learned and Shared: Seton Hall University, South Orange, New Jersey," in *Understanding Student Life at Catholic Colleges and Universities*, 182–83.

[46] Stewardship and care share many similarities, and a book on caring edited by Timothy Herrmann and Kirsten Riedel provides an in-depth exploration of what one could call the stewardship of students. See Herrmann and Riedel, *A Calling to Care*.

[47] Lisa L. Kirkpatrick, "Catholic Hospitality: The Foundation for Community in Catholic Higher Education," in *Student Life in Catholic Higher Education*, 80.

[48] Keiffer, Van Der Werf, and Wood, "More Than Just Getting Along," 120.

[49] Kirkpatrick, "Catholic Hospitality," 80.

[50] Goodwin, "Faith Matters," 84.

[51] Goodwin, "Faith Matters," 86.

[52] Beers, "Being Part of a Larger Purpose," in *Making a Difference*, 26.

[53] Sharia Brock, Angelica Hambrick, and Alexander Jun, "The Intersection of Christianity and Racial Justice Advocacy," *Growth* 15 (2016): 30.

[54] Alexander A. Astin, Helen S. Astin, and Jennifer A. Lindholm, *Cultivating the Spirit: How College Can Enhance Students' Inner Lives* (San Francisco: Jossey-Bass, 2010).

[55] James K. A. Smith, "Response by James K. A. Smith, in A Review of 'Imagining the Kingdom: How Worship Works,'" *Christian Higher Education,* 13, no. 2 (2014): 163.

[56] As referenced in the Introduction, Etienne Wenger, *Communities of Practice: Learning, Meaning, and Identity* (Cambridge: Cambridge University Press, 1999), 176.

Chapter Four: Who Are Our Students?

[1] Stanley J. Grenz, *The Social God and the Relational Self: A Trinitarian Theology of the* Imago Dei, 1st ed. (Louisville: Westminster John Knox Press, 2001).

[2] Arthur Frank Holmes, *Shaping Character: Moral Education in the Christian College* (Grand Rapids: Eerdmans, 1991), 59.

[3] American Council on Education, "The Student Personnel Point of View," Series 1 (Washington, DC: American Council on Education Studies, 1937), 1.

[4] Nancy J. Evans and Robert D. Reason, "Guiding Principles: A Review and Analysis of Student Affairs Philosophical Statements," *Journal of College Student Development* 42, no. 4 (2001): 370.

[5] For a rich theological exploration of this tension, see Marc Cortez, *Resourcing Theological Anthropology: A Constructive Account of Humanity in the Light of Christ* (Grand Rapids: Zondervan, 2017).

[6] Perry L. Glanzer, Nathan F. Alleman, and Todd C. Ream, *Restoring the Soul of the University: Unifying Christian Higher Education in a Fragmented Age* (Downers Grove, IL: InterVarsity Press, 2017), 152–53.

[7] Christian Smith, *To Flourish or Destruct: A Personalist Theory of Human Goods, Motivations, Failure, and Evil* (Chicago: University of Chicago Press, 2015), 28.

Chapter Five: The End of the Student Affairs Profession

[1] Robert M. Hutchins, "Education and Social Improvement: The Cults That Destroy," *Vital Speeches of the Day* 4, no. 16 (1938): 500.

[2] John of Salisbury, "Policraticus," in *The Great Tradition: Classic Readings on What It Means to Be a Human Being*, ed. Richard M. Gamble (Wilmington, DE: ISI Books, 2017), 274.

[3] Robert McGee, *The Search for Significance*, rev. ed. (Nashville: Thomas Nelson, 2003).

[4] Lawrence Kohlberg, *The Philosophy of Moral Development: Moral Stages and the Idea of Justice, Essays on Moral Development*, vol. 1 (San Francisco: Harper and Row, 1981), 9.

[5] Perry L. Glanzer and Nathan F. Alleman, *The Outrageous Idea of Christian Teaching* (New York: Oxford University Press, 2019).

[6] Perry L. Glanzer and Todd C. Ream, *Christianity and Moral Identity in Higher Education* (New York: Palgrave Macmillan, 2009); Perry L. Glanzer and Andrew J. Milson, "Legislating the Good: A Survey and Evaluation of Contemporary Character Education Legislation," *Educational Policy* 20, no. 3 (2006): 525–50.

Chapter Six: What Are We Trying to Teach Students?

[1] James K. A. Smith, *Desiring the Kingdom: Worship, Worldview and Cultural Formation* (Grand Rapids: Eerdmans, 2009), 157.

[2] David I. Smith, *Desiring the Kingdom.*

[3] Christopher Peterson and Martin Seligman, *Character Strengths and Virtues: A Handbook and Classification* (New York: Oxford University Press, 2004).

[4] See, for example, Peterson and Seligman, *Character Strengths and Virtues,* and Perry L. Glanzer and Andrew J. Milson, "Legislating the Good: A Survey and Evaluation of Contemporary Character Education Legislation," *Educational Policy* 20, no. 3 (2006): 525–50.

Chapter Seven: The How(s) of Christ-Enlivened Student Affairs

[1] Perry L. Glanzer and Nathan F. Alleman, *The Outrageous Idea of the Christian Teacher* (New York: Oxford University Press, 2019).

[2] David I. Smith, *On Christian Teaching: Practicing Faith in the Classroom* (Grand Rapids: Eerdmans, 2018).

[3] E. O. Jacobsen, *The Space Between: A Christian Engagement with the Built Environment* (Grand Rapids: Baker Academic, 2012).

[4] Of course, most Protestant Christians do not focus on building elaborate temples or even chapels because they take the biblical view that now the Holy Spirit resides in us. We are the temple of God (1 Cor. 6:19), and we are the body of Christ (1 Cor. 12:12).

[5] See, for example, George Marsden's description of the secularization of chapel in *The Soul of the University: From Protestant Establishment to Established Protestantism* (New York: Oxford University Press, 1994).

⁶Harold M. Best, *Music through the Eyes of Faith* (San Francisco: HarperSanFrancisco, 1993). See also James K. A. Smith, *Desiring the Kingdom* (Grand Rapids: Baker Books, 2009).

⁷Smith, *Desiring the Kingdom.*

⁸Smith, *Desiring the Kingdom*; Smith, *Imagining the Kingdom: How Worship Works*, Cultural Liturgies 2 (Grand Rapids: Baker Academic, 2013).

⁹Col. 1:17: ". . . in him all things hold together."

¹⁰Julie A. Reuben, *The Making of the Modern University: Intellectual Transformation and the Marginalization of Morality* (Chicago: University of Chicago Press, 1996).

Chapter Eight: How Christ Enlivens Residence Life

¹Rishi Sriram and Melissa McLevain, "The Future of Residence Life and Student Affairs in Christian Higher Education," *Christian Higher Education* 15, no. 1–2 (2016): 72–83.

²For more, see Michael O. Emerson and Christian Smith, *Divided by Faith: Evangelical Religion and the Problem of Race in America* (New York: Oxford University Press, 2000); Victor B. Saenz, "Breaking the Segregation Cycle: Examining Students' Precollege Racial Environments and College Diversity Experiences," *The Review of Higher Education* 34, no. 1 (2010): 1–37.

³For more, see Daryl G. Smith, *Diversity's Promise for Higher Education: Making It Work* (Baltimore: Johns Hopkins University Press); Zak Foste, "Reproducing Whiteness: How White Students Justify the Campus Racial Status Quo," *Journal of Student Affairs Research and Practice* 56, no. 3 (2019): 241–53.

⁴Dietrich Bonhoeffer, *Life Together* (New York: Harper & Row, 1954), 30.

Chapter Nine: How Christ Enlivens Student Conduct and Alcohol Education

¹Jennifer S. Fueglein, Kevin S. Price, Adriana Alicea-Rodriguez, Jan Wilson McKinney, and Anne L. Jimenez, "The E.P.I.C. Journey Sanctioning Model," *Journal of College and Character* 13, no. 3 (2012): 1–8.

²More on reimagining the cocurricular as a greenhouse in chapter 15 of Perry L. Glanzer, Nathan F. Alleman, and Todd C. Ream, *Restoring the Soul of the University: Unifying Christian Higher Education in a Fragmented Age* (Downers Grove, IL: InterVarsity Press, 2017).

³Perry L. Glanzer, "Building the Good Life: Using Identities to Frame Moral Education in Higher Education," *Journal of College and Character* 14, no. 2 (May 2013): 177–84.

⁴Glanzer, "Building the Good Life."

Chapter Ten: How Christ Transforms the Campus Racial Climate

[1] For more, see George A. Yancey, *Neither Jew nor Gentile: Exploring Issues of Racial Diversity on Protestant College Campuses* (New York: Oxford University Press, 2010); Michael O. Emerson and Christian Smith, *Divided by Faith: Evangelical Religion and the Problem of Race in America* (New York: Oxford University Press, 2000); Michael C. Smith, *Race, Rates, and Religion: The Relationship between Black Graduation Rates and Evangelical Religious Affiliation at Private Colleges and Universities* (Los Angeles: University of California, 2010); Kristin Paredes-Collins, "Cultivating Diversity and Spirituality: A Compelling Interest for Institutional Priority," *Christian Higher Education* 12, no. 1–2 (2013): 122–37; Kristin Paredes-Collins, "Campus Climate for Diversity as a Predictor of Spiritual Development at Christian Colleges," *Religion & Education* 41, no. 2 (2014): 171–93.

[2] Yancey, *Neither Jew nor Gentile*, 3–37.

[3] Smith, *Race, Rates, and Religion*.

[4] Joseph Crespino, *In Search of Another Country: Mississippi and the Conservative Counterrevolution* (Princeton: Princeton University Press, 2007), cited in Yancey, *Neither Jew nor Gentile*.

[5] Yancey, *Neither Jew nor Gentile*, 3–37.

[6] Emerson and Smith, *Divided by Faith*.

[7] Yancey, *Neither Jew nor Gentile*, 11.

[8] Smith, *Race, Rates, and Religion*, 132.

[9] See Yancey, *Neither Jew nor Gentile*.

[10] For example, see Smith, *Race, Rates, and Religion*; Paredes-Collins, "Cultivating Diversity and Spirituality: A Compelling Interest for Institutional Priority"; Paredes-Collins, "Campus Climate for Diversity as a Predictor of Spiritual Development at Christian Colleges"; Peter J. Hansen, *Perceptions of Campus Racial Climate as Predictors for Cross-Race Interaction at Christian Colleges and Universities: Differences by Race/Ethnicity, Sex, and Religiosity* (Los Angeles: University of Southern California, 2017); Yancey, *Neither Jew nor Gentile*.

[11] Hansen, *Perception of Campus Racial Climate as Predictors for Cross-Race Interaction at Christian Colleges and Universities*; Paredes-Collins, "Campus Climate for Diversity as Predictor of Spiritual Development at Christian Colleges"; Yancey, *Neither Jew nor Gentile*.

[12] Hansen, *Perception of Campus Racial Climate as Predictors for Cross-Race Interaction at Christian Colleges and Universities*; Yancey, *Neither Jew nor Gentile*.

[13] Damon A. Williams, *Strategic Diversity Leadership: Activating Change and Transformation in Higher Education* (Sterling: Stylus Publishing, 2013).

[14] J. Daniel Hays, *From Every People and Nation: A Biblical Theology of Race* (Downers Grove, IL: InterVarsity Press, 2003), 203.

[15] Samuel D. Museus and Uma M. Jayakumar, eds. *Creating Campus Cultures: Fostering Success among Racially Diverse Student Populations* (New York: Routledge, 2012).

[16] For similar concepts, see Sarah Shin, *Beyond Color Blind: Redeeming Our Ethnic Journey* (Downers Grove, IL: InterVarsity Press, 2017).

[17] Kristin Paredes-Collins, "Institutional Priority for Diversity at Christian Institutions," *Christian Higher Education* 8, no. 4 (2009): 280–303.

[18] For more on the importance of espoused and enacted mission, see George D. Kuh, Jillian Kinzie, John H. Schuh, Elizabeth J. Whitt, and Associates, *Student Success in College: Creating Conditions That Matter* (San Francisco: Jossey-Bass, 2010).

[19] Williams, *Strategic Diversity Leadership*.

[20] Marta Tienda, "Diversity ≠ Inclusion: Promoting Integration in Higher Education," *Educational Researcher* 42, no. 9 (2013): 467.

[21] Sylvia Hurtado, Jeffrey Milem, Alma Clayton-Pedersen, and Walter Allen, "Enacting Diverse Learning Environments: Improving the Climate for Racial/Ethnic Diversity in Higher Education," *ASHE-ERIC Higher Education Report* 26, no. 8 (1999): 1–140; Shaun R. Harper and Sylvia Hurtado, "Nine Themes in Campus Racial Climates and Implications for Institutional Transformation," *New Directions for Student Services*, no. 120 (Winter 2007): 7–24.

[22] For more see, Hurtado et al., "Enacting Diverse Learning Environments."

[23] Nathan F. Alleman and Perry L. Glanzer, "Creating Confessional Colleges and Universities That Confess," *Journal of Education and Christian Belief* 18, no. 1 (March 2014): 13–28.

[24] Alleman and Glanzer, "Creating Confessional Colleges and Universities That Confess," 15.

[25] Alleman and Glanzer, "Creating Confessional Colleges and Universities That Confess," 23–27.

[26] Jemar Tisby, *The Color of Compromise: The Truth about the American Church's Complicity in Racism* (Grand Rapids: Zondervan, 2018).

Chapter Eleven: The Stewardship and Redemption of Our Sexual Selves

[1] Beth Felker Jones, *Faithful: A Theology of Sex* (Grand Rapids: Zondervan, 2015), 16.

[2] Donna Freitas, *Sex and Soul: Juggling Sexuality, Spirituality, Romance, and Religion on America's College Campuses* (New York: Oxford University Press, 2011).

[3] Todd C. Ream and Perry L. Glanzer, *The Idea of a Christian College: Expanded for the Contemporary University* (Portland, OR: Cascade, 2013); Perry L. Glanzer and Todd C. Ream, *Christianity and Moral Identity in Higher Education* (New York: Palgrave Macmillan, 2009).

[4] Jones, *Faithful*, 33.

[5] C. S. Lewis, "The Inner Ring." First published in 1944. See https://www.lewissociety.org/innerring/.

Chapter Twelve: Sexual Justice in a Broken World

[1] 20 U.S.C. § 1681(a).

[2] Deborah Brake, *Getting in the Game: Title IX and the Women's Sports Revolution* (New York: New York University Press, 2010).

[3] Kate Shellnutt, "How Faith Changes Campus Sexual Assaults: Research Is Finding That Cultures of Restraint Fare Better Than Cultures of Mere Consent," *Christianity Today* 62, no. 7 (September 2018): 19–20.

[4] 20 U.S.C. § 1681(a)(3).

[5] Anthony Hoekema, *Created in God's Image* (Grand Rapids: Eerdmans, 1994); "So God created man in his own image, in the image of God he created them; male and female he created them" (Gen. 1:27).

[6] See US Department of Education, Office for Civil Rights, "Dear Colleague Letter to Title IX Coordinators," April 24, 2015, page 3, https://www2.ed.gov/about/offices/list/ocr/letters/colleague-201504-title-ix-coordinators.pdf.

Conclusion

[1] The distinction between espoused vision and enacted practices comes from George D. Kuh, Jillian Kinzie, John H. Schuh, Elizabeth J. Whitt, and Associates, *Student Success in College: Creating Conditions That Matter* (San Francisco: Jossey-Bass, 2010), xii.

[2] George D. Kuh and Association of American Colleges and Universities, *High-Impact Educational Practices: What They Are, Who Has Access to Them, and Why They Matter* (Washington, DC: Association of American Colleges and Universities, 2008); Kuh et al., *Student Success in College: Creating Conditions That Matter*.

[3] Perry L. Glanzer and Nathan F. Alleman, *The Outrageous Idea of Christian Teaching* (Oxford: Oxford University Press, 2019).

[4] Glanzer and Alleman, *The Outrageous Idea of Christian Teaching*.

[5] James K. A. Smith, *Imagining the Kingdom: How Worship Works*, Cultural Liturgies 2 (Grand Rapids: Baker Academic, 2013), 157.

[6] Perry L. Glanzer and Todd C. Ream, *Christianity and Moral Identity in Higher Education* (New York: Palgrave Macmillan, 2009), 188.

Appendix B: Research Methods

[1] For more on critical realism, see Philip S. Gorski, "What Is Critical Realism? And Why Should You Care?," *Contemporary Sociology: A Journal of Reviews* 42, no. 5 (2013): 658–70; Christian Smith, "Future Directions in the Sociology of Religion," *Social Forces* 86, no. 4 (2008): 1561–89; and Christian Smith, *What Is a Person?: Rethinking Humanity, Social Life, and the Moral Good from the Person Up* (Chicago: University of Chicago Press, 2010).

[2] Robert Benne, *Quality with Soul: How Six Premier Colleges and Universities Keep Faith with Their Religious Traditions* (Grand Rapids: Eerdmans, 2001).

[3] Barney G. Glaser and Anselm L. Strauss, *The Discovery of Grounded Theory: Strategies for Qualitative Research* (Hawthorne, NY: Aldine, 1967).

[4] Johnny Saldaña, *The Coding Manual for Qualitative Researchers*, 3rd edition. (Los Angeles: SAGE, 2016).

ABOUT THE AUTHORS

THEODORE F. COCKLE is a full-time doctoral student completing a PhD in higher education studies and leadership at Baylor University, and he serves as the editor of *Ideas*, an online publication of the Association of Christians in Student Development. He has also coauthored several peer-reviewed articles on Christian higher education. Theodore earned his BA and MA degrees from Wheaton College before serving as the Assistant Director of Wheaton's student activities office. He is currently completing a PhD in Higher Education Studies and Leadership at Baylor University. When he is not reading or writing, Theodore and his wife, Kate, enjoy spending time outside and reading to their three boys.

PERRY L. GLANZER is professor of educational foundations at Baylor University and a Resident Scholar with Baylor Institute for Studies of Religion. He is the coauthor, author, or editor of eleven books, including *The Outrageous Idea of Christian Teaching*. In addition, he has authored or coauthored over seventy-five journal articles and book chapters on topics related to moral education, faith-based higher education, and the relationship between religion and education. He lives with his wife and two boys in Hewitt, Texas.

BRITNEY N. GRABER is the director of institutional effectiveness at Trevecca Nazarene University. She earned her BS and MA from Taylor University, her MAT from Morningside College, and is completing her PhD in higher education studies and leadership at Baylor University. Her published works and research interests include Title IX policy and practice at Christian colleges, faith-based higher education, accreditation and assessment practices, and higher education law and policy.

ELIJAH G. JEONG is a full-time doctoral student completing a PhD in higher education studies and leadership at Baylor University. He also has served in various educational and ministry settings, including working as a high school teacher, a college administrator, and a pastor for an Asian American church. Elijah earned a BA from University of Washington, an MA from Wheaton College, and an MDiv from Reformed Theological Seminary. He has coauthored several peer-reviewed articles, and his research interest includes the intersection of race, religion, and higher education. Elijah loves spending time with his wife and son, playing basketball, and cooking Korean food.